Accession no.
36121011

KU-302-641

# THE OLYMPIC GAMES EXPLAINED

An awesome festival of sporting excellence and competition, the Olympic Games have now evolved into a major international event with great cultural, political, economic and social importance.

*The Olympic Games Explained* is an introductory guide to the history and meaning of the four-yearly phenomenon that is the modern Olympic Games. The book provides a comprehensive overview of 'Olympism' from its Ancient Greek origins through the beginnings of the International Olympic Committee to the global Olympic Movement in the twenty-first century.

Key topics include:

- Olympic history and modern Olympic case studies
- Britain in the Olympics
- The Paralympic Games
- Media and marketing at the Olympics
- Environmental impact of the Olympics
- Politics and organisation of the Olympics
- Ethical issues, doping and the Olympic spirit

Each chapter offers a range of study tasks and review questions to help students develop their understanding of key concepts in Olympic studies.

This book is supported by a dedicated website containing further material for learning and research into the Olympics at www.routledge.com/textbooks

**Vassil Girginov** is Senior Lecturer in Leisure and Sport Studies at the University of Luton, UK. **Jim Parry** is Senior Lecturer in Philosophy at the University of Leeds, UK, and is the founding Director of the British Olympic Academy.

# STUDENT SPORT STUDIES
General Editors: J. A. Mangan and Frank Galligan

## SERIES EDITORS' FOREWORD

This is a new series specifically for school, college and university students, written clearly and concisely by expert teachers. The series covers a range of relevant topics for those studying physical education, sports studies, leisure and recreation studies and related courses. Each volume is purposefully prepared for students facing specific course syllabuses and examinations and is sharply focused and written in plain English. The series is in response to repeated requests from students and teachers for accessible books concentrating on courses and examinations.

J. A. Mangan
Frank Galligan
2004

Other titles in the series

**The Story of English Sport**
*Neil Wigglesworth*

**In Pursuit of Excellence**
A Contemporary Issue
*Michael Hill*

**Acquiring Skill in Sport**
*John Honeybourne*

# THE OLYMPIC GAMES EXPLAINED

A Student Guide to the Evolution of the Modern Olympic Games

**VASSIL GIRGINOV AND JIM PARRY**

| LIS LIBRARY | |
|---|---|
| Date 3º/4 | Fund S |
| Order No 2108367 | |
| University of Chester | |

Routledge
Taylor & Francis Group

LONDON AND NEW YORK

To our families: Rossi and Katerina; Michelle, Jake and Eliot

First published 2005 by Routledge
2 Park Square, Milton Park, Abingdon, Oxon OX14 4RN

Simultaneously published in the USA and Canada
by Routledge
270 Madison Ave, New York, NY 10016

Transferred to Digital Printing 2006

*Routledge is an imprint of the Taylor & Francis Group, an informa business*

© 2005 Vassil Girginov and Jim Parry

Typeset in Zapf Humanist and Eras by
Keystroke, Jacaranda Lodge, Wolverhampton
Printed and bound in Great Britain by
TJI Digital, Padstow, Cornwall

All rights reserved. No part of this book may be reprinted or
reproduced or utilised in any form or by any electronic, mechanical,
or other means, now known or hereafter invented, including
photocopying and recording, or in any information storage or
retrieval system, without permission in writing from the publishers.

Every effort has been made to ensure that the advice and information
in this book is true and accurate at the time of going to press.
However, neither the publisher nor the authors can accept any
legal responsibility or liability for any errors or omissions that may
be made. In the case of drug administration, any medical procedure
or the use of technical equipment mentioned within this book,
you are strongly advised to consult the manufacturer's guidelines.

*British Library Cataloguing in Publication Data*
A catalogue record for this book is available from the British Library

*Library of Congress Cataloging in Publication Data*
A catalog record for this book has been requested

ISBN 10: 0-415-34603-7 (hbk)
ISBN 10: 0-415-34604-5 (pbk)

ISBN 13: 978-0-415-34603-0 (hbk)
ISBN 13: 978-0-415-34604-7 (pbk)

# CONTENTS

# FOREWORD

The Olympic Movement has an ancient history and a modern Charter that sets out high ideals:

 Olympism is a philosophy of life, exalting and combining in a balanced whole the qualities of body, will and mind. Blending sport with culture and education, Olympism seeks to create a way of life based on the joy found in effort, the educational value of good example and respect for fundamental ethical principles.

 The focus of the Olympic Movement is to contribute to building a peaceful and better world by educating youth through sport practised without discrimination of any kind and in the Olympic spirit, which requires mutual understanding with a spirit of friendship, solidarity and fair play.

Each National Olympic Committee is charged under the Olympic Charter with a specific educational role in both schools and universities. It is for this reason – amongst others – that the British Olympic Association has been co-operating with the authors in the preparation of this book.

There is a considerable amount of material available to the student of the Olympic Movement but we hope that this volume will be of particular value to the increasing number of students who have the opportunity to include an element of Olympic studies in their further education and/or degree courses.

A case can be made for the inclusion of Olympic studies as an example of an ancient institution which has adapted and modernised itself whilst retaining universal appeal to young people involved in sport and the application of its founding principles to the advantage of all mankind.

The student will find, chapter by chapter, the development of Olympism from the Ancient Games through their re-establishment as the 'Modern Olympic

Games' in 1896 to the organisation and impact of the world's greatest sporting event. The role of Britain in the modern history of the Games is chronicled in full and the authors have dealt with the greatly expanded problems of organising this complicated festival of sport in the twenty-first century.

Analysis is made of the increasingly complex relationships between the International Olympic Committee, the Games Organising Committees and modern media, the pressures of the commercial market place and the requirements of economic sustainability and environmental protection.

How these often-conflicting interests are dealt with by the Organising Committee can be the subject of individual studies especially where the overriding interests should be those of the athletes themselves. The challenge is enhanced with the relatively recent inclusion of the Paralympics and the opportunity to promote elite sport for those outstanding athletes who also have disabilities.

Throughout all these challenges – inevitably – the Olympic Movement must confront the world of politics, as there is now a general recognition that sport, as it grows in stature and importance, cannot stand aside from political involvement. Sport must also confront its own ethical standards, which are much wider than the huge challenge of doping in sport. In addition, Olympic sport should review its educational role and its association with culture.

In an attempt to link many of these themes, the book contains three case studies from the successful Olympic Games in Sydney, the equally successful Winter Olympic Games in Salt Lake City and, topically, the London bid to stage the Olympic Games in 2012.

There are many facets to the Olympic Movement and the organisational challenge in staging them is one of the most complex management problems of all. However, nothing seems to undermine the popularity of the Olympic principles and the attraction of the Games themselves.

The International Olympic Committee has had to face extreme pressures upon its own ethical standards in recent years and now seeks to make the Olympic Games themselves even more universal by reducing the ever-growing requirements on host cities.

Pressures exist across the whole movement: from the creation of new National Olympic Committees – now 202 in number; from sports wishing to join the programme of the Games; from increasing numbers of events or disciplines within individual sports; from ever-increasing standards of the athletes and the need to maintain the correct balance between participation of the elite and participation of all; from the number of cities applying to host the Games; and not least from the endless media scrutiny of the Olympic Movement and all its activities.

I hope first that this work by Vassil Girginov and Jim Parry will help to explain the many and varied relationships that exist because the Olympic Movement does much good. The Olympic Games themselves act as an inspiration for young arid old throughout the world. Olympic principles set out a philosophy of life that points to a better world and a wider understanding of all these in this modern world can do nothing but good.

Craig Reedie, CBE
Chair of the British Olympic Association and Member
of the International Olympic Committee

*Glasgow, 2004*

# PREFACE

## THE MODERN OLYMPIC MOVEMENT

The Olympic Games originated in Ancient Greece, emerging from the ritual practices of religious cults at the sacred site of Ancient Olympia somewhere near the beginning of the first millennium BC. Olympism, as a social philosophy, and the Olympic Movement, as a set of ideas, structures and competitions, are twentieth century phenomena.

The International Olympic Committee was established in 1894.

The purpose of the Olympic Movement and its highest manifestation, the Olympic Games, as set out by its founder Pierre de Coubertin in 1894, is to further the development of sport and to use sport to promote both personal and cultural change. This is a complex process which is based on several key principles.

The fundamental principles of Olympism, in simple value words, see the person as well-rounded, developing and striving. He or she exhibits leadership, ethics and fair play and treats others with dignity, respect and friendship in a community which is at peace and where sport is a right.

Drafted originally almost single-handedly by the French aristocrat Pierre de Coubertin and approved by representatives from a handful of nine Western countries (France, Great Britain, Belgium, Germany, Greece, Hungary, Russia, Sweden, and the USA), those principles and the values they assert have received virtually universal support from all 200 member-nations of the Olympic Movement throughout the twentieth century.

As Olympism grew in scale and popularity, its evolution inevitably evoked tensions between:

- amateur and commercial ethos
- mass participation and sporting excellence
- friendship and rivalry
- the pursuit of peace and nationalism (competition between national teams)
- Olympism as a social movement and the Olympic Games as a spectacle.

The most prevailing tension has been between the actions required to protect a commercial property (the Olympic symbols and the Games) and those required to nurture a global social movement for change.

Despite its efforts during the twentieth century, for geo-political, economic and cultural reasons, the Olympic Movement has failed to attend to the fundamental tensions described above. Additionally, malpractices within the Movement have exposed the Olympic idea to legitimate criticism. This yet again highlights the need to redress the balance and give prominence to the fundamental ethical values underpinning the Olympic ethos, which have helped the Movement to survive the political and economic turmoil of the twentieth century.

Plate 0.1 Jacques Rogge, President of the International Olympic Committee, opens the Games of the Small States of Europe, Malta, 2003

Furthermore, the growing interest in Olympism has led to a proliferation of literature, information sources and institutions. For example, some twenty years ago there were only 25 National Olympic Academies (NOAs) in the world, charged with the promotion of Olympic education. Today, there are more than 130 NOAs and at least one well-established Olympic Study Centre on each continent.

As a result, numerous competing explanations have been advanced about the role of Olympism in history and in modern society. The variety of practices and explanations makes writing a book on Olympism a daunting task. As Segrave (2000) commented:

> the older Eurocentric conception of Olympic internationalism as universal humanism is no longer sufficient by itself to mediate even the European, much less the global experience. Requisite for the formation of a viable neo-modern Olympism is the recognition that an ontology rooted in European traditions can no longer curry enough political favour to persuade the rest of the world that it is superior to any one of a whole multiplicity of ontologies that organize human experience.

Whatever the cogency of such a relativistic stance, people's experience of Olympism in the twenty-first century, in terms of Games, images and discourse, will be quite different from that of the first 110 years of its history.

This is not merely a convenient statement issued at the beginning of the new millennium. The Olympic Movement is undergoing massive transformations. The catalyst for the reforms was the bribery scandals of February 1999 with respect to Salt Lake City's bid to host the Winter Olympic Games in 2002. The resultant enquiry exposed unethical behaviour by some members of the International Olympic Committee (IOC) and flaws in the selection procedures of Olympic host cities. The reforms which the enquiry triggered have had far-reaching effects and required a thorough re-evaluation of structures, policies and representations of the Olympic Movement. This time the process is global and comprehensive, and involves representatives from all stakeholders of the Olympic Movement – athletes, officials, government agencies, national and supra-national structures, the media, commerce and academics.

The reforms were approved by the IOC's extraordinary 110th session in Lausanne on 11–12 December 1999, and changed the Olympic Movement forever. The key changes adopted aim to ensure that the Olympic Movement in the twenty-first century will be value-driven and athlete-centred. This is to be achieved by putting in place a new decision-making process based on the following principles:

- responsibility
- inclusiveness
- transparency
- accountability
- democracy.

Most of the ideas for reform are not new and had previously been promoted with varying degrees of success by various stakeholders. For example, the debates during the Tenth (1973) and Eleventh (1981) Olympic Congresses provide ample evidence for that (Lekarska, 1986).

A broad view of the evolution of the Olympic Movement, from 1894 to the present, suggests that it has gone through several turning points, each marking a decisive transformation:

- transforming from a religious (ancient) to a secular (modern) character of the Games
- moving from being a Western European concern, with 13 participating countries in the first modern Olympic Games in 1896 in Athens, to a world project with 201 countries in the 2004 Athens Olympics
- abandoning key tenets, e.g. women's participation in sport; amateurism
- joining the 'real' world, when the Eleventh Olympic Congress in Baden-Baden in 1981 approved the commercialisation of the Olympics
- moving towards a value-driven and athlete-centred movement.

The novelty now is that the Olympic Movement in the twenty-first century is set to be truly 'value- and athlete-centred'. This orientation should shape an environment dominated by concerns about athletes and actions promoting good values, an environment that has democratic structures, shares a culture of transparency and accountability, and provides leadership for sports development throughout the world. Achieving these ideals in reality is not unproblematic, and this is what provokes different interpretations and treatments in the literature. Hence, to avoid ambiguity and bias, it is important to clarify our approach in this book.

Plate 0.2   The Olympic flag over Sydney, 2000

## THE APPROACH OF THE OLYMPIC GAMES EXPLAINED

In his lifetime Pierre de Coubertin, the founder of the modern Olympic Movement, produced over a thousand publications – books, articles and speeches. Today, to the best of our knowledge (which is by no means complete), there are about 17,000 volumes, numerous articles and papers, over 100,000 web pages and 100 films on Olympism, not to mention still images. Since the IOC presence on the Internet began in 1995, its website contains currently more than 700,000 words, 7000 images and 1200 audio and video files.

Clearly, over the past century and more the amount and the content of information have increased in complexity and structure. This has turned Olympism into a rich content domain which, with a few notable exceptions (e.g. video and film services provided by the Olympic Television Archive Bureau), is not well organised.

The traditional approach to Olympic education relies on linear media, e.g. textbooks and lectures (or 'safe' multimedia educational packages such as *Olympic Themes*, 2000), is teacher-led, offers little feedback to the learner, and is informational rather than developmental.

The use of linear media for education (or closed media, with a beginning, middle and end, e.g. books, audio or video) would have been less problematic if the subject matter of Olympism was simple and well structured. However, it is not and this is why we have developed *The Olympic Games Explained* not just as a traditional book, but as a text accompanied by a dedicated website. Such an approach allows for greater flexibility, interactivity and explorations of various Olympic themes.

*The Olympic Games Explained* seeks to introduce the complexity of modern Olympism by viewing it as a historical, cultural, social, political and economic phenomenon. The aim of the book, therefore, is to offer a comprehensive understanding of the fundamental principles, dimensions and historical developments of the modern Olympic Movement, on the one hand, and the nature of the tensions that evolved in the process of its formation, on the other. These two aspects are intertwined into a logical whole in which the former supports the comprehension of the latter, and vice-versa. In doing so, this book presents fifteen fundamental chapters for comprehending modern Olympism in its entirety. No attempt is made to promote a particular point of view: rather, different interpretations of theories and events have been put forward, and the reader is invited to evaluate them critically.

The principal function of *The Olympic Games Explained* is to create a learning environment which enables the reader to use and explore a combination of text, graphics, images, the Internet, independent study and assessment. It is an open book, complemented by additional texts and study activities on the website. Following your own pace, you can explore and critically evaluate various aspects of Olympism in an interactive way, get in touch with fellow students and experts, share ideas and develop skills.

Each chapter is a self-contained unit that can be studied independently. However, accounting for the complexity of Olympism, and in order to facilitate better understanding, there are many cross-references between chapters. The navigation system on the book's website is user-friendly and has been thoroughly tested.

We invite you to explore the fascinating world of the modern Olympic Movement and to share your views with us.

## THE OLYMPIC GAMES EXPLAINED ON THE INTERNET

*The Olympic Games Explained* is accompanied by a dedicated website. It has been designed to enhance your Olympic experience, and will enable you to explore further various topics through reference material, tables, pictures and video footage. Modules are included to enhance your writing and presentation skills.

Please take a minute to register on the book's website by visiting <www.routledge.com/textbooks/isbn>. The site is easy to navigate – just click on the relevant chapter to get access to the additional materials, or follow suggestions to other websites or other specific resources.

Enjoy your Olympic journey.

*Vassil Girginov, Luton*
*Jim Parry, Leeds*
*2004*

# ACKNOWLEDGEMENTS

Naturally, a book such as this has drawn on many sources and influences, but the authors wish to recognise their special debts to the following.

The International Olympic Academy (IOA), where they first met in 1985 at the 25th Main International Session.

The friendship and encouragement offered by the late President Nikos Nissiotis, President Nikos Filaretos and Dean Kostas Georgiadis.

The continuing and enriching contact with colleagues at the various Sessions of the IOA, and at various National Olympic Academies, especially those of Great Britain and Bulgaria.

The assistance and collaboration of: The British Olympic Association, The International Olympic Committee, The Olympic Television Archives Bureau, The London 2012 Bid, The International Paralympic Committee.

The particular expertise of: Cleanthis Palaeologos and Nikos Yalouris (Chapter 2), Sam Mullins and John MacAloon (Chapter 3), Don Masterson (Chapter 13), Daryl Siedentop (Chapter 14), and Don Anthony.

In production and general support: Tony Mangan, Frank Cass, Frank Galligan, Samantha Grant.

## CHAPTER ONE

# THE IDEA OF OLYMPISM

## Chapter aims:

- to introduce the Olympic Idea
- to develop the Idea as a universal social philosophy, with reference to the ideas of Pierre de Coubertin
- to develop the philosophy as a philosophical anthropology.

After studying this chapter you should be able to explain:

- the nature of Olympism
- the ideas of de Coubertin
- the way in which ancient and modern ideas can contribute to an idealised conception of the human being.

## INTRODUCTION

## STUDY ACTIVITY 1.1

Before you begin this chapter think about the meaning of the terms 'Olympic', 'Olympism' and 'Olympiad'. What do they mean to you?

For most people, the word 'Olympic' will conjure up images of the Olympic Games, either ancient or modern. The focus of their interest will be a two-week festival of sport held once every four years among elite athletes representing their countries or city-states in inter-communal competition.

1

Most people will also have heard of an 'Olympiad'. Although this term is sometimes thought to refer to a particular Games, it refers in fact to a four-year period, the opening of which is celebrated by a Games, and during which a Games may or may not be held. So, the Athens 2004 Games are properly referred to not as the XXVIII Games (since there have been only twenty-five, three having been cancelled owing to world wars) but as the Games of the XXVIII Olympiad.

Fewer people, however, will have heard of 'Olympism', the philosophy developed by Pierre de Coubertin. This philosophy has as its focus:

■ not just the elite athlete, but everyone
■ not just a short truce period, but the whole of life
■ not just competition and winning, but the values of participation and co-operation
■ not just sport as an activity, but also as a formative and developmental influence contributing to desirable characteristics of individual personality and social life.

## Olympism – a universal social philosophy

Olympism is a social philosophy that emphasises the role of sport in world development, international understanding, peaceful co-existence, and social and moral education. De Coubertin understood that, as physical activity grounded in rule-adherence, sport was apparently 'universalisable' – providing a contact point across cultures.

By definition a universal philosophy applies to everyone, regardless of nation, race, gender, social class, religion or ideology. The Olympic Movement has worked for a coherent universal representation of itself – a concept of Olympism that identifies a range of values to which each nation can sincerely commit itself. At the same time it is necessary to find a form of expression for the idea that is unique to itself, generated by its own culture, location, history, tradition and projected future.

De Coubertin, being a product of late nineteenth-century liberalism, emphasised the values of equality, fairness, justice, respect for persons, rationality and understanding, autonomy, and excellence. These are values that span nearly 3000 years of Olympic history, although some of them may be differently interpreted at different times. De Coubertin (1906, p. 16) said:

But now Olympia . . . has been rebuilt or rather renovated under forms which are different because modern, yet steeped in a kindred atmosphere.

The contemporary task for the Olympic Movement is to further this project: to try to see more clearly what its Games (and sport in wider society) might come to mean. This task will involve both ideas and action. If the practice of sport is to be pursued and developed according to Olympic values, the theory must strive for a conception of Olympism that will support that practice. The ideal should seek both to sustain sports practice against unjust criticism (where it exists) and to lead sport towards a vision of Olympism that will help to deal with the challenges that are bound to emerge.

---

## STUDY ACTIVITY 1.2

Before reading the next section, find the Olympic Charter at <www. olympic.org/uk/organisation/missions/charter_uk.asp> and read the sections on Fundamental Principles and the Olympic Movement.

---

## CONCEPTIONS OF OLYMPISM

Let us try to set out some of the many modern attempts there have been to capture the meaning of Olympism, to try to give a flavour of the idea in all its complexity. We will in the main simply report the position of others, but give occasional comment on some theme, where it might be necessary or useful.

### Contemporary official sources

The first words of the Olympic Charter (IOC, 2003) state simply the nature and goals of Olympism. Fundamental Principle 2 says:

> Olympism is a philosophy of life, exalting and combining in a balanced whole the qualities of body, will and mind. Blending sport with culture and education, Olympism seeks to create a way of life based on the joy found in effort, the educational value of good example and respect for universal fundamental ethical principles.
>
> (Fundamental Principle 2, IOC, 2003, p. 10)

The goal of the Olympic Movement is to contribute to building a peaceful and better world by educating youth through sport practised without discrimination of any kind and in the Olympic spirit, which requires mutual understanding with a spirit of friendship, solidarity and fair play.

(Fundamental Principle 6, IOC, 2003, p. 11)

### Pierre de Coubertin

Now let us remind ourselves of the considered ideas of the founder of the modern Olympic Movement, Pierre de Coubertin (Plate 1.1). His mature article 'The Philosophical Foundations of Modern Olympism' (1935) clarifies the idea of Olympism. It is:

(i) *A religion of sport* (the *'religio athletae'*).

I was right to create from the outset, around the renewed Olympism, a religious sentiment (transformed and widened by Internationalism, Democracy and Science) . . . This is the origin of all the rites which go to make the ceremonies of the modern Games.

(De Coubertin, 1935, p. 131)

Plate 1.1 Pierre de Coubertin

Roesch (1979, p. 199), however, argues that this is to misunderstand the nature of religious life:

> Religious life and cultic expressions take part in other forms and contents, such as gesture, attitude, ritual dance, prayer, speech and rites. The individual athlete, no matter what his religion, denomination or ideology, lives and acts according to his religious conviction as a Christian, Moslem, Buddhist, Jew and so on . . . 'Olympism' can't take the place of that.

Roesch calls the ritual elements of Olympism consciously created by de Coubertin 'pseudo-cultic' expressions and proposes four central values of Olympism, which seem to be entirely secular: freedom, fairness, friendship, peace.

This insistence on the secular nature of Olympic values seems entirely correct; but Roesch creates his contrast only by failing to take account of what de Coubertin means by 'religion', and of what he repeatedly says about the *religio athletae*. Again, the core of de Coubertin's concern here is the moral value of sport.

(ii) *An aristocracy, an elite* (but egalitarian and meritocratic). De Coubertin's political views were forged in a political context in which liberal capitalism was under threat from the rising forces of socialism. Under the influence of the sociologist Le Play, he championed the cause of the nationalist and royalist bourgeoisie. This brought with it a tendency to see the benefits of the marriage of aristocratic and meritocratic virtues.

(iii) *Chivalry* (comradeship and rivalry, and the suspension of exclusively national sentiments). Looking back to medieval times, de Coubertin saw in the ethic of chivalry a prefiguring of the modern virtues of fair play and respect for one's opponent.

(iv) *Truce* (the temporary cessation of quarrels, disputes and misunderstandings). Mimicking the ancient practice, de Coubertin (1935, p. 132) thought that the modern Olympics provided an opportunity for nations '. . . to interrupt their struggles for a moment in order to celebrate loyal and courteous muscular Games'.

(v) *Rhythm* (the Olympiad). Given its beginnings as an agrarian religious chronology, the idea of the Olympiad is tied to its function as a marker of the eight-yearly rhythms of the movements of the moon. An Olympiad marks each rhythm and half-rhythm, echoing the natural progression of season upon season, year upon year (Gardiner, 1955). De Coubertin saw the value of replicating such predictable rhythms for the Games.

(vi) *The young adult male individual*. 'It follows from what I have said that the true Olympic hero is in my view the adult male individual . . .' (De Coubertin, 1935, p.133), who alone should be able to enter the Altis, or sacred enclosure. This means that team games will be at best secondary, taking place outside the modern Altis ('. . . fittingly honoured, but in the second rank'). It also means that women 'could also take part here if it is judged necessary', although de Coubertin himself thought that they had no place even in the second rank. He says:

> I personally do not approve of the participation of women in public competitions, which is not to say that they must abstain from practising a great number of sports, provided they do not make a public spectacle of themselves. In the Olympic Games, as in the contests of former times, their primary role should be to crown the victors.
>
> (De Coubertin, 1935, p. 133)

De Coubertin is at least consistent on this:

> I still think that contact with feminine athletics is bad for him (the modern athlete) and that these athletics should be excluded from the Olympic programme.
>
> (1934, p. 129)

> As to the admission of women to the Games, I remain strongly against it. It was against my will that they were admitted to a growing number of competitions.
>
> (1928, p. 106)

There are very important corollaries of this kind of statement. For example, those who simply disparage the Muslim doctrine of 'separate but equal development' should notice the echoes of that view in de Coubertin's work, in the practice of the Ancient Olympics, and in the educational ideology of single-sex schooling throughout Europe. And those who, on other issues, call upon the authority of the thoughts of de Coubertin or of ancient practices to support their views should notice that such 'authority' does not necessarily derive from justifiable principle, and does not necessarily support their other views.

(vii) *Beauty* (artistic and literary creation). De Coubertin (1935, p. 133) was in favour of 'intellectual manifestations organised around the Games', so as to promote 'civilisation, truth, and human dignity, as well as . . . international relations'.

(viii) *Peace* (promoted by mutual respect based on mutual understanding). This is related to the ancient idea of truce, but without the modern preoccupation with the dangers and waste associated with warfare.

(ix) *Participation and competition*. Let us also add the complementary ideas of participation and competition. De Coubertin (1908, pp. 19–20) said in London at the close of the 1908 Games:

> Last Sunday, in the course of the ceremony organised at St Paul's in honour of the athletes, the bishop of Pennsylvania recalled this in felicitous words: 'the important thing in these Olympiads [sic] is less to win than to take part in them.' . . . Gentlemen, let us bear this potent word in mind. It extends across every domain to form the basis of a serene and healthy philosophy. The important thing in life is not victory but struggle; the essential is not to have won but to have fought well.

In saying this, de Coubertin gave credit to the bishop for a sentiment that was often on his own lips. Fourteen years earlier he is quoted as exhorting an audience at the Parnassus Club in Athens to support the revival of the Games (1894b, p. 10), and '. . . not to let their enthusiasm be cooled by the thought that they might be beaten by strangers. "Dishonour," he said, "would not lie in defeat, but in failure to take part."'

---

**STUDY ACTIVITY 1.3**

Do you think that these elements of Olympism still exist into the twenty-first century? Should they?

---

### Avery Brundage

Just to show how things change over a very short period of time, consider the views expressed by the former President of the International Olympic Committee (IOC), Avery Brundage, in terms that remained fairly standard (although under threat) into the 1980s:

> The first and most important of these rules, for good reasons, was that the Games must be amateur. They are not a commercial enterprise

and no-one, promoters, managers, coaches, participants, individuals or nations, is permitted to use them for profit.

(Brundage, 1963, p. 30)

How dramatically outdated this dogma now seems. As we have already remarked, if this were the first and most important of Olympic values the Games would have collapsed by now. However, the Olympic Games were revived by Baron de Coubertin, according to Brundage (1963, p. 39), in order to:

- bring to the attention of the world the fact that a national program of physical training and competitive sport will not only develop stronger and healthier boys and girls but also, and perhaps more important, will make better citizens through the character building that follows participation in properly administered amateur sport;
- demonstrate the principles of fair play and good sportsmanship, which could be adopted with great advantage in many other spheres of activity;
- stimulate interest in the fine arts through exhibitions and demonstrations, and thus contribute to a broader and more well rounded life;
- teach that sport is play for fun and enjoyment and not to make money, and that with devotion to the task at hand the reward will take care of itself – the philosophy of amateurism as contrasted to that of materialism;
- create international amity and good will, thus leading to a happier and more peaceful world.

**IN BRIEF**

## JUAN ANTONIO SAMARANCH

In an editorial for the *Olympic Review*, the former President of the IOC, Juan Antonio Samaranch (1995), appealed to six 'basic elements' of Olympic ethics:

1 tolerance
2 generosity
3 solidarity
4 friendship
5 non-discrimination
6 respect for others.

In the same editorial he also says that the principles that inspire the Olympic Movement are based on:

1 justice
2 democracy
3 equality
4 tolerance.

## THE PHILOSOPHICAL ANTHROPOLOGY OF OLYMPISM

What are we to make of this bewildering welter of ideas, offered by various writers as values, aims, goals or principles of Olympism, the Olympic Movement or the Olympic Games? The ideas so far presented are highly suggestive, but they are not systematic or coherent, and it has been possible thus far to discuss only a fraction of them – and only at a relatively superficial level.

We need to try to find a way to organise our thoughts in relation to all these ideas so that they can be pulled together into a framework that renders some version of them systematic and coherent.

A guiding thought lies in the status of Olympism as a social, political and educational ideology. Any such ideology necessarily appeals to a philosophical anthropology – an idealised conception of the human being towards which the ideology strives in its attempted social reproduction of the individual.

Social anthropology is the investigation of whole cultures, which are preferably (from the point of view of the researcher) quite alien to the researcher's own society. A social anthropologist investigates the diversity of human nature – the quite different kinds of human nature that are to be found around the world – practically, scientifically, through observation and social scientific methodology.

A philosophical anthropologist, however, tries to create a theory about human nature by thinking about human beings at the most general level. Hoberman (1984) writes about the differing political conceptions of sport, but finds it necessary to refer to several levels of explanation and theorising:

[Different societies] . . . have distinct political anthropologies or idealised models of the exemplary citizen which constitute complex answers to the fundamental question of philosophical anthropology: 'What is a human being?'

9

In order to try to fill out just what were the ideas that have been handed down from classical times, to be reinterpreted and re-specified (by de Coubertin and others) we need to examine two central ideas.

### The ideas of Kalos K'agathos and Arete

The idea of Kalos K'agathos was the guiding ideal of the ancient Athenian conception of education – being a person both good and beautiful. 'Good' (*agathos*) referred to moral development and 'beautiful' (*kalos*) referred to physical beauty, and together they referred to the ideal of a fully developed mind in a superb body, later echoed in Juvenal's dualistic tag: *mens sana in corpore sano*.

Lenk (1964, p. 206) says:

> Many representatives of the Olympic movement combine these values together to form a picture of the human being harmoniously balanced intellectually and physically in the sense of the Greek 'kalos k'agathos'.

This is also a theme in Nissiotis (1984, p. 64):

> . . . the Olympic Ideal is what qualifies sport exercise in general as a means for educating the whole man as a conscious citizen of the world . . . The Olympic Idea is that exemplary principle which expresses the deeper essence of sport as an authentic educative process through a continuous struggle to create healthy and virtuous man in the highest possible way ('*kalos k'agathos*') in the image of the Olympic winner and athlete.

Eyler (1981) pursues the meaning of the Olympic virtue of excellence in performance and in character, through Homer, early philosophers, Pindar and Pausanias. He concludes:

> In summary, arête has several meanings – distinction, duty (primarily to oneself), excellence, fame, glorious deeds, goodness, greatness, heroism . . . valour and virtue. Some of the many implications of these meanings contextually are: man is born, grows old, and dies; performance is not without risks; winning is all; man achieves by his own skills . . . human

performance is the quintessence of life; and finally, man is the measure of all things and the responsible agent.

(Eyler, 1981, p. 165)

He quotes Kitto (1951, p. 166):

... what moves a Greek warrior to heroism is not a sense of duty as we understand it, i.e. duty towards others, it is rather a duty towards oneself. He strives after that which we translate virtue or excellence, the Greek 'arête' (The Right Stuff).

Lenk (1982, p. 166) emphasises the centrality of the ideas of action and achievement:

The Olympic athlete thus illustrates the Herculean myth of culturally exceptional achievement, i.e. of action essentially unnecessary for life's sustenance that is nevertheless highly valued and arises from complete devotion to striving to attain a difficult goal.

Palaeologos (1982, p. 63) echoes the mythical origins of the Ancient Games in the deeds of one of the great heroes of antiquity, Hercules:

With the twelve labours depicted by the bas-reliefs on the two metopes of the Temple (of Zeus), the world is presented with the content of the moral teachings which Olympia intended with the Games.

As has been noted, the idea is that the sculptures of the demi-God Hercules in Olympia performed a morally educative function, standing as role models, especially for the athletes who were there to train for the Games, of physical, moral and intellectual virtue:

... Hercules is shown bearded, with beautiful features, ... a well-trained body, fine, proportioned muscles, ... as a representative of the 'kalos k'agathos' type, where the body is well-formed and harmonious, the expression of a beautiful soul, and the face radiates intelligence, kindness and integrity.

(Palaeologos, 1982, p. 67)

Nissiotis (1984, p. 66) concludes:

> The Olympic Idea is thus a permanent invitation to all sportsmen to transcend . . . their own physical and intellectual limits . . . for the sake of a continuously higher achievement in the physical, ethical and intellectual struggle of a human being towards perfection.

So, a philosophical anthropology is an idealised conception of the human. If we ask ourselves what the Olympic Idea is, it translates into a few simple phrases that capture the essence of what an ideal human being ought to be and to aspire to. From the above, and drawing on conceptions of Olympism presented in the previous section, It might be suggested that the philosophical anthropology of Olympism promotes ideals:

- of individual all-round harmonious human development
- towards excellence and achievement
- through effort in competitive sporting activity
- under conditions of mutual respect, fairness, justice and equality
- with a view to creating lasting personal human relationships of friendship,
- international relationships of peace, toleration and understanding, and
- cultural alliances with the arts.

That is the general idea – a conception of the human being who is capable of being and doing those things. This idea will have consequences for views on both the ethical issues affecting sport and on the nature of Olympic Education, to which we now turn.

---

## STUDY ACTIVITY 1.4

Do you find this conception of the human being attractive? Do you think it could form the basis of an educational ideology to which people could commit themselves?

---

## PRACTICES, VIRTUES AND PHYSICAL EDUCATION AS OLYMPIC EDUCATION

Thus far it has been the intention to show how philosophical anthropology, ethical principle and ethical practice can and should cohere. It now remains to provide an indication as to how this might translate into the educational situation. At this point, let us remind ourselves of a thought of de Coubertin's (1894b): '. . . character is not formed by the mind, but primarily by the body. The men of antiquity knew this, and we are painfully relearning it'.

The idea is that sport itself is educative – that games, for example, are laboratories for value experiments. Students are put in the position of having to act, time and time again, sometimes in haste, under pressure or provocation, either to prevent something or to achieve something, under a structure of rules. The settled dispositions which it is claimed emerge from such a crucible of value-related behaviour are those that were consciously cultivated through games in the public schools in the last century.

The suggestion is that physical education activities should be seen as 'practices' that act as a context for the development of human excellences and 'virtues' and the cultivation of those qualities of character that dispose one to act virtuously.

In an oft-quoted passage, MacIntyre (1981, p. 194) describes a 'practice' as:

> Any coherent and complex socially established co-operative human activity through which goods internal to that form of activity are realised in the course of trying to achieve those standards of excellence, and human conceptions of the ends and goods involved are systematically extended.

An educational curriculum, then, should be organised in terms of 'significant practices'. However, just which practices constitute a flourishing life, or just which practices are to be deemed significant, remains open to debate. This chapter has attempted to sketch out some considerations in favour of sport as a significant practice.

Practices, then, promote those human excellences and values that constitute a flourishing life. But, more than that, practices are the very sites of development of those dispositions and virtues which serve us in our quest for self-development. It is by participating in a practice (and by practising its skills and procedures) that one begins to understand its standards and excellences, and the virtues required for successful participation.

We do not become virtuous by learning rules. We gain virtue, and hence learn to make right decisions, by cultivating certain dispositions. This is the importance of the education of character, for the acquisition of these dispositions does not come naturally, but must be taught.

13

We acquire dispositions by first of all acting as if we had them – we train ourselves to do the right things, and gradually we gain a standing disposition to do them.

The suggestion here is that the way forward for physical education lies in the practice of sport that is influenced or informed by the philosophical anthropology (and the ethical ideals) of Olympism, providing a specification of a variety of human values and excellences which:

- have been attractive to human groups over an impressive span of time and space
- have contributed massively to our historically developed conceptions of ourselves
- have helped to develop a range of artistic and cultural conceptions that have defined Western culture
- have produced a range of physical activities that have been found universally satisfying and challenging.

Although physical activities are widely considered to be pleasurable, their likelihood of gaining wide acceptance lies rather in their intrinsic value, which transcends simple pleasure. Their ability to furnish us with pleasurable experiences depends upon our prior recognition in them of opportunities for the development and expression of valued human excellences.

In claiming that Olympic ideals may be seen not merely as inert 'ideals', but living ideas that have the power to remake our notions of sport in education, it follows that we should see sport not as mere physical activity but as the cultural and developmental activity of an aspiring, achieving, well-balanced, educated and ethical individual.

## OLYMPISM

1   Explain the main features of the idea of Olympism, and show how they may (or may not) be relevant today.
2   Evaluate the contribution of de Coubertin to our understanding of the significance of the Olympic Games.
3   Critically assess the coherence and relevance of the philosophical anthropology of Olympism as set out in this chapter, and illustrate with contemporary examples.
4   Set out a conception of physical education in schools, including a suggested outline curriculum, which you would endorse as an Olympic conception.

## CHAPTER TWO

# THE ANCIENT OLYMPIC GAMES

## Chapter aims:

- to explore the mythical origins of the ancient Games
- to describe the ancient site of Olympia
- to describe the ancient Games and their organisation
- to explain the significance of the Games for over a thousand years.

After studying this chapter you should have a much clearer picture of:

- the origin and evolution of the ancient Games
- the nature of the programme and the organisation of the Games
- the significance of athletics in the ancient world
- the demise of the Games.

## THE GODS, MYTH AND THE ORIGINS OF THE GAMES

The origins of the Olympic Games in Ancient Greece are shrouded in myth and historical interpretation.

The Ancient Greeks lived and worked in the open. For them, nature was alive and familiar, close and deeply felt. Their gods were found in nature, and they believed in the complete harmony of the natural and spiritual world. Olympia, in the district of Elis on the Pelopponesian peninsula, was always a sacred place, and its oldest temple belonged to the Great Mother Rhea, the earth goddess. Gradually, in parallel with religious ceremonies and celebrations, there developed a set of athletic contests, which came to have extraordinary meaning and significance in the political and everyday lives of citizens of the Greek city-states.

## The myth of Pelops

There are many myths that seek to explain the origin of the Olympic Games, always with reference to events that occurred under the eyes of the gods. One is the myth of Pelops, after whom the peninsula is named.

The story is that Oenomaus, King of Pisa, challenged all suitors for his daughter Hippodamea to a chariot race. During the race, he would kill each of his adversaries and then place their heads among his trophies.

Naturally, this discouraged young men from seeking his daughter's hand. But then arrived Pelops, son of Tantalus, King of Phrygia. He was both fortunate, because Hippodamea fell in love with him at first sight, and also clever, because he realised what was going on. He conspired with Oenomaus' charioteer, Myrtilus, and during the race managed to throw Oenomaus from his chariot. Oenomaus was killed and Pelops won both Hippodamea and the kingdom, but he killed Myrtilus for his treason.

To appease the gods for his bold wrong-doing, Pelops established the Olympic Games.

The myth of Pelops echoes down to the twentieth century, when George Orwell (quoted in Goodhart and Chataway, 1968, p. 3) described modern sport as 'war minus the shooting', and Chris Chataway, an Olympic athlete, co-authored a book called *War Without Weapons* (Goodhart and Chataway, 1968). The earlier form of contest was that of mortal combat, in which the triumph of the victor meant the death of the adversary. In the Olympic Games, however, contest took on the nobler form of rule-governed and disciplined athletic competition. The instinct for murder was 'civilised' and became the drive for victory on the athletic field.

The chariot race of Pelops and Oenomaus was to be the last deadly incident in the sacred site of Olympia. From that time in Olympia – after the death of the murderous and arrogant Oenomaus – a black ram was sacrificed instead of a human victim. This shift from primitive bloody antagonism to fair and peaceful competition constitutes the starting-point of the Olympic Games.


## The myth of Hercules

Another myth sees Hercules as the heroic founder of the Games. Of the Twelve Labours of Hercules, six took place on the Pelopponese, and the next six all over the rest of the known world, including the underworld, where he wrestled Cerberus, the guard-dog, and brought him to Mycenae.

The Fifth Labour, the Cleaning of the Augean Stables, was staged in Elis. The King of Elis, Augeas, owned vast herds of cattle, but had been remiss in cleaning out their stables, which were full of the dung of thousands of animals.

The problem was two-fold: the local fields were becoming infertile because the dung had not been spread on them, and the filth of the stables threatened to pollute the whole of Elis. Hercules cleverly solved both problems by diverting the rivers Peneus and Alpheos, whose currents both washed out the stables and deposited the dung on the fields. However, Augeas did not keep his promise to Hercules to reward him with a tenth of his kingdom, so Hercules deposed him, gave his kingdom to his successor, and established the Olympic Games to celebrate his victory.

Notice that Hercules' labour was achieved not just by brute force, but also by intelligence: a marriage of muscle and mind. Also, his goals were honourable: the aim of his struggle was to serve the people of Elis. He represents the nobility of physical strength in the rational pursuit of the good: a model of the ideal Olympic hero.

The Twelve Labours of Hercules were depicted in twelve bas-reliefs on the façades of the temple of Zeus in Olympia, as reminders to athletes and others of the virtues to which they ought to aspire. More will be said of the meaning of these sculptures for the Olympic Idea in Chapter 13.


## THE OLYMPIC FESTIVAL AND THE EVOLUTION OF THE GAMES

There was a prehistoric Iron Age settlement at Olympia in the twelfth century BC following the invasion of the Dorians from the north, and remains suggest a particular role for the strategically placed hamlet.

Olympia has been a sacred place since very early times. Thousands of votive offerings have been found there dating from at least the tenth century BC, left by a fertility cult associated with an oracle of Rhea, the earth goddess.

But Zeus was the supreme Greek god, and the grove known as the Altis at Olympia became his most sacred place, beautifully situated at the foot of Mount Kronos and named after the husband of Rhea and the father of Zeus. As the cult of Zeus gained ground, people used the grove for worship at altars and for hanging offerings from the trees: primitive figures of people and animals made from terracotta or even bronze have been found there.

However, local disputes interrupted celebrations, which some say included games and contests, until 884 BC, when local rulers King Iphitus of Elis, lawgiver Lycurgus of Sparta and Archon Cleosthenes of Pisa, made a truce and revived the festival.

The terms of this sacred truce were engraved on a bronze disc, which still existed in the time of Pausanias the traveller and chronicler, who described it in the second century AD; however, we have no specific record of any games that might have taken place.

## STUDY ACTIVITY 2.1

See if you can find the work of Pausanias in your library and search for his accounts of Olympia.

Find a book on Pindar and read one of his Victory (Epinician) Odes. Does it impress upon you the significance of the contest and of victory for the ancient Greeks?

The Olympic festival marked the beginning (and later also the middle point) of a Great Year of eight years. Thus an Olympiad was a period of four years, with each Olympiad celebrating one Games. This became a standard way of marking the calendar in ancient times.

It was a festival of Zeus, held in early autumn, a season of rest from agricultural work and celebration of fertility – a sort of Harvest Festival. Gardiner (1925) also saw it as a festival of 'lustration', involving ceremonies of purification by making offerings to the gods.

The ancient Olympic Games, so far as we know, began at Olympia in 776 BC. Some authorities say that the first official event, a simple straight sprint race of about 192 metres, originated in a race to light the flame that would have been used for the sacrifice to Zeus.

This festival to the greatest of gods attracted athletes and citizens from all over the Greek city-states and colonies, which meant most of the known world at the time. It meant a truce from war and an opportunity for all Greeks to meet on neutral and sacred territory. This truce established Olympia not as one amongst many of the Greek city-states, but as a place apart – both neutral and sacred – a place where Greek society and culture could attain and represent its self-awareness and self-identity.

And of course the greatest of Games were held, at which only free-born warriors of the Greek tribes might compete. As Swaddling (1980) says:

> there is no modern equivalent for Ancient Olympia. It would have to be a site combining a sports complex and a centre for religious devotion – something like a cross between Wembley Stadium and Westminster Abbey.

The Games were held every four years until they were banned by the Roman Emperor Theodosius I in AD 394. The last Games, the 293rd, were held in AD 393, and so they had been held continuously for 1168 years. This astonishing record in itself demands the attention of students of history. Apart from the rituals of some of the major world religions, what other human institution has lasted as long?

## THE SITE AT OLYMPIA

An Englishman, Richard Chandler, rediscovered Olympia in 1766 and a team of French archaeologists visited the site in 1829. But in 1875 full-scale investigations were begun by the German government of Kaiser Wilhelm I, under the supervision of Professor Ernst Curtius of the University of Berlin, and with the permission of the Greek authorities. Excavations continue to the present day, but the general contours of the site and its principal buildings and treasures are now well understood.

### The great altar of Zeus

This altar is thought to have existed from the tenth century BC. It was built from the ashes of sacrificed animals which, when mixed with water from the river Alpheus, formed a cement-like paste, thus building to a height of seven metres.

## The temple of Zeus

This huge temple took ten years to build and was completed in 456 BC (Plate 2.1). It had thirty-four columns and a roof made of Pentelic marble (from a famous quarry near Athens, 300 kilometres away). Among its many great sculptures were those occupying the two triangular pediments to front and rear of the roof, where two mythical scenes were depicted.

Although many of the sculptures are lost, the modern museum at Olympia provides an impressive attempt at reconstruction. Around the temple were innumerable altars, statues, offerings, pillars, temples, arcades, galleries and buildings. Pausanias counted 69 altars and Pliny counted 3000 statues.

## The statue of Zeus

The temple's main function was to house the cultic statue of the god, which was one of the seven wonders of the ancient world. It was 13 metres high, built

Plate 2.1 The ruins of the temple of Zeus

by Pheidias from the best and most expensive materials available. Pausanias describes it to us from his visit in the second century AD:

> The god is seated on a throne. He is made of gold and ivory, and on his head is a wreath representing sprays of olive. In his right hand stands a figure of Nike, also of gold and ivory . . . The sandals of the god are of gold, and so is his robe . . . The throne is adorned with gold, precious stones, ebony and ivory; it is painted and carved with figures.
>
> (Pausanias, *Description of Greece*, V, II.1–2, 9)

### The Temple of Hera

This temple is the earliest remaining building in Olympia, built to honour Zeus's wife, Hera, whose cult pre-dates the Olympic cult of Zeus. The Heraia were Games held in her name, exclusively for women, with only one event, the foot-race (Plate 2.2).

Plate 2.2 The Temple of Hera, where the Olympic flame is born

## Pheidias' workshop

This is where Pheidias designed and constructed the statue of Zeus, so it was built to the same proportions as the interior of the temple. Fragments of gold, ivory, glass and precious stones were excavated here, together with a cup inscribed, 'I belong to Pheidias'.

## The Nike of Paionios

This statue of Victory has largely survived, and a reconstructed version impressively dominates the modern museum. She looked down, as if hovering, from a nine-metre pedestal in front of the Temple of Zeus, which is still standing today.

## Treasuries

A row of treasuries existed at the foot of Mount Kronos, built by colonies to represent their status to the motherland, and to house precious objects and money.

## The stadium

Originally, races were run within the Altis, or sacred precinct, and the finishing line was close to the Altar of Zeus, in whose honour they were held. Later, in the fourth century BC, a new stadium was built outside the Altis, with a 32-metre-long connecting tunnel, which still exists. The length of the track is 600 Olympic feet (as myth has it, measured by the feet of Hercules), or 192 metres. Embankments were built so as to allow a view for over 40,000 spectators.

## Gymnasium and palaestra

The Gymnasium was built for training and indoor practice. It had a track exactly the same size as the stadium track within it as well as space for throwing events. The palaestra was a training facility for combat and jumping events, and also a kind of social club for the athletes.

### Baths and swimming-pool

Bathing facilities existed from the fifth century BC, with hot and cold running water, and the swimming pool, 24 metres long, 16 metres wide and 1.6 metres deep, was unique in Ancient Greece.

Of course, there were many other buildings on the site, but clearly this was a substantial and well-equipped facility, whose construction and maintenance would have been very expensive.

---

**STUDY ACTIVITY 2.2**

See the site at Ancient Olympia at <http://www.culture.gr/2/21/211/21107a/e211ga02.html>.

Apart from the athletics facilities, what evidence is there of other cultural activity at the site? Visit the website <http://www.forthnet.gr/olympics>.

---

### THE EVENTS AND THE PROGRAMME

Events held at the ancient Games over more than a millennium varied considerably over such an extended period of time.

In the beginning (776 BC is the earliest recorded date) only the 'stade' was run, or at least was officially recorded. The stade was one length of the stadium, which at Olympia was approximately 192 metres. It is still possible to place one's feet in the marble starting blocks at one end of the excavated stadium at Olympia, and to run the full stade.

It is thought that initially (for the first 13 Olympiads) only the stade event was held, but other events were added over time. The *diaulos* was introduced in the 14th Olympiad and in the 18th *wrestling* and the *pentathlon* were added. Boxing was included in the 25th Olympiad along with the *tethrippos* (four-horse chariot race) and the 30th Olympiad saw the inclusion of the horse race and the *pankration*. This last event was a kind of all-in wrestling in which only biting and gouging were not allowed and in which strangling and submission moves often brought victory. Later the *hoplite* race was added, which was a long-distance running event in armour.

For quite a period (as long as there were few events) it was possible to complete the programme in one day. But as more events were added an additional day was required until finally the whole of the festivity lasted five days.

IN BRIEF

## A TYPICAL OLYMPIC PROGRAMME

*Day 1*
Ceremonies and a contest for heralds and trumpeters

*Day 2*
Chariot races in the morning
Pentathlon in the afternoon

*Day 3*
Sacrifice to Zeus in the morning
Footraces in the afternoon

*Day 4*
Wrestling
Boxing
Pankration
The hoplite race (in armour)

*Day 5*
Prize-giving ceremony
Ceremony of thanksgiving
A banquet

Three days only were devoted to the holding of the Games themselves, whilst the first and last days were necessary for the great religious rituals and sacrifices.

## Day 1

The first day was taken up with the opening of the festival in the Altis, and the oath-taking ceremony, which took place in front of the statue of Zeus. The athletes, their relatives and their trainers were required to swear over the entrails of a boar that they would not cheat at the Olympic Games. The athletes then gave a further oath to the effect that they had carefully prepared for the games over a period of ten months. The judges, who determined the eligibility of the participants for their respective events, were also required to give a solemn oath that they would deliver their verdicts honestly and would refuse all bribes.

After 396 BC a contest for heralds and trumpeters was the first event at the Games, the winning trumpeter starting the events and the winning herald declaring the verdict of the judges.

## Day 2

In the early days of the festival the equestrian events consisted of chariot races with teams of four. At first they were fully grown horses but subsequently colts were also used and for a while even mules. In 480 BC races with two-horse teams were introduced. These were also initially for fully grown horses but were subsequently extended to include colts. The horse racing was probably four stades in length, or 769 metres; the four-horse chariot races for fully grown horses was 9229 metres; the two-horse chariot races was 6153 metres.

The pentathlon consisted of:

- the discus
- the long jump
- the javelin
- running (the stade)
- wrestling.

The second day closed with the obsequies (funeral rites) for Pelops, which were held at nightfall and reinforced the relationship between religion and sport, which was always a feature of the ancient Games.

## Day 3

The sacrifice to Zeus – the main sacrifice at the Games – involved a procession to the altar of Zeus where one hundred bulls were sacrificed.

The foot races in the afternoon included:

- the *stade* (one length of the stadium or 192 metres)
- the *diaulos* (two stades or 384 metres)
- the *dolichos* (probably 24 stades or 4614 metres).

Some authorities suggest that the third day of the festival closed with a ritual banquet, at which the guests ate the meat of the sacrificial animals.

## Day 4

The events held on this day were:

- wrestling
- boxing
- pankration
- hoplite (race in armour).

## Day 5

Once the prize-giving ceremony and banquet were over, the delegations and citizens, teams and individuals, athletes and spectators, would turn their minds to the preparations required for the sometimes very long journeys back to the furthest edges of the Greek Empire.

## THE ORGANISATION

### The spondophori

Ten months before the Games, the Olympic heralds, accompanied by a colourful retinue, set out to all parts of the land, to proclaim that the rituals for the ceremonials of the Olympic Games were starting. They arrived at city-states as official representatives of the region of Elis, while the nobles of the cities received them with honours and accepted the proclamation. From that moment the operation of the truce (ekecheiria) was in force, as also was the ten-month compulsory training period for athletes.

### The ekecheiria

The truce was a sort of armistice, a cessation of hostilities. Warfare ceased until the completion of the Games, and this was a major contribution not only to the organisation of a Games with authority over the whole of Greece, but also to the unification of the various Greek states and colonies.

27

## The theoriae

Each city receiving the proclamation considered itself honour-bound to send a delegation to the Games. These *theoriae* represented the greatness of their cities, which vied with each other in the splendour of their delegation, and the great value of the gifts they brought for Zeus and the rulers of Elis.

The tremendous expense of the organisation of the Games, of the building and upkeep of temples and altars, was such that the people of Elis could not undertake them on their own, but only with the willing and rich contribution of the whole of Greece. All the expenses of the Games were covered by the rich votive offerings given by spectators, by the presents made by delegations, and by fines imposed on athletes or cities contravening the rules.

## The hellenodicae

The whole organisation of the Games, the maintenance of the regulations, judging and the general supervision of the Games were in the hands of the judges. The *hellenodicae* were elected from among the highly esteemed citizens of Elis, ten months before the Games, and the eldest was the chairman. Their decisions were final and there was no appeal.

## THE RULES

The whole of this great festival was governed by traditions maintained by the Elians, who trained the judges for each Olympic Games.

The regulations and instructions that governed the Olympic Games are referred to by the poet Pindar as the Ordinances of Zeus.

The contestants were required to:

- be free-born Greeks – participation was not permitted to slaves and non-Greeks
- be male – women were prohibited even from attending the Games; only one woman could enter the stadium and she was the priestess of the Temple of Demetra, who had a special seat at an altar opposite the seats of the judges. Separate games were held for women, such as the Games of Hera, but there was only a foot race, with the distance of the stade shortened by one-sixth

- not have been declared as dishonourable or convicted of ungodliness
- prove that they had trained for ten months prior to the Games
- appear a month prior to the start of the Games in front of the panel of judges and remain for a month in training at Olympia
- appear in their set places in the stadium naked.

## Penalties

Penalties were imposed for rule-breaking, and included flogging, fines and exclusion of the athlete and even of his home city from the contests. Floggings often took place on the spot and were administered by the rod-bearers, who carried sticks or wicker canes and were under the orders of the judges.

## The prize

The prize was called the *athlon* and was a head-wreath of *cotinus* (a branch of wild olive). The significance of the prize was incalculable. The Games were a matter of pride and honour and were contested with fair play and with dignity in order to obtain a plain wreath-crown treasured more than anything else. This would be offered as a priceless decoration by the victor to his household, city or nation, to his ancestors and to the gods.

Of course, this does not mean that successful athletes were not also rewarded in other ways. As Young (1984) has conclusively demonstrated, Olympic champions received not only cash and other prizes at non-Olympic competitions, but also a number of sometimes very substantial benefits from their home communities, upon whom they had brought such honour and prestige.

## THE ATMOSPHERE AND THE SIGNIFICANCE

In addition to the athletic events, there would be religious activities, including the ritual sacrifice of animals: we have already mentioned the hundred bulls that were sacrificially roasted, and the amount of time during the Games devoted to ritual and ceremony. Remember that attendances in this rural location were said to have exceeded 40,000, so let us absorb the descriptions of Palaeologos (1985, p. 68):

Olympia's glory was extraordinary. Large crowds used to come every four years to worship at the sanctuaries, admire the great works of art, listen to historians, poets and rhapsodists and watch the statuesque men, well-built boys and wingfooted horses competing in fascinating contests. For many centuries, Olympia had become a panhellenic centre . . . In Olympia the great Themistocles was acclaimed, Herodotus read a part of his history, Plato spoke and Demosthenes, Ippias, Prodicus, Anaximenes, Pindar, Simonides, Thucydides, Polus, Gorgias, Anaxagoras, Diogenes the cynic, Lucian came as spectators.

Olympia, centre of a cult of Zeus, enveloped in mystic ceremony, with gatherings of thousands on neutral territory, ameliorated political discord and led to a belief in common values and a common consciousness, contributing to the unity of the Greek world.

These pan-Hellenic festivals were much more than athletic meetings, since Olympia became the meeting-place of the whole Greek world. As we have noted, many cities – some of them from overseas colonies – sought to secure themselves a permanent standing at the sanctuary by dedicating little temples or treasuries. Thus the site became immensely richer than could have been produced or sustained from local resources alone.

## STUDY ACTIVITY 2.3

Imagine a time with no Olympic Games, no football World Cup and no athletics World Cup. What benefits can you see in the introduction of such events, especially the Olympic Games?

## THE GOLDEN YEARS, AS CELEBRATED BY PINDAR

Pindar is one of our richest sources for understanding the qualities of Olympic (and other) Games. His 'Epinician Odes', which commemorate the success of a winner in the Games or other athletic meetings, are his only works to have survived almost intact, although the fragments show that he wrote much besides. His career as a writer of victory odes spans at least 52 years.

What Pindar catches is the joy beyond ordinary emotions as it transcends and transforms them. It can be found in athletic success, convivial relaxation, song and music, friendship and love, in many natural sights and sounds, in prayer and hymns. He is a religious poet . . . the poet's task is to catch and keep the fleeting divine moment and to reveal to men what really matters in their busy bustling lives.

(Bowra, 1969, p. xvi)

The fact that such an eminent national poet worked to so many athletic commissions is evidence of the supreme importance of athletic success and fame to the Greeks.

However, it was also noticed that moral and political benefits were to be had. In Lucian's dialogue between Solon and Anarcharsis, Solon says:

We compel them to train and tire their bodies not only for the sake of the games and of winning prizes – because very few of them achieve such high performances so as to obtain them – but because we expect that a much greater good will ensue for the city-state and for themselves.

(West, 1753, p. 220)

Those few victors were shown as examples worth following, so that young men were encouraged to exercise their bodies. Later, formal intellectual education also became a part of the compulsory education of a young man, as the 'gymnasium' was infiltrated by academics. Aristotle still maintained that:

The legislator's first and foremost task is to see to it that the city's men grow strong and to choose the best means to enable them to lead an excellent life.

(Politics 2, 13)

Right from the start the legislator must see to it that the bodies of young men become excellent.

(Politics 2, 14)

## ANCIENT ATHLETICS

Of the development of athletics in ancient times, Gardiner (1955) says:

The story of ancient athletics is the story of Greek athletics. The Greeks, as far as we know, were the only truly athletic nation of antiquity. To them we owe the word 'athlete' and the ideal that it expresses.

Gardiner distinguishes between the love of play, which he considers to be universal, and the love of athletic competition.

> The child plays till he is tired and then leaves off. The competitor in a race goes on after he is tired, goes on to the point of absolute exhaustion; he even trains himself painfully in order to be capable of greater and more prolonged effort and of exhausting himself more completely. Why does he do this? Why does he take pleasure in what is naturally painful?
>
> (Gardiner, 1955, p. 1)

He identifies four main ideas in Ancient Greek athletics:

- effort (derived from the same root as the word for athlete)
- contest or competition, excellence and honour
- the real prize is the honour of victory, and the motivation that turns the athlete's effort into joy
- the desire to put to the test his physical powers, to rise above the ordinary; the desire to excel, to be the best that a human can be.

The Ancient Greeks were serious about their athletics: this was no mere play. They were the first amongst humans to institutionalise play-like activities into 'athletics' – competitions as important to them as their art, their religion and their morality, in which a man could achieve distinction through his excellence against all others in equal competition.

We hope that we have shed some light on how the Games originated, and provided some hints as to what relevance they might have for us today. In understanding the role played by athletic contests in the lives of the Ancient Greeks and in wondering what produced their motivation to effort, competition and excellence, we come to understand a little more about the society upon whose ideas and achievements so much of Western civilisation is based.

## THE DEMISE OF THE GAMES

Some believe that the decline in importance of the Games after the fourth century BC can be traced to a single cause: the decline of the Olympic religion after the Pelopponesian War when its teachings and conventions came under challenge.

Others consider that there is a more complex story to be told, with reference to a series of political and economic changes, including the threat from German tribes to the north, and the influence of the Roman Empire. But, whatever the reasons for the decline and eventual demise of this long tradition, it was also long forgotten. After twelve centuries of celebration of sport and religion at the ancient Olympics there then followed another thirteen centuries during which the physical remains and, along with them, the moral and spiritual legacy of Olympia, were destroyed and then buried.

The first ravages were at the hands of the Goths in AD 393, and the Christians who wanted to destroy the idols. A few years earlier, the magnificent ivory and gold statue of Zeus had been transported from the temple of Olympia to Constantinople, where it was destroyed in the great fire that broke out in the city in AD 475. After the Goths, destruction after destruction followed. A large fire, in 426, destroyed the temple of Zeus and other buildings. Then came earthquakes in 522, 551 and the biggest in 580, destroying everything that had remained standing.

Christians used the marble to build a church and the Byzantines completed the damage by erecting a wall. Then followed the great flood of the Kladeos River, which covered everything under five metres of water. On the other side the Alpheus covered the hippodrome and the stadium, so that the whole site was covered in metres of silt.

It would be many centuries before the flame was rekindled.

---

### STUDY ACTIVITY 2.4

Do you think that the Ancient Greek ideal still has something to say to modern people all over the world?

# THE ANCIENT OLYMPIC GAMES

1   It is often difficult to see how 'modern' practices have developed from ancient (even mythical) origins. Try to provide an explanation of how the ancient Olympic Games might have developed from prehistoric times.

2   Explain the attraction of the Olympic Games to Ancient Greeks, and critically assess the benefits they saw in practising athletics.

3   Try to reconstruct a typical celebration of the ancient Olympic Games in its most developed and successful period.

4   The ancient Games were held for nearly 1200 years. Why did they end?

## CHAPTER THREE

# REVIVAL OF THE MODERN OLYMPIC GAMES

**Chapter aims:**

- to illustrate the links between ancient and modern versions of the Games
- to stress the importance of revivalist efforts in the nineteenth century
- to show how de Coubertin's idea built on and developed those efforts into a modern edition of the Games in 1896.

After studying this chapter you should be able to explain:

- the relative absence of organised sport in the Middle Ages
- the nature of the 'pseudo-Olympic' revivals
- the role of de Coubertin in re-establishing the Games.

## SPORTING ACTIVITY ACROSS THE CENTURIES

For thirteen centuries Olympia lay buried and forgotten, but physical and sportive contests did not. Although the Christian Emperor Theodosius I abolished the Games in AD 394, and the last gladiatorial contests were held in Rome in 404, chariot races and beast fights continued into the sixth century. Elsewhere in Europe, Celtic Games were held from the seventh to the twelfth centuries, and the 'Highland Gatherings' of Scottish Celts (Gaels) were established by King Malcolm the Sixth in 1040. Contests included a 2000-yard race, a cross-country race, high jump, long jump, triple jump (with both standing and running starts), and stone- and hammer-throwing.

35

The popularity of such events is well attested to in Britain throughout the eleventh to seventeenth centuries and, additionally, the chivalric education of the knightly classes throughout the Middle Ages involved robust preparation for hand-to-hand combat, including well-regulated contests. Folk feasts and festivals for the people were often accompanied by contests such as races and jumping competitions, sometimes with very exact local rule specifications.

By the mid-seventeenth century, the practice of 'pedestrianism' had developed. Gentlemen employed 'footmen' to take messages for them, since they were often faster and more efficient than other methods, and trained them up for the purpose. Soon, the footmen were participating in contests upon which their gentlemen were betting. Prizes were high, and the competitions developed into great events. Many gentlemen took up training themselves and entered into challenge matches and other contests. Names and performances were recorded, and watches were made that timed to the half-second. Later, in 1731, the first stopwatch was made, and the first races timed by three separate watches.

So, pedestrianism led to the era of modern athletics. Athletics clubs were set up in Britain and the USA in the first half of the nineteenth century, and schools, colleges and universities ran track and field meetings. In Britain, the first national championships in athletics took place in 1866, and the Football Association Challenge Cup competition began in 1871. Many sports received their definitive rule codes during a short period towards the end of the nineteenth century.

From this we can see that the value and attraction of the physical and sporting contest was alive and well – and that, by the end of the nineteenth century, the world was ready for international competition.

---

## STUDY ACTIVITY 3.1

Visit the website <http://www.aafla.com> and search for articles on pedestrianism. From the 'home page' click 'search', enter 'pedestrianism' and check the first tick-box, 'search whole site'. What evidence can you find that pedestrianism was a precursor of modern athletics?

---

### OLYMPIA REDISCOVERED

Meanwhile, the Europe-wide renaissance of interest in Ancient Greek thought and life brought travellers to the region.

As described in the previous chapter, the site of Olympia was destroyed by two major earthquakes in the late fourth century AD, which brought down the massive columns and destroyed the walls of the sanctuary. The river Kladeos burst its banks and washed away the gymnasium, and in the late Middle Ages the river Alphaeos changed course and flooded the area, covering it with silt to an average depth of four metres. The site was hidden and became forgotten.

But in 1766 an English traveller, Richard Chandler, rediscovered the site while on a mission from the Society of Dilettanti, and a team of French archaeologists investigated further in 1829. However, it wasn't until 1875 that full-scale excavations were carried out by the German archaeologist Curtius with the support of the German government, and with the consent of the Greek authorities. Early reports of their work must have made an impression on the young de Coubertin. In 1936 the German Institute of Archaeology began detailed work that continues to this day.

Today it is possible to visit the remains at the ancient site of Olympia and to recreate in the mind the splendours of the past. To assist the imagination, the local museum next to the archaeological site contains a model reconstruction. The rivers Kladeos and Alpheos follow their modern courses, and the hill that is Mount Kronion may be climbed with a brief but steep walk.

## 'PSEUDO-OLYMPICS' – SEVENTEENTH TO NINETEENTH CENTURY REVIVALS

As we have seen, deprived of the legacy of Ancient Greece, the Middle Ages in Europe saw very different forms of physical competition from those of Olympia, including chivalric tournaments and many forms of folk games and contests.

However, a series of attempts to recreate the Olympic Games was initiated from the beginning of the seventeenth century, illustrating the rediscovery of Olympic ambitions. Redmond (1988) refers us to many attempts at re-establishing the Olympic Games prior to 1896:

**1604** Revival of the Cotswold 'Olympick Games' by Robert Dover: lasted intermittently until 1857, revived in 1952

**1819** Celtic Highland Games revived in St Fillans, Scotland, and spread by emigrants to Australia, Canada, New Zealand, South Africa and the USA

37

**1839** An Olympic Games in Sweden

**1844** An Olympic Games in Montreal

**1849** Much Wenlock Olympian Games in Shropshire, England, organised by William Penny Brookes

**1853** Franconi's Hippodrome in New York featured 'many of the most attractive games of ancient Greece and Rome'

**1853** The Boston Caledonian Games

**1856** The New York Caledonian Games

**1859** Evangelis Zappas attempts to revive the Olympic Games in Athens

**1862** First Olympic Festival in Liverpool, England – the Athletics Club of Liverpool

**1866** First Olympic Festival of the Athletic Society of Great Britain in Llandudno, Wales

**1866** First National Olympian Games in London

**1870** Second attempt to revive the Olympic Games in Greece (Athens)

**1875** Third Olympic Games at Athens

**1888/89** Fourth Olympic Games at Athens

**1892** An 'Anglo-Saxon Olympiad' proposed by J. Astley Cooper: unsuccessful but initiated the idea of the British Empire Games, later known as the Commonwealth Games.

These many and varied attempts at reviving the idea of ancient Olympic competition, or at least claiming the appellation 'Olympic' to dignify their proceedings, are also evidence of a revival of interest in the underlying values and virtues of organised sport.

Despite the fact that most of these attempts were unsuccessful in the long run, they nevertheless provided a link between the ancient and the modern forms of sport, and between the ideas of the ancients and of such revivers as de Coubertin.

Some of the notable Olympic revivals in Britain – Robert Dover's Cotswold Games, the Much Wenlock Games of William Penny Brookes, and the Liverpool Olympic Festival – are described in detail in Chapter 4. Doubtless there are many more such manifestations awaiting discovery by historians.

## ZAPPAS' GREEK OLYMPIC GAMES

During the nineteenth century there were developments in Greece also. In 1856, a wealthy Greek expatriate, Evangelis Zappas, a landowner in Romania, was enthused by an article he had read about the revival of the Olympic Games and offered to pay for a games to be held in Athens.

The offer, made to King Othon, was passed to the foreign minister, Alexander Rangarbe, who thought the offer ridiculous, given the pressing economic and social needs of Greece. Nevertheless, he was reluctant to turn the offer down, but insisted that the games should be held together with industrial and commercial exhibitions.

The games were eventually held in November 1859, but were considered to be of a poor standard and badly organised. Events held were:

- the stade (one length of the stadium)
- the diablos (two stades)
- the dolichos (seven stades)
- the high jump
- the long jumps
- the discus
- the javelin.

Curiously, the discus had events for distance and height, and the javelin had events for distance and accuracy.

Some note the comical finale: a contest of climbing the greasy pole. A tall pole had been smeared with soap, and prizes hung on the top, including a silk belt, some silk handkerchiefs, two bottles of wine, a dozen spoons and two silver-plated candlesticks. The first contestant failed to reach the top, but carried away with him most of the soap, so that four finally reached the top and took the prizes.

When Zappas died in 1865 he left his fortune to his cousin Constantine on condition that it be spent on the project of reviving the Games. Another Games was held in 1870, when many thousands of spectators attended events at the Panathenian stadium, and two more followed in 1875 and 1888/89.

When Constantine Zappas died in 1892, the Romanian government refused to allow the execution of his cousin's will to continue, and the Greek government had to pay for the completion of the Zappeion Hall. The renovation of the

Panathenian stadium had to wait until 1896 for completion. (For a detailed account of the background from a Greek perspective, see Georgiadis 2004.)

---

**STUDY ACTIVITY 3.2**

On Zappas and other Greek revivalists, see <http://www.forthnet.gr/olympics/>.

On British revivalists, see the article by Mullins (1984) at <http://www.ioa.leeds.ac.uk>. Compare the different emphases you find, and try to assess the relative contributions of the various actors to the eventual revival of the Games in 1896.

---

### PIERRE DE COUBERTIN'S IDEA

The French aristocrat Pierre de Coubertin, encouraged by the success and vision of William Perry Brookes, inspired by the role of sport in the English public school (see Chapter 3), and motivated by the discoveries of the German archaeologist Curtius, who had uncovered the ancient stadium in Olympia (see Chapter 2), sought to reinstate the Games as an international multi-sport festival.

Believing that the Ancient Greek heritage remained at the core of Western civilisation and that modern sport in its moral characteristics (though not in its techniques, organisation or programme) was largely continuous with Ancient Greek athletics, de Coubertin began to dream of a 'revival' of the Olympic Games on an international basis.

In the late 1880s and early 1890s, de Coubertin devoted much of his energy and personal finances to laying the groundwork for the revival. He founded and directed the Union des Societes Francaises de Sports Athletiques and the Revue Athletique, organising local and bi-national competitions, and identifying foreign allies in his travels. De Coubertin travelled to the USA in 1889 and again in 1893 where he met many politicians, academics and physical educators. One of them, William M. Sloane, a professor of political science at Princeton, became instrumental in the success of the Olympic project. Throughout this period, de Coubertin drew upon the tradition of international expositions and world congresses that were such an important part of late nineteenth-century Euro-American cultural life.

40

Aware of the political and economic power possessed by both the USA and Great Britain at the time, de Coubertin put himself, Charles Herbert and William Sloane at the head of the organisation for the Sorbonne Congress.

This 'immoveable trinity' was selected for geopolitical reasons and each member was entrusted with the responsibility of ensuring support from different regions of the world:

- Herbert for Great Britain and the British Empire
- Sloane for the American continent
- De Coubertin for France and Continental Europe.

The first Olympic Congress was convened at the University of the Sorbonne on 23 June 1894, with 79 delegates from 14 countries and 49 athletic societies. It was at this congress that the International Olympic Committee was born, with eight honorary members elected from each of the four 'home countries'.

The first seven agenda items addressed the topical and important issue of amateurism, and the eighth suggested the possibility of the re-establishment of the Olympic Games. The Congress approved de Coubertin's suggestions, and agreed that the first Games should be held in 1896.

The resolutions included four-year intervals for the Games, exclusively modern sports, exclusion of competitions for children, the movement of the Games from site to site, and a permanent International Olympic Committee whose members would represent Olympism in their respective countries (Plate 3.1).

Despite originally planning on Paris as the venue, de Coubertin agreed with his Greek colleague, Vikelas, that a symbolic link with the past would be created by holding the first modern Games in Athens, and they were organised for April 1896 (Plate 3.2). Shortly after the Paris Congress, de Coubertin visited Olympia. In his essay 'Olympia', written many years later in 1929, de Coubertin says:

> I therefore invite you . . . to come and sit on the wooded slopes of Mount Kronion at the hour when beyond the Alpheus the rising sun begins to touch the swelling hills with gold and to lighten the green meadows at their feet . . .

> On a morning in November 1894 I became aware in this sacred place of the enormity of the task which I had undertaken in proclaiming five months earlier the restoration of the Olympic Games after an interruption of fifteen hundred years; . . .

Plate 3.1 Members of the International Olympic Committee in Athens, 1896. Standing (left to right): W. Gebhardt (Germany), Guth-Jarkovsky (Czechoslovakia), F. Kemeny (Hungary), V. Balck (Sweden); seated (left to right): P. de Coubertin (France), D. Vikelas (Greece), A. de Butovsky (Russia) (Frank Cass Library)

> From this lovely pine forest which climbs Mount Kronion . . . it is possible to recreate in imagination the long avenues of plane trees along which there once came the athletes and pilgrims, the embassies and the commerce, all the traffic and all the ambition . . .
>
> Altis – the sacred precinct – immediately reveals itself as a religious focus, the centre of a cult. Among this people and above all at this time it is difficult to imagine a religion not based upon a positive philosophical conception.
>
> Let us therefore look for this basis. And if there really was a religion of athletics . . . let us find out why it is in Greece that it took shape, and whether the Greek ideal . . . is still suited to the rest of humanity.
>
> (p. 107)

Plate 3.2 Poster for the Athens Games, 1896 (British Olympic Association Library)

## STUDY ACTIVITY 3.3

On the role of Pierre de Coubertin, see <http://www.olympic.org/uk/passion/museum/permanent/coubertin/index/uk.asp>.

Write an account of his contribution to reviving the Olympic idea.

**IN BRIEF**

## KEY FEATURES OF THE REVIVAL OF THE OLYMPIC GAMES

- The general developments of sports and athletic contests in the nineteenth century
- Archaeological advances in Olympia

43

- The commitment of Greeks such as the Zappas cousins
- The many revival attempts, including those of W.P. Brookes
- The ideas of Pierre de Coubertin
- The institution of the International Olympic Committee in 1894
- The links between Great Britain, France and Greece

## THE FIRST GAMES OF THE MODERN ERA: ATHENS, 1896

Perhaps surprisingly, there was opposition from the Greek government to proposals to hold the Olympic Games. The country's President, Tricoupis, and his party thought that Greece should concentrate on its social and economic problems rather than on attempts to reconnect with the glories of the past.

The opposition party of Delyannis was influenced by the ideology of 'Hellenism', and took the view that such dramatic 'encounters' with the ancient past as the Olympic Games would both deepen the spirit of ethnos among contemporary Greeks and draw good will and resources from foreign powers.

The royal family, who were not Greek but northern European in origin, constantly sought to demonstrate its 'Greekness' to the Greek people. Often, this effort took the form of the identification of the sovereign with his people through symbols of their 'shared' classical past. The royal family had previously patronised the Zappas Olympics, and it chose now to support the new effort mandated by Coubertin's Paris Congress.

Tricoupis fell from power, and organisational and financial obstacles were overcome, the latter through the generosity of 'Hellenistic' citizens at home and abroad. The Games were financed by the sale of souvenir stamps and coins and by a donation of one million drachmas by a wealthy businessman, Georgios Averoff.

The mass of Athenian citizens turned out to be enthusiastic supporters and hosts of the 1896 Games, and the impact of the Games on national consciousness came to be felt widely throughout Greece. As MacAloon (1984) says, the very first modern Olympics show us how the Games can fully engage the national consciousness of a host people and all the conflict as well as the consensus within it. It will be interesting to see, when the social history of Greece in the early twenty-first century comes to be written, what interpretation is put upon the role and influence in wider events of the return of the Games in 2004 to the place of their modern revival.

LIBRARY, UNIVERSITY OF CHESTER

In April of 1896, 245 male athletes from 13 nations took part in 43 events and 9 sports.

The competitions were well received by the large audiences which were overwhelmingly Greek, although the results were modest in terms of international representation and technical standard. Among the thirteen countries represented, only Greece fielded a full team up to the standard of sports development in the country and chosen by anything remotely approximating a national selection process.

No world records were broken in the nine sports contested multi-nationally, and performances rarely approached contemporary standards. However, this hardly detracted from the drama of the competitions or from the glory of the first Olympic Champions in over 1500 years.

A German, Carl Schuhmann, won medals in gymnastics and wrestling, as well as being placed third in weightlifting and fourth in the shot put, whilst a Frenchman, Paul Masson, won three of the six cycling events. Two American brothers, John and Sumner Paine, competing in the military revolver shooting, became the first siblings to finish first and second in the same event.

But the hero of the 1896 Games was Spiridon Louis, a 24-year-old Greek shepherd from the village of Amarousion. There was no event that the Greek hosts wanted more to win than the 26-mile marathon race, which was created to honour the legend of Pheidippides, who allegedly carried the news of the Greek victory at the Battle of Marathon in 490 BC by running from Marathon to Athens.

On 10 April Louis set off from Marathon with 16 other runners, took the lead two miles from the Panathenian Stadium and, to the great joy of the 100,000 spectators in and around the stadium, won the race.

He became a hero, partly because his was the only Greek win of the Games, and partly because, as an illiterate peasant, he represented the triumph of the native ability of the ordinary worker over the leisured classes so well represented elsewhere in the victors' lists.

The victory of a Greek in the first marathon race ever run provided these Games with their one truly epic victory.

The Greek population took a great interest in the 1896 Olympic Games, and we may well ask why. MacAloon suggests that one answer may lie in their con-sciousness of their heritage, doubtless encouraged in part by news of discoveries at excavation sites in Greece, and by the only partial success of the efforts of the

Zappas cousins. Another suggestion is that the project of reviving Olympism drove to the heart of Greek national consciousness, in a way re-evoking the role of Olympia in ancient times.

In any case, the first steps had been taken. The revival was a reality. But de Coubertin realised that there was still much to be achieved. To be assured that the experiment had succeeded would require not one or two editions of the Games, but at least half a century of development, and in this he was quite right, given the difficulties he faced in Paris in 1900 and St Louis in 1904.

---

## STUDY ACTIVITY 3.4

Visit the website <http://cbs.sportsline.com/u/olympics/2000/history/>. It gives statistical data and other information for over 100 years of the Olympic Games. What patterns of development can you discern over the years?

---

## THE MODERN OLYMPIC GAMES

1   We call our Games 'Olympic', but do they really share any significant similarities with the ancient Olympic Games, or with pre-twentieth-century 'revivalist' attempts? Compare and contrast the various versions.
2   Provide an account of either Robert Dover's games, or those of W.P. Brookes.
3   Examine the process by which the Olympic Games were revived in 1896, with reference to significant actors and events.
4   Explain the developing significance of the modern Olympic Games in social and cultural terms, with reference to the ideas of Pierre de Coubertin.

## CHAPTER FOUR

# BRITAIN IN THE OLYMPIC MOVEMENT

## Chapter aims:

- to map out the British Olympic heritage
- to examine the evolution of the British Olympic Association
- to offer an understanding of some social and political issues faced by Britain and the Olympic Movement.

After studying this chapter you should be able to explain:

- the key historical factors responsible for nurturing the Olympic idea in Britain
- the role of the British Olympic Association in the Olympic Movement
- some of the main issues surrounding the position of Britain in the modern Olympic Movement.

## INTRODUCTION

The emergence of the modern Olympic Movement has been documented in Chapter 3. Here we will briefly revisit some of these early events from a British perspective, before continuing the story into the twentieth century.

Despite the growing popularity of sport world-wide at the end of the nineteenth century, only a handful of European countries, and the USA, took part in 1894 in establishing a modern Olympic Movement and its leading institution, the International Olympic Committee (IOC). Britain was one of those founding countries. Owing to its political, economic and cultural position in the world,

47

Britain has played an important role in promoting the Olympic ideals throughout the past century.

## OLYMPIC FORERUNNERS IN BRITAIN

The precise beginning of the connection between Britain and the ancient Olympic ideas and Games is difficult to pinpoint. The Anglo-Greek connection has long been present in the English language and the arts. The word 'Olimpical' is seen as early as 1432, 'Olympicad' appears in 1553 and the word 'Olympic' in around 1600.

In 1753, Gilbert West brought out an edition of the Odes of Pindar, with an accompanying Volume II that included 'a Dissertation on the Olympick Games' of some 203 pages, which is a rich source of information on the ancient Games.

In 1883, Charles Waldstein, Director of the Fitzwilliam Museum in Cambridge, published an influential paper on the effect of athletics on Greek art. Similar examples abound but history testifies that there have been three major events that have had a significant bearing on the British position in the modern Olympic Movement.

Although pre-modern Olympic festivals had also been organised in other European countries, the events referred to below ensured a re-birth of ancient Olympic ideas and served as a catalyst for their revival in the late nineteenth century.

### Robert Dover's Olimpicks, 1612–1850

In 1612 Robert Dover started his 'Olimpick Games', which were held in the Cotswolds above Chipping Camden in north Gloucestershire.

The name 'Olimpick' appears in the publication *Annalia Dubrensia*, a collection of thirty-three poems about the Games. The subtitle of the work 'Vpon the yeerely celebration of Mr Robert Dover's Olympick Games vpon Cotswold-Hills' shows clearly the use of the term.

Furthermore, eighteen contributions make reference to the original Olympic Games. One of them, a poem by William Denny, provides a graphic account of the variety of activities at Dover's Games:

Oh most famous Greece!
That for brave Pastimes, wert earths Master-peece!
Had not our English DOVER, thus out-done
Thy foure games, with his Catswoldion one.

The activities at Dover's Games included horse-racing, coursing, hunting, wrestling, throwing the sledge and spurning the bar.

More importantly, the Games enjoyed the blessing of James I as they were held on Thursday and Friday of Whit-week. They generated great enthusiasm and drew participants from all segments of society. Largely unknown to the rest of the country, the scale of these Games and the standard of activities were very different from the Games of today.

One of the major contributing factors to the longevity of Robert Dover's Games was the heroic status – almost equal to that of the Greek Olympics – conferred upon them by various literary publications and theatrical plays.

The Games were closed in 1852, nearly 250 years after they had first begun, by which time they had paved the way for a British Olympic tradition that was continued by the organisers of the Much Wenlock Olympian Games in 1850.

Robert Dover's Olimpicks were revived in 1951, almost 100 years after they had been closed because of the rowdyness of visitors. The tradition continues today in Chipping Camden in the form of a recreational festival held each year during the last week of May.


**The Liverpool Olympics, 1862–1867**

Another important part of the nineteenth-century British sporting tradition was the Liverpool Olympics. In 1862 Charles Pierre Melly and his friend John Hulley initiated a series of six 'Grand Olympic Festivals'. That same year these two enthusiasts founded the Liverpool Athletic Club for the encouragement of physical education.

It is worth noting that the programme of the first modern Olympic Games in 1896 was almost identical to the programme of the Liverpool Olympics between 1862 and 1867 with the exception of shooting, cycling, the marathon and lawn tennis, the last of which had not at that time been invented. Predictably, women were not allowed to participate.

49

The Liverpool Games grew rapidly in popularity, drawing between 7000 and 10,000 spectators in the first year. In 1863 this number rose to between 12,000 and 15,000.

A year later, some twenty policeman sent to control the event found themselves completely powerless against a huge crowd and this led the *Liverpool Mercury* to warn its readers:

> We hope these attempts to revive the games of the Olympiad will not alarm the fearful and timid, or beget an apprehension that we are retrograding towards the Paganism of the ancient Greeks. The sports may, in a modified form be similar . . . but the festival has no religious significance . . . How strikingly does this revival of the Olympic games illustrate the proverb 'There is nothing new under the sun'.
>
> (Quoted in Anthony, 1999, p. 47)

There are many today who may wish to disagree with this comment in the *Liverpool Mercury*. Whilst there were certain similarities between the Ancient Greek and nineteenth-century English Games, the Liverpool Olympics were symptomatic of a major transition from the ancient to the modern world of sport.

Spectators were charged two shillings [10p] admission fee and the organisers promoted the entertainment value of the Olympic Festival. The Liverpool Olympics challenged two of the main pillars of the ancient Olympic ideal: its religious character, and its symbolic meaning. The former was substituted with a secular event, whilst the latter added a new dimension to the Olympics – as a source of profit.

### The Much Wenlock Olympian Games, 1850–1895

Much Wenlock is a small village in Shropshire, but its significance in the revival of the modern Olympic Games is widely acknowledged.

The founding of the Games at Much Wenlock is due largely to the efforts of Dr William Penny Brookes, who was an outstanding educator, politician and an advocate of health and sport for ordinary people.

Brookes was born in Much Wenlock in 1809 and after studying medicine in London and Italy he returned to his place of birth and devoted his energies to the prosperity of its people.

His contributions to the well-being of the local community included the railway, the gasworks, the Much Wenlock Agricultural Reading Society and, of course, the Wenlock Olympian Society, established in 1850.

> Object of the Society: To promote the moral, intellectual and physical improvement of the public, by the encouragement of out-door recreation, and the award of prises, annually, for literary and fine-art achievements, and for skills and strength in athletic exercises.
>
> (Anthony, 1999, p. 6)

William Brookes admired the Ancient Greek heritage and was a great believer in the importance of physical education for the harmonious development of man. The Much Wenlock Olympian Society organised the early Olympian Games and continues to do so today, over 150 years later.

The programme of events at the Games included various disciplines such as the running high leap, the running long leap, the running quarter of a mile, putting the 32lb shot and rope-climbing.

Brookes was also active at a regional level and in 1859 founded the Shropshire Olympian Society, which staged the highly successful Shropshire Olympian Games from 1860 until 1864.

In 1861 the Society introduced the idea of moving of the Games from town to town – an idea subsequently borrowed by Baron Pierre de Coubertin in developing the 'host city' concept of the modern Olympic Games.

Dr Brookes was aware of the wider implications of his athletic and moral vision. He raised the possibility of an international Olympian Games at an early date, as revealed by his correspondence with Greece. In 1859 a prize of £10 was sent by the Wenlock Olympian Society to Zappas' Greek Olympic Games (see Chapter 3) and the recipient Petros Velissarios, winner of the long foot race (4200 feet), was made an honorary member of the Society. In return, in 1877, George I King of the Hellenes sent Brookes a silver trophy for presentation at the National Olympian Association Games at Shrewsbury. In 1881 the Greek newspaper *Clio* reported:

> Dr Brookes, the enthusiastic Philhelline, is endeavouring to practice an international Olympia festival to be held in Athens.

It comes as no surprise to discover that Brookes was also instrumental in the creation of the National Olympian Association in 1866. This organisation was composed of various Olympian societies, clubs and associations and staged the First National Olympian Games in London on 31 July 1866 in front of some 10,000 spectators.

In a recent study, Anthony (2000) reveals that the National Olympian Games were not just a domestic affair, but truly 'international and open to all comers' and represented 'grand national contests against the flower of the youth of France, Russia, Germany, and the world at large'.

> . . . and of the Olympic Games which modern Greece has not yet revived, it is not a Greek to whom one is indebted but rather to Dr W. P. Brookes . . . still active, organising and animating them . . . Athletics does not count many partisans as convinced as W.P. Brookes.
>
> (De Coubertin, 1888, p. 15)

Between the early days of the Much Wenlock Olympian Society in 1850 until the founding Congress of the International Olympic Committee in 1894 Dr Brooks made some eighteen interventions of an 'international' Olympian nature and his ideas and experience critically influenced the visions of Pierre de Coubertin, founder of the modern Olympic Movement.

De Coubertin first heard about Brookes in 1889 as a response to his call for an International Congress on Physical Training in Paris. De Coubertin visited Much Wenlock in October 1890, when a special Games was organised in his honour. The co-operation between these two men quickly matured and resulted in Britain's full support for the inaugural congress of the International Olympic Committee in 1894 and the revival of the modern Olympic Games in 1896.

**IN BRIEF**

## BRITAIN IN THE PRE-MODERN OLYMPISM

Britain's contribution was instrumental in the revival of the modern Olympic Movement. It could be summarised in the following points:

- Historically – in forging links and appreciation of Ancient Greek heritage
- Ideologically – in providing the concepts of fair play, amateurism and the value of physical education for general education

- Organisationally – in offering the expertise of the British sport-governing bodies in running sporting events and members of the first International Olympic Committee
- Technically – in pioneering the codification of various recreational activities into systematic charters, rules and regulations
- Personally – in inspiring Pierre de Coubertin, the founder of the modern Olympic Movement.

## DE COUBERTIN, THE INTERNATIONAL OLYMPIC COMMITTEE AND THE BRITISH CONNECTION

William Penny Brookes provides a direct link with the founding of the International Olympic Committee and the revival of the Olympic Games in 1896.

Another major influence on de Coubertin's Olympic philosophy came from the educational theories of Thomas Arnold, headmaster of Rugby School. De Coubertin first came across these ideas in 1875 after reading the novel *Tom Brown's Schooldays* by Thomas Hughes.

It was Arnold's philosophy at Rugby that helped de Coubertin realise the potential of physical education in general education and for the wider socialisation of the individual. In 1883 he visited Rugby and other schools in order to obtain better insights into English public school education.

Pierre de Coubertin's encounters with the English educational system and organisation of sport were part of the preparation for the founding of the Olympic Congress at the Sorbonne in Paris (see Chapter 3).

### STUDY ACTIVITY 4.1

Study the article 'Coubertin, Britain and the British – A Chronology' by D. Anthony on the book's website. Identify the ideological, organisational, technical and personal links that existed between de Coubertin and Britain.

Lord Ampthill and Charles Herbert were the first two British members of the International Olympic Committee (IOC). British membership of the IOC in its formative years was continued with three new appointments in 1897, 1901 and 1906.

A small delegation from Britain also took part in the first Olympic Games in Athens in 1896. The crew of HMS *Howe*, which was in port at Pireus at the time, went along as spectators.

Britons competed in the discus throw, athletics, cycling, tennis, weight-lifting, wrestling and rope-climbing and they also officiated, managed other teams and worked as correspondents for various newspapers in England.

Thomas Cook, a British travel organiser, made inroads in bringing sport and commerce together by obtaining a franchise from the IOC for tourism at the Games. The company was advertising tours to 'The Olympic Games in Athens', with 'side tours' at a cost of £40 for 26 days' travelling.

During the opening ceremony in Athens, George Robertson, a hammer-thrower from New College, Oxford, presented the King of Greece with a copy of the Pindaric Ode published in England in 1745. This book also contains one of the first in-depth studies of the ancient Games, written by Gilbert West.

---

**STUDY ACTIVITY 4.2**

Do you know who was Britain's first Olympic Champion?

Read the article by Ian Buchanan on the book's website to find out about this extraordinary person.

---

### THE BRITISH OLYMPIC ASSOCIATION IN THE MODERN OLYMPICS

The British Olympic Association (BOA) grew out of the National Olympian Association and the influence of the International Olympic Committee. It was formed at the House of Commons on 24 May 1905 with Lord Desborough elected first Chairman.

The Council of the Association consisted of the British members of the IOC and twenty-eight governing bodies, including various unions, associations and clubs. From its inception the BOA was set up to play an active role in the modern Olympic Movement. Its objectives were:

54

to secure that the views of our great governing associations shall have due weight in the organisation of all future Games.

(Anthony, 1999)

Over nearly 100 years of its existence, the role of the BOA has grown in both complexity and scope. The first salaried official was Sandy Duncan in 1949, one of the organisers of the 1948 Olympic Games in London, who took over as general secretary. Today, the BOA is a unique blend of elected officials and over 80 professional staff working in nine departments.

---

**STUDY ACTIVITY 4.3**

Visit the BOA website at <http://www.olympics.org.uk> and study the work of each department. Draw up a list of services available to athletes, which will help you to understand the role of the BOA and the support available to elite athletes in Britain.

---

The BOA is funded privately by commercial sponsorship and public appeals. It receives no government funding. As Neil Townshend, BOA Vice-Chairman, put it:

Indeed we fund the Government in that we have the dubious privilege of being the only National Olympic Committee in the world that pays tax.

(Townshend, 1995)

The IOC called on the BOA to save the Games on two occasions: in 1908 when Rome withdrew due to political and economic problems; and in 1948 after the Second World War. On both occasions British organisers were given only two years to prepare, but managed to stage successful Games and even made profit. What is more, the 1908 Games set standards of organisation to be followed in the future. This was due largely to the considerable practical experience of British sports governing bodies such as the Amateur Athletic Association and the stewards of the Royal Henley Regatta (Plates 4.1 and 4.2).

Britain is one of only five countries to have attended every Olympic Games. Of these only France, Great Britain and Switzerland have been present at all Winter Olympic Games. Table 4.1 shows the participation of Great Britain at the modern Olympic Games and Figure 4.1 shows Great Britain's medal share from 1948 to

Plate 4.1  Poster for the 1908 London Games

Plate 4.2  Poster for the 1948 London Games

2000. It can be seen that Britain's medal share has been diminishing gradually since the Second World War.

The unique position of the BOA as a politically independent voluntary organisation is rooted in the democratic traditions of society. The amateur and fair play ethos, which had underpinned British sport for nearly two centuries, were at times, however, at odds with global developments in the Olympic Movement: for example, the promotion of physical education and Olympic sports, not for their own sake but as a form of entertainment in the case of early Olympics, or their use as a source of profit in the case of Thomas Cook's tours. Other problems, such as nationalism, amateurism and professionalism, transcended national boundaries. The views of the BOA and other public institutions on these issues therefore constitute an inseparable element of the British participation in the Olympic Movement.

Two examples illustrate these complex developments. As early as the 1908 London Games, the British interpretation of fair play came under heavy criticism from the Americans. The BOA had to defend what were, in effect, the underlying

*Table 4.1* British participation at the Olympic Games, 1896–2000

| Olympic Games | No. nations participating | No. athletes competing | No. in British team | No. medals won* | |
|---|---|---|---|---|---|
| 1896 Athens | 13 | 311 | 8 | 7 | (5) |
| 1900 Paris | 23 | 1330 | 103 | 35 | (3) |
| 1904 St Louis | 12 | 687 | 1 | 1 | (10) |
| 1908 London | 23 | 2035 | 721 | 145 | (1) |
| 1912 Stockholm | 28 | 2545 | 293 | 41 | (3) |
| 1920 Antwerp | 29 | 2607 | 231 | 43 | (3) |
| 1924 Paris | 44 | 3092 | 247 | 34 | (4) |
| 1928 Amsterdam | 46 | 3014 | 211 | 20 | (11) |
| 1932 Los Angeles | 37 | 1408 | 71 | 16 | (9) |
| 1936 Berlin | 49 | 4066 | 205 | 14 | (10) |
| 1948 London | 59 | 4099 | 313 | 23 | (12) |
| 1952 Helsinki | 69 | 4925 | 257 | 11 | (18) |
| 1956 Melbourne | 67 | 3342 | 189 | 24 | (7) |
| 1960 Rome | 83 | 5348 | 253 | 29 | (13) |
| 1964 Tokyo | 93 | 5140 | 205 | 18 | (10) |
| 1968 Mexico | 112 | 5531 | 223 | 13 | (10) |
| 1972 Munich | 122 | 7147 | 308 | 18 | (12) |
| 1976 Montreal | 92 | 6085 | 225 | 13 | (13) |
| 1980 Moscow | 81 | 5353 | 230 | 21 | (9) |
| 1984 Los Angeles | 141 | 7078 | 362 | 37 | (11) |
| 1988 Seoul | 159 | 9421 | 386 | 24 | (12) |
| 1992 Barcelona | 172 | 10563 | 387 | 20 | (13) |
| 1996 Atlanta | 197 | 10319 | 304 | 15 | (36) |
| 2000 Sydney | 199 | 10651 | 321 | 28 | (10) |
| 2004 Athens | 201 | 10500 | 271 | 30 | (10) |

Source: Nichols, 1996, and own statistics

Note: * Numbers in parentheses represents Britain's position in the overall medal table

values of Olympism in a special publication entitled *Replies to Criticism of the Olympic Games*.

The truly amateur status of British athletes was becoming ever more untenable. The 'defeat' at the 1912 Stockholm Games caused widespread anxiety as it was clear that to win at international level British athletes had to turn professional. This was in sharp contrast with the amateur ethos, which was the essence of British sport.

The amateur–professional tension escalated to the point that in the run-up to the 1920 Antwerp Games, Theodore Cooke, a leading English sport administrator, published a letter in *The Times* calling for complete withdrawal from the Olympic movement.

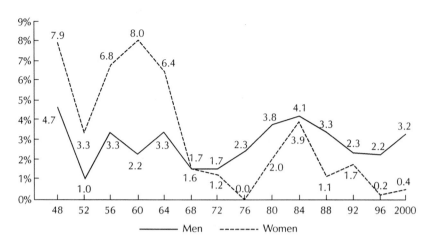

Figure 4.1 Britain's Olympic medal share for men and women, 1948–2000

Source: Shibli, 2003

> The country has made it perfectly clear that the whole Olympic movement has become entirely alien to English thought and character. England had utterly refused to give our representatives sufficient money to give them any chance of showing their best form. The Secretary of the British Olympic Committee should inform the International Olympic Committee that this country will not be represented at any future games and so say farewell to the Olympic movement as it is presently conducted.
>
> (Wigglesworth, 2002, p. 63)

Cooke's was not an isolated voice and some forty-five members of the BOA echoed his concerns. It took the IOC more than 50 years after his letter to resolve the amateur–professional dilemma. In 1972 the term 'amateur athlete' was removed from the Olympic Charter.

The uncertainties within the British sporting community were matched by a lack of interest about the Olympics on the part of the general public. The 1948 London Games proved to be a testing ground for the future of the Olympic Movement both internationally and nationally. 'The Austerity Games' as they remained in history due to post-world war shortages, presented the London organisers with problems of communication as well as economics. Fears about the 'parochialism' of British sporting interests were real and causing growing concern. As Sir Noel

Curtis-Bennett, Vice-Chairman of the British Olympic Association, observed on 18 June 1947 in *The Times*:

> Few people in this country realise the intense reverence in which the Olympic spirit is held throughout the world.

Educating the public therefore became more important than the technicalities of the Games. A last-minute marketing and public relations campaign eventually paid off as huge numbers turning out to watch the events boosted ticket sales and made them profitable.

> In a summer scattered with sporting festivals like plums in a pudding, the five Test Matches against Australia still take first place in domestic affection and interest and not even the international and record breaking rivalries of the coming Olympic Games can stir up the same delightful anxieties.
>
> (*The Times*, June 1948)

Related to amateurism was the issue of international understanding and peace. The Olympic Games were seen as a model of peaceful coexistence and appreciation of cultural differences even before they started. In his last letter to de Coubertin in 1894, Dr Brooks reinforced his belief that the Athens Games in 1896 would lead to peace between nations. As Chapter 10 demonstrates, the global appeal of the Games has been used by various regimes for political gains. The American-led boycott of the 1980 Moscow Olympic Games is a case in point. The British government supported the boycott and Mrs Thatcher's administration put a great deal of pressure on the BOA not to send a national team.

This was not simply a domestic issue. At stake was the integrity of the Olympic Movement. Owing to its contribution to the Olympic Movement, the position of the BOA was crucial for the message it was going to send to the rest of the world. The BOA stood behind the Olympic principles and defeated the government by sending a British team to Moscow. Although several countries backed down to American pressure, others followed the British lead and also took part.

Philip Noel-Baker, an Olympic silver medallist, a statesman, and a Nobel Peace Prize recipient, was appalled by the double standards used by governments in making sport a hostage to political interests. While condemning the Soviet aggression in Afghanistan, which led to the boycott, he equally disapproved of aggression irrespective of whether the aggressor is the host to the Games or another nation taking part.

In a letter to *The Guardian* on 16 June 1980, Noel-Baker made a direct reference to the USA's ongoing aggression in Vietnam and Laos in two Olympic years of 1968 and 1972 respectively. Noel-Baker argued:

> Why British Athletes Should Go To Moscow:
>
> If this policy prevails it will mean that politicians are free to use sport for short-term political objectives, in some cases, as now, for nothing nobler than catching votes in a forthcoming election.

Britain was a founding member of the modern Olympic Movement and has contributed significantly to the spread and enhancement of its key conceptual, organisational, technical and cultural aims.

This co-operation continues in the twenty-first century in a number of different ways. Four Britons serve as IOC members and many more on various IOC commissions and functional departments.

Many outstanding scholars have studied and disseminated Olympic knowledge. The BOA has been very active in publishing widely on Olympism (see the BOA website).

Two of the Olympic Movement strategic agencies, the Olympic Television Archive Bureau and All Sport (now part of Getty Images), responsible for preserving, producing and promoting the visual images and messages of Olympism, are based in London.

**IN BRIEF**

## BRITAIN'S CONTRIBUTION TO THE OLYMPIC MOVEMENT

In the twentieth century Britain has contributed to the Olympic Movement:

- *Ideologically* – in continuing to promote the concept of amateurism and fair play; athletes, experts and academics played critical role in drafting 'The Oath' document which was used by the IOC as a blueprint for the reforms of the Olympic Movement in 2000
- *Organisationally* – London hosted two Olympic Games in 1908 and 1948 in turbulent times for the Movement; British athletes have taken part in all Olympic Summer and Winter Games

> ■ *Technically* – in pioneering advances in various summer and winter sports; maintaining a key role in the fight against doping in sport.

## BRITAIN IN THE OLYMPIC MOVEMENT

1   Describe in your own words the importance of Britain's pre-modern Olympic festivals to the future of the Olympic Movement.
2   How has the role of the British Olympic Association changed over the past 100 years?
3   Discuss the relationship between the British Olympic Association and the professionalisation of Olympic sport.
4   Examine the topics covered by the BOA publications and identify underinvestigated areas, which in your view need to be covered.

## CHAPTER 5

# THE PARALYMPIC GAMES

### Chapter aims:

- to analyse the relationship between disability and sport
- to trace the emergence and development of Paralympic sport
- to consider the Paralympic Movement as a model for change.

After studying this chapter you should be able to explain:

- the nature of the 'medical' and 'social' model of disabled sport
- the key factors responsible for the construction of the modern Paralympic sport
- the contribution of the Paralympic Games for changing societal perceptions about people with disabilities.

## DISABILITY AND SPORT: THE WIDER CONTEXT

Sport for people with disability is a relatively recent concept, and even more so is the participation of disabled athletes in a Paralympic Games, which started in 1960 in Rome. However, individuals with impairments have always been present in society and attitudes towards them have varied across time and from one culture to another. As asserted in previous chapters, the Olympic Movement is an inseparable part of the world we live in and sport and society are mutually constructive. This implies that a better understanding of the Paralympic Games can be obtained if attention is given to wider environmental factors affecting their constitution.

The participation of people with disability in sport is depicted by a variety of terms: 'special needs sport', 'wheelchair sport', 'handicapped sport', 'disabled sport' or 'adopted sport' are amongst the most prevalent terms. The use of different terms reflects the specificity of both the individuals involved and the activity practised. Furthermore, this variety is indicative of the existence of a range of specialised sports-governing bodies at local, national and international levels and the diverse issues they have to deal with.

Disability revolves around three major concepts:

> *Deficiency* corresponds to the loss, in substance or alteration, of a function or a psychological, physiological or anatomical structure;

> *Incapacity* corresponds to any, partial or total reduction (result of a deficiency) of the capacity to accomplish an activity in a normal way or a way considered normal for a human being;

> *Handicap* is a social disadvantage for a person, a result of his deficiencies or incapacity which limits or prevents the accomplishment of a role considered as normal taking into account age, sex and socio-cultural factors.

> (Auberger *et al.*, 1994, p. 163)

This chapter follows the contention of DePauw and Gavron (1995) about the term disability sport 'to refer to sport that has been designed for or specifically practised by athletes with disability'. The notion of disability covers any physical, sensory and mental impairments of the individual. Disability sport also emphasises clearly the importance of the person, to which sport comes second.

## Historical attitudes

Historically, the typical perception of individuals with disability has been one of difference and 'otherness'. The firm divide between able-bodied and disabled had been originally established on biological and physiological grounds. In many early societies for example the survival of the family unit was critical and infanticide (the demise of newly born with impairments) had been a regular occurrence. The Greeks and the Romans had similar practices but these were 'justified' by concerns about the safety and protection of the state from enemies. After all – physically unfit individuals did not make good soldiers.

Gradually, the increased value placed on human life put a stop to the purposeful dismissal of the disabled. They also introduced a range of policies and institutions to regulate the participation of this category of people in society. The nineteenth century saw the first steps beyond the 'separation and isolation' attitude towards disabled individuals. The pioneering work of Jean Mark Itard in this area demonstrated that people with impairments are not doomed and they can be taught, treated and their conditions improved.

## Twentieth-century perceptions

The twentieth century witnessed an increased interest on the part of medical science and a proliferation of residential institutions for the treatment of individuals with disability. The two world wars played a major role in advancing medical and social understanding and, more importantly, in stimulating a growing acceptance of the disabled in the community. There were two major reasons for this. First, the number of veterans who had been disabled during these wars urged societies to take a different view on this issue. Second, the introduction of a compulsory military physical examination in the USA and Europe discovered numerous cases of 'hidden' disability. These were persons who had some form of physical impairment but who had not been classed as disabled.

The British government is credited as having been the first to recognise the problem and in 1944 opened the Spinal Injury Centre at Stoke Mandeville Hospital in Aylesbury. This is where the neuro-surgeon Sir Ludwig Guttmann introduced sport to patients as a form of rehabilitation for the first time. Both Guttmann and Stoke Mandeville proved instrumental for the future of disability sport:

> sport is invaluable in restoring the disabled person's physical fitness, i.e., his strength, coordination, speed and endurance . . . restoring that passion for playful activity and the desire to experience joy and pleasure in life . . . promoting that psychological equilibrium which enables the disabled to come to terms with his physical defect, to develop activity of mind, self-confidence, self-dignity, self-discipline, competitive spirit, and comradeship, mental attitudes . . . to facilitate and accelerate his social re-integration and integration.
>
> (Sir Ludwig Guttmann, quoted in Thomas and Smith, 2003)

Developments in social integration were accompanied by a number of legislative measures and practical policies, which helped both change and reinforce the

64

segregation of people with disability. The formal recognition of those with disability as a dependent group inevitably imposed certain limitations on their participation in life. Naturally, these limitations were extended to sport and separate provision for impaired individuals had to be put in place by public and voluntary agencies alike.

## STUDY ACTIVITY 5.1

Study the chapter on 'Disabled People and Sport' (pp. 19–22) of Sport England's policy document *Making English Sport Inclusive: Equity Guidelines for Governing Bodies*. Identify the key measures that mainstream sport organisations need to implement to make their sports equally accessible to participants with impairments. The document is available at <http://www.sportengland.org/resources/pdfs/people/equity.pdf>.

**IN BRIEF**

## ATTITUDES TO DISABILITY

Historically, societal attitudes and treatment of individuals with disabilities reveal a pattern of rejection, followed by a reluctant acceptance, and more recently concerted attempts to increased independence and full integration. However, there is still a great deal of work to be done. As the British Social Attitudes Survey (1998) showed, three in four Britons thought there was prejudice against disabled people.

Traditionally, a popular functionalist perception about disability and sport has been established. It sees sport as having only a positive effect on individuals with disability. Hence, sport for the disabled is presented along a continuum with therapeutic (rehabilitative) sport at one end and elite sport at the other. This is a limited picture as it fails to recognise sport as a more complex phenomenon, which can produce both positive and negative effects for individuals and communities. A similar picture could also be seen as divisive as it differs from the presentation of sport for the able-bodied where the opposite pole to competition is recreational sport.

# THE PARALYMPIC MOVEMENT: FROM THERAPY TO ATHLETICISM

Perhaps the earliest evidence for organised sport for individuals with disabilities is from 1888 when the first sports club for the deaf was founded in Berlin. The concept of segregated competition was pioneered in Paris in 1924 with the first International Silent Games. The British Deaf Sport Council further developed it in 1930 before Sir Ludwig Guttmann brought it to public notice after the Second World War and inspired the disabled sports movement in Britain.

In 1948 Guttmann organised the first International Wheelchair Games at Stoke Mandeville Hospital to coincide with the Opening Ceremony of the London Olympic Games. On 28 July 1948, fourteen paraplegic men and two women competed in archery. The health and productivity benefits associated with sport urged its conceptualisation as a form of rehabilitation. This view is indicative for the medical model of disability. It sees the individual as a passive victim suffering a pathological condition, who is in need of treatment and rehabilitation. Interestingly, one of the first ever fully accepted wheelchair athletes to take part in an Olympic Games was Neroli Fairhall, who competed in the 1984 Los Angeles Games for New Zealand in archery.

The role of treatment and physical exercise, however, was limited to restoring some basic neuromuscular functions in order to facilitate disabled adaptation to the world of the able-bodied. Subsequently these therapeutic activities were prescribed and administered by medical doctors, nurses and therapists and their intensity and effect on athletes' performance was rather restricted. Key elements such as the process, the opportunities and the conditions of participation were hardly ever considered.

## A social model of disability

As general and medical attitudes developed, a social model of disability emerged which challenged the dominant medical view. This alternative model defines disability in terms of the barriers and limitations which society imposes on people with impairments. These include, among others, prejudice, exclusion, lack of planning and lack of adequate access and provision. The social model of disability argues that, 'the limitation of activity is not caused by impairments but is a consequence of social organisation'.

Historically images of disability have been generated by non-disabled people, and there have been more about the prejudices and decision of mainstream society than the reality of the disabled experience.

(French and Hainsworth, 2001, p. 36)

It goes on to suggest that disability is a result of the failure of society to provide the adequate material and social environments within which the needs of people with disability can be met. This kind of thinking has been the driving force behind landmark legislation such as the Disability Discrimination Act (1995) in Britain and the Rehabilitation Act (1973) in the USA. These and other similar legislation have made it illegal to discriminate on the basis of disability or to deny the access of disabled persons to sport facilities and programmes or to physical education.

Despite changes, the tension between medical and social models of disability in sport still remains. This is partly because of the very nature of sport performance in disability sport. Athletes' medical conditions have to be established in order to classify them in particular categories of competition. The foundations of a medical sport classification system for athletes with disabilities were laid down in England in the 1940s.

After a number of refinements, currently this type of functional classification includes paraplegics, tetraplegics, amputees, blind and cerebral palsied individuals, 'les-autres' (the others) and those with an intellectual disability. Within each of these groups there are a number of subcategories. The present classification system with its focus on fairness of competition is far from ideal. Ironically, it enhances both integration and segregation of athletes with disability because it loses sight of the wider issue of integration with the mainstream Olympics and other championships. Hence, it is a subject of continuing debate.

## The International Paralympic Committee

The variety of functional disabilities gave rise to a myriad of specialised sports-governing bodies around the world. As the number of sport organisations and events for athletes with impairment grew so did the complexity of co-ordinating and managing the disabled movement. In the 1980s disparity and fragmentation crippled the Paralympic Movement. Out of this, however, on 22 December 1989 came unity in the form of a new world organisation of sport for athletes with disability – the International Paralympic Committee (IPC). In 1995 the

International Deaf Sports Association (CISS) withdrew from the International Paralympic Committee and continued to run its own World Games.

The International Paralympic Committee developed its visions along the course of four interrelated objectives:

1  The highest ideals of Olympism as laid down by Pierre de Coubertin some 100 years ago. The Paralympic Games have become a unique testing ground for overcoming difficult barriers and severe limitations. The Paralympic Games have become a stepping-stone for self-expression, self-realisation and self-actualisation. And, the Paralympic Games have become an open stage for a remarkable demonstration of enthusiasm, energy, confidence, courage and skills of our athletes.

2  Overcoming barriers as they relate to human rights, integration, tolerance and acceptance.

3  Introducing social change by permeating the public consciousness and serving as a catalyst for the emergence, recognition and acceptance of a person with a disability into sport and into society.

4  Above all, becoming a symbol of unification of all disabilities, all athletes, all sports from all nations.

(Steadward, 2001)

The creation of a world organisation of sport for athletes with disability was not just an act in consolidation of power within the framework of the medical model of disability. In the words of Dr Robert Steadward, the first President of the IPC (1989–2001): 'since 1989 there has been a fundamental paradigm shift, and our focus has been on athleticism, sport excellence and high level of competition'. These visions mark a transition to the social model of disability that sees sport as a form of self-expression and achievement. It also uses sport as a means to promote the wider cause of disability in the world.

The essence of this change of models is well depicted by the childhood experiences of Tanni Grey-Thompson, Olympic wheelchair road racer champion:

> . . . doctors were obsessed with me walking. Their attitude was, I must stay on my feet as long as possible . . . Everything the doctors did was about keeping me on my feet when it should have been about finding the best way for me to be mobile.
>
> (Thomas and Smith, 2003, pp. 167, 172)

**Paralympic Games**

## The Paralympic Games

The success of the Stoke Mandeville Games and other major tournaments paved the way for the first Paralympic Games, which were held in Rome in 1960. These were followed by the first Paralympic Winter Games in Ornskoldsvik, Sweden, in 1976. The Paralympic Games are the equivalent of the Olympics for elite athletes with a physical disability, mental disability or visual impairment. Inroads were made in 1984 in both Summer and Winter Olympic Games in Los Angeles and Sarajevo respectively, where disability sports were included in the programme as demonstration events (Plates 5.1 and 5.2).

Since the 1988 Seoul Olympic Games a trend has been established to stage both the Winter and Summer Paralympic Games in the same location as the main Olympics to take advantage of facilities, technology and expertise. Demonstrating unity in developing sport for the able-bodied and the disabled is now part of candidate cities' strategies as demonstrated by the London bid to host the 2012 Olympic and Paralympic Games.

Plate 5.1  A paralympic athlete in action (International Paralympic Committee)

Plate 5.2 The Winter Paralympic Games (International Paralympic Committee)

**IN BRIEF**

## THE PARALYMPIC GAMES

The word 'paralympic' comes from the Latin prefix *'para'* as in parallel, or the Greek *'para'* for 'next to'. It is a misconception that it derives from the word 'paralysed' or 'paraplegic'. The Paralympic Games are the *parallel* games to the Olympic Games.

As both Olympic and Paralympic movements aspire to achieve the same objectives and to advance human progress, in the past 15 years there has been a growing fusion between the respective committees. The grounds for this are not only practical but as Fernard Landry (1995, p. 131) writes:

> In terms of the primary process through which a man or a woman advances on the road to, or up the ladder of relative perfection, there is little philosophical difference indeed between 'Olympism' and 'para-lympism', between an 'Olympic' athlete and a 'paralympic' athlete.

Over the years the Paralympic Games have grown in size, standard of performance and inclusion of different disabilities. For example, the Sydney Paralympic Games were larger in size than the 1956 Melbourne Olympics (67 National Organising Committees and 3178 athletes) and the 1998 Nagano Winter Olympics. Table 5.1 documents the history of the Paralympic Games. Figure 5.1 shows some statistics for the British Paralympic team in Sydney, 2000. The programme grew from four sports in 1960 to eighteen sports in 2000 Sydney Paralympic Games. Of these only four sports – bocca, goalball, powerlifting and wheelchair rugby – are not on the Olympic programme.

*Table 5.1* Chronology of the Paralympic Games

| Paralympic Summer Games | | | Paralympic Winter Games | | |
|---|---|---|---|---|---|
| | No. nations participating | No. athletes competing | | No. nations participating | No. athletes competing |
| 1960 Rome | 23 | 400 | | | |
| 1964 Tokyo | 22 | 390 | | | |
| 1968 Tel Aviv | 29 | 750 | | | |
| 1972 Heidelberg | 44 | 1000 | | | |
| 1976 Toronto | 42 | 1600 | 1976 Ornskoldvik | 14 | 250+ |
| 1980 Arnhem NL | 42 | 2500 | 1980 Geilo | 18 | 350+ |
| 1984 Stoke Mandeville & New York | 42 | 4080 | 1984 Innsbruck | 22 | 350+ |
| 1988 Seoul | 61 | 3053 | 1988 Innsbruck | 22 | 397 |
| 1992 Barcelona | 82 | 3020 | 1992 Tignes-Albertville | 24 | 475 |
| 1996 Atlanta | 103 | 3195 | 1994 Lillehammer | 31 | 1000+ |
| 2000 Sydney | 123 | 3843 | 1998 Nagano | 32 | 571 |
| 2004 Athens | 141 | 4000 | 2002 Salt Lake City | 36 | 416 |

Source: International Paralympic Committee website <www.paralympic.org/games/0201.asp>
and DePauw and Gavron, 1995

131
medals

———————

214 athletes in
18 sports make up
the Great Britain team

———————

Over 60,000 athletes with
disability take part in sport

———————

10 million Britons have a disability

UK population 58 million

**Figure 5.1** A sport pyramid: British athletes and medal winners at the 2000 Sydney Paralympic Games

---

## STUDY ACTIVITY 5.2

Visit the International Paralympic Committee website <http://www.paralympic.org> to read about four unique sports for athletes with disability:

- bocca
- goalball
- powerlifting
- wheelchair rugby.

Write a short description of each sport. Try to find local clubs where these sports are practised. Talk to athletes and find out how long it takes to excel in their sport, the nature of competition nationally and internationally and the support they need to achieve their dreams.

---

### SPORTS WITHOUT LIMITS: THE PARALYMPIC MOVEMENT AS A MODEL OF SOCIAL CHANGE

'Sport without limits' was the theme of the Barcelona 1992 Paralympic Games. It encapsulates both the extraordinary achievements of athletes with disability and their continuing struggle to raise awareness of the need for more integration.

The underlying mission of the Paralympic Movement is social change in all aspects of life. Since its inception after the Second World War three periods can be discerned in the history of the movement:

72

- therapy
- athleticism
- development.

The first of these periods (1948–1989) was dominated by visions of the use of sport for therapeutic purposes. Significant progress in medicine, legislation and general attitudes had been achieved.

Athleticism (1989–2003) has advanced the idea of the human potential of individuals with impairment and promoted sport as a form of self-actualisation.

By choosing a top-down approach, the IPC have used the elite athletes as models to be emulated by other people and institutions. To that end, the Paralympic Games have served three important purposes:

- As a unique ground for overcoming difficult barriers and severe limitations;
- As golden opportunities and stepping stones for self-expression and self-realisation; and
- As an open stage where truly remarkable levels of enthusiasm, energy, confidence, audacity, courage, skills and remarkable achievements can be (and have been repeatedly) demonstrated.

(Landry, 1995, p. 131)

Sport development is the focus of the third period (2003 to present day) in the Paralympic Movement. This means undertaking a massive task of building on the legacy of the Paralympic Games to make a difference at grass roots level.

**IN BRIEF**

### DID YOU KNOW?

| Discipline | Paralympic record | Olympic record |
| --- | --- | --- |
| Men's 100m | 10.72 sec (arm amputee) | 9.84 sec |
| Men's high jump | 1m 96cm (single leg amputee) | 2m 38cm |
| Swimming (blind) women's 100m butterfly | 1min 7.07 sec | 58.62 sec |
| Women's 1500m wheelchair | 3min 45.3 sec | 3min 52.47 sec |

As Phil Craven, the IPC President, states:

> This new centre of attention has to be seen as twofold: first, sport development in a sense of developing sport opportunities for people with disability on a grass root level. It is important for an international representative organisation of sport for people with disability to cover all aspects of sport . . . Secondly, sport has to be seen as a means to promote global development.
>
> (Craven, 2003, p. 1)

The three periods – therapy, athleticism, development – are not just convenient labels for what appears to be a complex social, political and economic phenomenon. Rather they reflect the irony inherited in the progress of disability sport.

Whilst the therapeutic period brought about better understanding of disability and practical policies for solving real problems it was, at the same time, imposing conceptual constraints that hindered change. Athleticism, for its part, addressed this issue and introduced, among other things, glamour, spectacle and commercialisation into the movement. In order to counter excesses, the notion of ethics is now an essential part of the IPC vocabulary.

With its focus on elitism, athleticism inevitably embraced the philosophy of business and entertainment. The IPC's first encounter with the corporate world of images and rights was with the International Olympic Committee (IOC) after its creation in 1989. The IOC asked the IPC to change its logo as it was felt to be too similar to the IOC's five rings making it difficult to market the two organisations.

The 1992 Games in Barcelona witnessed the first doping violation and there were more in Sydney 2000. In 1995 an American athlete launched a legal challenge for $20 million discrimination charges against the IPC rules, which prevented him from participating in the Games. In the same year the split between the IPC and the International Deaf Sports Association was announced. It would be difficult to justify this step other than on grounds of power and vested interests.

Poor organisation of the Games in Atlanta in 1996 caused widespread concerns among athletes and officials about the future.

Throughout the three periods outlined above, the Paralympics and the whole movement have been promoted as:

■ a *conduit* for the development of positive attitudes towards people with a disability, and to integration and inclusion

- a *window* through which one can view the abilities of people with disability
- a *showcase* for the progress people with disability have made in the latter half of the twentieth century
- a *catalyst* for future opportunities for people with disability and for the movement to inclusion
- a *manifestation* of the truly ethical sports environment – sportsmanship as a moral category.

As we have seen, the pursuit of various ideals has not been without drawbacks. To fulfil its social mission the Paralympic Movement has increasingly had to seek the assistance of major institutions such as governments and the media. The most recent example is the agreement signed between the IPC, the European Paralympic Committee and the European Disability Forum, which aims to promote and expand the opportunities of people with disability to play a more active role in society.

It is hoped that the proclamation of 2003 as European Year of People with Disability will give impetus to practical developments. Another avenue vigorously pursued by the Paralympic Movement is the inclusion of selected full medal events for athletes with disability in major international competitions including the Olympic Games.

Similar efforts at a higher political level, however, are countered by old attitudes and stereotypical images portrayed by the media. As the majority of people gain their perspective about disability sport through the media they become exposed to selected presentations and representations. Two recent independent studies on the media coverage of the 1996 Paralympic Games in Atlanta and 2000 Games in Sydney support this conclusion.

Schell and Duncan's (1999, p. 29) analysis of the CBS TV coverage of the 1996 Paralympics argued that:

> Media portrayals cast disability as an individual problem, one that can only be solved at the individual level. These portrayals do not address the fact that disability is a societal problem, one that is not susceptible to individual solutions. The greatest obstacle for people with disability is not the physical or mental limitation but society's attitudes toward disability and the ensuing discrimination.

Thomas and Smith's (2003, p. 172) study of the British media coverage of the 2000 Paralympics echoes this concern. They found that nearly one-quarter of the articles in the national newspaper depicted athletes as 'victims or courageous people who suffer from personal tragedies'.

The Paralympic Movement and its practical manifestation, the Games, possess the social, political and economic power to change this situation. The 1988 Paralympics in Seoul are a case in point. With very little background in disability sport the Koreans staged a landmark event, which served as a blueprint for the future.

However, prior to the Games they regarded disability as a major social catastrophe in the family and decided not to use the Olympic Village for the Paralympic athletes and constructed alternative accommodation. They feared that the traditional cultural perception of disability would adversely influence sales of the flats after the Games. Fortunately the success of the 1988 Paralympics markedly changed traditionally negative attitudes.

**REVIEW QUESTIONS**

## THE PARALYMPIC GAMES

1   Explain the nature of the medical and the social models of disability and their implications for the organisation of sport.
2   Visit a major sporting event for athletes with disabilities staged locally and study the national/local press coverage of it.
3   Compare and contrast the results achieved by men and women in five sports at the Paralympic Games in Sydney 2000 and Athens 2004. What trends can you identify in terms of these sports' geography, participation, level of competition and results?

76

## CHAPTER SIX

# THE OLYMPICS AND THE MASS MEDIA

## Chapter aims:

- to explain the role and functions of the mass media for society and the individual
- to elaborate on the evolving relationship between the media and the Olympics
- to analyse how the media coverage of the Olympics is constructed.

After studying this chapter you should be able to explain:

- the role of the media, and television in particular, in transforming Olympic sport
- how the media shape attitudes, knowledge and beliefs
- the chief considerations in designing the Olympic coverage
- the nature of the media/Olympic relationship.

## INTRODUCTION

Before examining relationships between the Olympics and the mass media we need to establish an understanding of the media. As the mass media are in the business of communication, attention also has to be given to the general characteristics of the process of communication.

Whether we are talking to a friend, sending an email, watching television or reading the morning newspaper, we are constantly involved in the process of communication. Human movements, particularly in a game or contest, also act as a symbolic form of communication. This language, however, has a limited

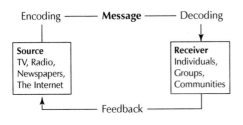

Communication channel
(medium: e.g. words, sound and light)

Encoding ——— **Message** ——— Decoding

| **Source**<br>TV, Radio,<br>Newspapers,<br>The Internet | | **Receiver**<br>Individuals,<br>Groups,<br>Communities |

——— Feedback ———

**Figure 6.1** The communication process

capacity and whilst most people do not need an interpreter to explain what is happening on the athletics track, they will nonetheless find it difficult to do without a narrator. This role (sports commentator) guides the audience through the history, statistics, preparation of athletes, personal dramas and the nature of the competition that is being covered.

In general, the communication process involves several components (see Figure 6.1):

- a *source* to initiate the process (an individual, organisation or an event)
- *encoding* (putting thoughts and ideas in a form that may be perceived by the senses)
- a *message* (human speech, a TV or radio programme, a sport contest)
- a *channel* (the way in which a message travels from the source to the receiver)
- *decoding* (reading, writing or listening – to decode messages)
- *receiver* (the target of the message – an individual or a larger audience)
- *feedback* (responses of the receiver that alter subsequent messages).

## WHAT IS THE MASS MEDIA?

The media provide the fourth component in the communication process. According to Dominick (1990, p. 27):

> a medium is a channel through which a message travels from the source to the receiver ('medium' is singular, 'media' is plural).

Consequently, when discussing the transmission of major international events such as the Olympic Games to large global audiences we are dealing with mass

78

communication. For this to occur there must be channels along which messages are carried, referred to as the mass media.

In the context of this chapter the various forms of mass media will be interpreted as both the transmission device and the organisation, the people (a source) and policies responsible for the construction and transmission of messages.

The most important mass media are newspapers, radio, television, film, books, magazines, recorded sound and the Internet. They are large and complex institutions, operate in a highly competitive market, employ thousands of people, and have great impact upon large audiences. It is possible to study the functions and uses of mass communication at two levels. A wider perspective suggests that we could consider these functions in terms of society as a whole. This is known as a macro-level of analysis, which focuses on the work of the mass media and the nature of its content.

A more in-depth look into individual receivers of the media content would concentrate on how they use mass media. This approach is referred to as the micro-level of analysis. Ideally, the mass media would have wanted the receiver to use the media content as intended by the source, but this is not always the case.

## MASS MEDIA FUNCTIONS IN SOCIETY

Despite their specificity and mode of operation, most mass media share certain commonalities. They have multiple 'gatekeepers' – people who have control of the production and transmission. Almost everyone in a media institution – porter, journalist, programme director, president of the corporation – can be seen as a gatekeeper. The job of the gatekeeper is to:

- make profit
- shape values and norms in which we believe or which we obey
- provide service to the public
- build their own reputation as credible sources of information
- express themselves in unique, artistic form.

Society has certain communication needs, which are satisfied by media functions. These functions are influenced to a degree by common characteristics shared by most mass media. In respect of the Olympic Movement they can be interpreted as:

- *Surveillance* – the news/information role: feeds us with sound, text and pictures about the Games, athletes' performances, records, scores, events, transport links, tickets, weather conditions, etc.
- *Interpretation* – information on the meaning and significance of the Olympic events. Not everything that happens is transmitted to people in all countries. The media select the events and stories and how much prominence they are to be given. Thus, the audience gains an added perspective on the news stories. The Games in Sydney set a record of 3500 hours of broadcast sporting action. In the UK the BBC showed only 318 hours of coverage (9 per cent of the total) which allowed an average viewing of 10 hours per viewer.
- *Linkage* – the Olympics bring together culturally and geographically diverse groups of people who share a common interest in sport. Also, the Olympic Games are one of the few events to draw together all members of a family. The advertising of Olympic sponsors' products is another example as it links them to the needs of buyers.
- *Transmission of values* (socialisation functions) – refers to the ways in which an individual adopts the behaviour and values of a group. Sport and the Olympics in particular present many examples of desirable values, such as excellence, friendship and positive role-models.
- *Entertainment* – coverage of the Olympics is a prime example of entertainment, the most obvious function of the media. Television, most radio stations, and a significant proportion of newspapers devote up to three-quarters of their content to entertainment. Another view of different functions of the media is offered by Morrow (1987) in Table 6.1.

*Table 6.1* Detailed categorisation of various functions performed by the media

| Primary functions | Secondary functions | Compounding functions |
| --- | --- | --- |
| Inform | Flavour | Frequency topic |
| Report | Sentiment | Subject reporting |
| Publicise | Sensationalise | Prominence of topic/subject |
| Promote | Highlight | |
| Criticise | Reinforce | |
| Illustrate: | 'Stories' | |
|   pictorially | | |
|   verbally | | |
| Reflect: | | |
|   public opinion | | |
|   image | | |
|   nationalism | | |

Source: Morrow, 1987

*Table 6.2* Differences between the print and broadcast media: the case of sport coverage

| Print media | Broadcast media |
| --- | --- |
| • Emphasis on news, analysis, and special features<br>• Summaries of events that have already occurred<br>• Broad scope of tangible information<br>• Success depends on credibility<br>• Diverse coverage aimed at distinct audience groups<br>• Content likely to provide criticism of sport and sport personalities | • Emphasise entertainment in the form of action and drama<br>• Play-by-play descriptions and interpretations<br>• Immediacy in coverage of on-the-spot action<br>• Success depends on generating hype<br>• Focused coverage aimed at large single audience<br>• Content likely to provide support for sport and sport personalities |

The functions of the media and the extent of their usage in the Olympic coverage will vary for different media. Coakley (1990) offered a useful distinction between the print and broadcast media (see Table 6.2).

As most people do not have the chance to attend the Olympic Games in person, it is the media that form the bridge between the Olympics and us. In doing that the media are performing the dual role of offering opportunities for getting new information but also of limiting our perspective on the Olympics. This is because the reality brought to us through the media is always edited and 're-presented' by those who control them – the producers, sponsors, editors, programme directors and commentators. Reality is thus 'mediated' to us. For example, Plate 6.1 shows a Trans World Sport journalist interviewing 89-year-old Arthur Podesta, a Maltese water-polo player who took part in the 1936 Berlin Olympic Games. Podesta answered questions for about 60 minutes but what viewers saw six weeks later was some 120 seconds of his recollections.

## STUDY ACTIVITY 6.1

Look at *Communicating Atlanta 1996 Olympic Games* on the book's website. What do you think would be the message about the Olympic values, which the Games were likely to convey to the world?

Plate 6.1  A Trans World Sport journalist interviews Arthur Podesta, 2003

### How people use the mass media

While an understanding of the media is essential, it is equally important to consider why people use the mass media. Broadly speaking, there are four main needs satisfied by the media (so-called 'media gratification'):

- *Cognition* – this is the act of coming to know something. People use the media to learn about the Olympics or the performance of their favourite teams and athletes.
- *Diversion* – the media as a means of stimulation, relaxation and emotional release. Olympic competitions provide tension and suspense, as well as many pleasant moments of high quality performance, pride and satisfaction.
- *Social unity* – we often use the media to strengthen our contacts with family or the community. By following Olympic coverage, people share many hours together and get involved in various activities, from cheering their team to eating and drinking together.
- *Withdrawal* – conversely, we can use the media to create a barrier between us and other people or their activities. Watching the finals of Olympic athletics might be a good excuse not to go to a birthday party, or to clean the car.

## OLYMPICS AND THE MASS MEDIA: AN EVOLVING RELATIONSHIP

At the dawn of the modern Olympics in 1896 neither the term mass media nor the radio, television or Internet existed. The lack of technologies, widespread illiteracy and other factors confined the meaning of the mass media primarily to newspapers. In Athens that year only eleven journalists ventured to attend the Games and reported the revival of Olympic tradition. Several British athletes as well as competitors from other countries took an active part in the making of Olympic history by writing articles for national and local newspapers. Today newspapers remain a powerful medium. In July 1992 the city of Barcelona was on the front page of more than 15,000 newspapers around the world with a total estimated circulation of more than 500 million copies.

For some 25 years newspapers enjoyed a monopoly for coverage of the Olympic Games. Interestingly, the arrival of new media forms has always been perceived as a threat and usually had to face strong opposition. In 1920 the first radio station, KDKA, went on air in Pittsburgh, USA. KDKA is also credited with broadcasting the first ever sporting event (a boxing match) in 1921.

Broadcasting services in Great Britain started in 1922 with the establishment of the British Broadcasting Corporation (BBC). Sports commentary, however, was not permitted until 1925. Radio commentators were covering the Olympic Games in Paris (1924), Amsterdam (1928) and Los Angeles (1932), but due to technical limitations this medium remained local and regional until 1936. The advent of the radio and its interest in sport was considered as a threat by the rest of the media. Newspapers and the Hollywood movie industry in particular put strong pressure and demanded regulation and restrictions of this medium.

---

### STUDY ACTIVITY 6.2

Read the articles 'Radio Sports Broadcasting in the United States, Britain and Australia, 1920–1956 and its influence on the Olympic Games' (J. McCoy, 1997) and 'Changing partners: the relationship between the mass media and the Olympic Games' (J. Slater, 1998) on the book's website. Discuss the key factors responsible for the changing relationship between radio, TV and the Olympic Games.

---

83

## Television

By the time that the radio made its genuine debut as an international communication medium at the 1936 Berlin Olympic Games, television had already made its appearance. The first regular television services began in Germany in 1935, followed by Britain in 1936, France in 1937, the former USSR in 1938 and the United States in 1939.

However, it was not television but the cinema which was responsible for making the first moving pictures of an Olympic Games: in 1900 in Paris and a special feature on the Olympics in 1912 in Stockholm. These developments in cinematography had an impact on the TV coverage of the Games, which began in 1936 in Berlin.

---

**IN BRIEF**

### *OLYMPIA*

The first film produced about an Olympics, *Olympia*, is about the 1936 Games in Berlin. The film:

- was directed by Leni Reifenstahl
- was commissioned by the Nazi government
- was 225 minutes long, and took 2 years to edit
- was in two parts: *Festival of Nations* and *Festival of Beauty*
- took 1.4 million feet of film
- took 150 troops to shoot it.

Filming involved many innovations, with cameras:

- on rails to follow the sprints
- on horses to cover equestrian events
- in tethered balloons for overhead views.

---

Of the twenty-four cameras used to broadcast the Games only three were electronic, thus capable of producing video signal. The remaining cameras had to use a complex technological process to convert images into video signal, so the coverage was not completely 'live'.

*Table 6.3* Chronology of TV rights in the Summer Olympic Games

| Olympic Games | TV rights (US$) | Broadcast hours | Audience |
|---|---|---|---|
| 1936 Berlin | Not paid | 136 | 162,000 |
| 1948 London | 1000 | 64.5 | 500,000 |
| 1960 Rome | 200,000 | 102 | n/a |
| 1964 Tokyo | 1.5 M | n/a | n/a |
| 1968 Mexico | 4.5 M | 938.5 | 60 M |
| 1972 Munich | 7.5 M | 1266 | 900 M |
| 1976 Montreal | 34.9 M | n/a | n/a |
| 1980 Moscow | 88 M | n/a | n/a |
| 1984 Los Angeles | 286 M | 1300 | 2000 M |
| 1988 Seoul | 402 M | 2230 | 10,400 M |
| 1992 Barcelona | 600 M | 20,000 | 16,600 M |
| 1996 Atlanta | 900 M | 25,000 | 19,600 M |
| 2000 Sydney | 1331 M | 29,600 | 36,100 M |

Source: Lines and Moreno, 1999, and other IOC statistics

Note: M = million

The Second World War interrupted advances for some 12 years, but it was clear that the Olympic coverage would never be the same. Both newspapers and radio had to reinvent their role in relation to the Games.

Table 6.3 shows the evolution of the Olympic TV broadcast. It can be seen that the prominence of television sport has been growing steadily. However:

> What some people forget is that television got off the ground because of sport. Today, maybe, sports need television to survive, but it was just the opposite when it first started. When we put on the World Series in 1947, heavyweight fights, the Army–Navy football game, the sales of television sets just spurted.
>
> (Neal-Lunsford, 1992, pp. 59–60)

---

**IN BRIEF**

## RADIO, TELEVISION AND SPORT IN BRITAIN

- In 1950 there were 343,882 TV licences, covering 2 per cent of British households
- In 1954 there were 3.2 million television sets

85

- In 1962 82 per cent of the population had access to television
- In 2000 32 per cent of British households had more than three television sets
- Radio provided the major coverage of the 1948 London Olympics with 8 radio stations and 32 channels, 15 commentary positions and 16 open positions in the stadium and the swimming pool respectively; Lines reached 30 Olympic venues and BBC commentators supplied coverage in 40 languages.

## The Internet

Sixty years after the appearance of television, the Internet, a new medium, joined the contest for the coverage of the Olympic Games. In 1996 the first official website of the Atlanta Organising Committee <www.atlanta.olympic.org> was launched.

During the 16 days of the Games this website received a total of 185 million visits. Since the International Olympic Committee presence on the Internet began in 1995, its website has been revamped several times. Currently, with more than 700,000 words, 7000 images and 1200 audio and video files it serves as a powerful gateway to the Olympic Movement.

The Internet presents a new medium which combines the processes of production and diffusion of information. In fact, it is a multi-medium allowing the use of data, images, texts and real-time textual, audio and video communications. In addition, the Internet offers a range of other services. For example, 76 per cent of tickets for the Sydney 2000 Games and 80 per cent for the 2002 Salt Lake City Winter Olympics were sold on-line, and 90 per cent of volunteers for the Salt Lake City Games were recruited on-line from over 67,000 applicants. Table 6.4 demonstrates the growing popularity of the Olympics on the Internet.

Predictably, the arrival of the Internet caused a range of problems for the rest of the mass media and for the Olympic Movement particularly. Prior to the Sydney 2000 Games the International Olympic Committee (IOC) complained to the World Intellectual Property Organisation (WIPO) about the unauthorised use of Olympic insignia by some 2000 websites. Most threatened by the arrival of the Internet, however, was television. At present the IOC prohibits the broadcasting of Olympic images on the Internet in order to protect the rights of the major networks, which in turn have been critical of the financial stability of the Olympic

*Table 6.4* Olympic Games website statistics, 1996–2002

| Olympic Games | No. hits (16 days) | No. hits per day | Max. no. hits per minute | Pages of content |
|---|---|---|---|---|
| 1996 Atlanta | 185.8 M | 11 M | no data | no data |
| 1998 Nagano | 634 M | 39.7 M | 110,414 | 48,493 |
| 2000 Sydney | 11,300 M | 70.6 M (874.5 M in one day) | 1.2 M | no data |
| 2002 Salt Lake City | 325 M | 3 M | no data | no data |

Source: de Moragas Spa, 1995; IOC *Marketing Matters*, Nos 18–20
Note: M = million

Movement over the past 20 years, a period during which it has received some US$5 billion from the sale of media rights.

## Symbolic associations

Over the years the relationship between the Olympics and the media has evolved into three intertwined symbolic associations – economic, promotional and passional.

The *economic association* is based on the economic interests of the two parties: TV companies pays fees for rights but at the same time derive profit because of the advertising revenue from sponsors.

The *promotional association* suggests that sport is a major source of revenue and programme content. It is therefore in the best interest of the media to sustain and promote a positive image of the Olympics. Some of the most popular international sports events, such as the Tour de France, the European Football Cups or the Skiing World Cup were created by the French newspapers *L'Auto* and later *L'Equipe*.

The *passional association* stems from the media dual responsibility to inform, analyse and comment, and to be a counter-authority. Despite their economic interest in sport, it is in the nature of the media to keep a distance from it, to maintain their credibility, and to serve the truth and their audience. Table 6.5 shows the role of television in promoting the Olympic Games around the world. Its role in this respect is guided by the IOC policy for granting the TV rights of the Olympic Games. This policy is based on two major criteria: exclusivity per country/territory, and free coverage to the largest possible audience. The higher

*Table 6.5* Countries televising Summer and Olympic Winter Games

| Summer Games | | No. countries | Winter Games | | No. countries |
|---|---|---|---|---|---|
| 1948 | London | 1 | 1948 | St. Moritz | 2 |
| 1960 | Rome | 21 | 1972 | Sapporo | 20 |
| 1972 | Munich | 63 | 1980 | Lake Placid | 40 |
| 1980 | Moscow | 58 | 1984 | Sarajevo | 100 |
| 1984 | Los Angeles | 156 | 1992 | Albertville | 86 |
| 1992 | Barcelona | 193 | 1994 | Lillehammer | 120 |
| 1996 | Atlanta | 214 | 1998 | Nagano | 160 |
| 2000 | Sydney | 220 | 2002 | Salt Lake City | 160 |

Source: Lines and Moreno, 1999; IOC *Marketing Matters*, Nos. 19, 20

bidder is not necessarily awarded the rights as in the case of Sky TV for the 2000 Olympics.

A practical result of the economical, promotional and passional association is the support which the major TV networks give to the IOC promotional campaign 'Celebrate Humanity' (see Chapter 7). For example, the US broadcasters NBC, MSNBC and CNBC, the European Broadcasting Union (EBU), Eurosport, Australia's Seven Network and several Asian broadcasters have been airing it to millions of households around the world.

## STUDY ACTIVITY 6.3

Read Whannel's (1986) article 'The unholy alliance: notes on television and the remaking of British sport 1965–85' on the book's website. Compare and contrast the traditional with the entrepreneurial approach to sport and the role of television in changing the organisation of sport.

## THE OLYMPIC GAMES: FROM NEWS TO A MEDIA EVENT

The interaction between the Olympics and the mass media resulted in a transformation of the Games from being merely a sporting competition for an 'aristocratic elite', in de Coubertin's words, to a special genre appealing to millions.

When the organisers of the 1956 Melbourne Olympic Games demanded remuneration for the right to televise the competitions, this unprecedented decision was met with a massive outcry from the networks. They put forward the argument that the Olympic Games were a news event and, similarly to the print media, television should also have free and open access. The organisers insisted that the Olympics were an entertainment event and therefore subject to a rights fee, before contests could be included in television programming. This episode proved critical for the development of the Olympic Games as a media event.

The term 'media event' was coined to indicate a series of emerging scientific, political and sporting occurrences with the status of being public time markers:

> these broadcasts integrate societies in a collective heartbeat and evoke
> a renewal of loyalty to the society and its legitimate authority.
> (D. Dayan and E. Katz, 1992, quoted in Puijk, 1997, pp. 28–30)

The Olympic Games clearly fit into this category as they are unique, follow a regular four-year pattern of occurrence and involve the participation of nations from all over the world. Moreover, a sports competition has all the characteristics of a good story:

- conflict
- dramatic development towards the resolution of the conflict
- suspense by the retention of information
- the possibility of involvement and identification.

---

**STUDY ACTIVITY 6.4**

Consider the brief history of Olympic coverage by television on the book's website and examine the impact of technological innovations on viewers' experiences of the Olympics.

---

### A special media experience

D. Dayan and E. Katz's (quoted in Rivenburgh, 1999 pp. 143–144) analysis helps us to understand the main characteristics of the Olympics as a special genre of media experience:

- they are televised and rely on the impact of visual images
- the Games interrupt daily routines and at times virtually bring the life in a country to a halt
- the Olympics are monopolistic in the sense that all channels focus on the event, and it is very close to being watched at nearly all times
- Olympic competitions are live and unfolding
- the Olympics are organised in a location outside the media, by the IOC and the host city
- the Olympic Games are complex in structure both to organise and to broadcast
- the Olympics are not only spontaneous but pre-planned, announced and advertised in advance
- the Olympics as a media event emerge from celebration but they also involve rivalry and tension
- the Olympics promote idealised values – they remind us how the world should be
- the Olympics have unusual and unprecedented audiences who are drawn to watch television individually, as a family, a group of strangers in front of a street screen, as a small community in the pub, or a virtual community on the Internet.

Table 6.6 shows the ever-increasing number of media representatives at the Olympic Games who contribute greatly to their construction as a media event. Since the 1984 Los Angeles Olympics the number of accredited journalists at the Olympic Games has surpassed the number of participating athletes.

Table 6.6 Accredited media representatives and technical staff at the Games

| Olympic Games | | Press | Radio and TV | Total |
| --- | --- | --- | --- | --- |
| 1960 | Rome | 1146 | 296 | 1442 |
| 1964 | Tokyo | 1507 | 2477 | 3984 |
| 1972 | Munich | 3300 | 4700 | 8000 |
| 1984 | Los Angeles | 4000 | 4200 | 8200 |
| 1988 | Seoul | 5380 | 10,360 | 15,740 |
| 1992 | Barcelona | 4880 | 7951 | 12,831 |
| 1996 | Atlanta | 5000 | 12,000 | 17,000 |
| 2000 | Sydney | 5298 | 14,292 | 19,590 |
| 2004 | Athens | 5500 | 16,000 | 21,500 |

Source: IOC *Olympic Marketing Fact File* No. 67, 1996; www.athens2004.org

the Olympics and the mass media

## SYDNEY OLYMPIC GAMES AS A MEDIA EVENT

- 29,600 hours of TV coverage
- 17-day event (average of 1741 hours per day)
- 220 countries and territories world-wide receiving the signal
- nine out of every ten individuals on the planet with access to television watched some part of the Olympics
- a global audience of 3.7 billion viewers tuned in to watch
- 15,600 accredited broadcast and press journalists from all over the world.

The above characteristics of the Olympic Games as a media event portray them as a social construct, which is achieved through the contribution of three main actors:

- the IOC and the host city (news promoters)
- TV networks (news disseminators)
- the global TV audience (consumers).

It is important to note here that the social construction of the Games has economic consequences, one of which involves the transformation of the audience from sport followers to a commodity with an economic value expressed in terms of its size and composition.

Subsequently, audience demographic reports and media usage patterns become crucial for the commercial success of the media and of the Olympic Games. Millions of dollars are paid for broadcasting rights but broadcasters charge their advertisers tens of thousands of dollars per second of airtime. Such profits are, however, contingent upon the delivery of certain viewing figure levels and failure to achieve these could result in huge losses for the media companies. NBC had to refund some US$ 90 million to its advertisers as compensation for the low ratings achieved by their coverage of the Barcelona Games of 1992.

## MEDIA CONSTRUCTION OF THE GAMES

Further scrutiny of the Olympics as a media event reveals that TV coverage is built around two vectors – as a social system and a performance system (Plate 6.2). The broadcasts of the 1984 Los Angeles Games as a *social construct* included eleven building blocks and tens of frames (Meadow, 1987).

1. *The sports events*

   ▪ medal events
     (30 per cent of Olympic broadcasting time)
   ▪ qualifying or trial heats
     (24 per cent of Olympic broadcasting time)
   ▪ highlights
     (2.06 per cent of Olympic broadcasting time)
   ▪ explanations
     (1 per cent of Olympic broadcasting time)
   ▪ locker room interviews
     (1.5 per cent of Olympic broadcasting time)

2. *The athletes*

   ▪ up close and personal in-depth look
     (1.8 per cent of Olympic broadcasting time)

Plate 6.2 Watching the Games

3. *Sports trivia*

   ■ the Olympic encyclopaedia
   (1 per cent of Olympic broadcasting time)

4. *Ceremony*

   (4 per cent of Olympic broadcasting time)

5. *Education*

   ■ lessons of history
   (sport and Olympics in particular)
   ■ international studies
   (political/trade relations between countries)
   ■ sociology lessons
   (of the Games and around the Games)
   ■ geography lessons
   (location of different countries/cultures)
   ■ snapshots
   (photos of arenas where events are held)
   ■ sports psychology and physiology lessons
   (mental training of athletes)
   ■ fitness lessons
   (role of training and nutrition for athletes)
   (1.7 per cent of Olympic broadcasting time)

6. *Hosting*

   ■ audio/video hosting
   ■ table of contents
   ■ review (what has already been shown)
   (4 per cent of Olympic broadcasting time)

7. *News*

   ■ Olympic news
   ■ Newsbreaks
   (1 per cent of Olympic broadcasting time)

8. *Entertainment*

   ■ Olympic montage (a video essay to stir and excite the audience)
   (1 per cent of Olympic broadcasting time)

93

9. *Talk show*

   ▦ interviews and guests
   (3 per cent of Olympic broadcasting time)

10. *Graphics*

    ▦ flying banner
    ▦ montage banners
    (200 minutes of Olympic broadcasting time)

11. *Commercials*
    (25 per cent of Olympic broadcasting time)

The Olympic broadcast as a *performance system* includes four building blocks:

1 *Physical performance of the body*
  Emphasis on athletes' skills, abilities and determination to win

2 *Individuals symbolising a whole nation*
  Athletes viewed as typical representatives of whole nations and their physical and moral qualities attributed to it; the nation seen as a single sentient being, a metonym

3 *Presentation of national teams*
  Scores, medals and ranking

4 *Representation*
  Of Olympic heroes/heroines and stereotypical images.

These general vectors of Olympic broadcasting, however, will vary in different countries depending on a number of cultural, technical, economic and political factors. In a multi-national comparative study of the TV broadcasts of the 1992 Games in Barcelona, de Moragas Spa (2001) identified four key Olympic programming models. There were broadcasters:

▦ that dedicated all their programming to the Olympic Games without altering their regular programming strategies (Eurosport or Canal Plus, France)
▦ that dedicated a large part of their programming to the Olympic Games but were unable to offer their audiences adequate alternatives (Cuba and China)
▦ that dedicated a large part of their programming to the Olympic Games whilst retaining some of their usual programming (French A2, FR3, NBC, BBC)

■ from the same country offering complementary programming strategies (Germany, Greece, Russia, Japan).

The Olympic programming in some countries was timetabled in different blocks and parts of the day. According to Nicholas Schiavone, Senior Vice-President of NBC, its Olympic programming principles interpret the Olympics as:

■ a story
■ linkage – gluing the viewer to the Games alone
■ reality in the form of unscripted drama
■ credibility – marked with trust between the media and the audience
■ a metaphor for life and possibilities
■ identity – allowing people to see themselves in the Games
■ idealistic – with purity and honour being the essence of the Games
■ a patriotic celebration.

The lessons from broadcasting suggest that the Olympic television 'experience' differs for viewers around the world, and this in turn influences our understanding of the Olympics.

Finally, the media influence our knowledge and attitudes. Most people's experience, limited to media text and pictures, affects their perceptions, attitudes and beliefs about Olympic sport and its values. This is achieved in a number of ways, two of the most obvious being the use of stereotypes and discourses. Additionally, because of their huge audience-drawing potential, the Olympics are much sought-after for commercial advertising, the ultimate objective of which is to develop consumer skills.

---

**STUDY ACTIVITY 6.5**

Look at the note on 'Stereotypes and Discourses' on the book's website. Read a newspaper article on the Opening Ceremony of the 2004 Athens Olympics. Can you identify at least one popular discourse about the home country?

---

The Olympic media is a complex phenomenon and a field of production that incorporates a variety of ideological, economic, cultural, technological and organisational aspects. The future success of the Olympic Games is unthinkable without television, but the notion that the Olympics are purely a media event, and that the broadcasting authorities are motivated only by profit, would be misleading.

---

IN BRIEF

## COMMUNICATING THE ATLANTA 1996 OLYMPIC GAMES

In July 1996 there were 1242 Atlanta Olympic Broadcasting employees compared to 39 in 1993. The Games creative theme was 'Supporting the Dream'. Live broadcasts were expected to attract viewers, with action spontaneous and unrehearsed.

*Creative theme*

The creative theme of the Atlanta 1996 Games, aimed at conveying the notion of the Olympics as the world's biggest sporting forum where only the best athletes come to compete and achieve their dreams, was based on a well-formulated communication strategy and a key message developed by the Organising Committee of the Olympic Games (AOCOG).

*Communications strategy*

> To implement a regular flow of information worldwide, across a range of media, that provides detail about the business of Olympics. An increased effort, on heightening awareness of the TOP sponsor companies, will be implemented during the Olympic Games.
>
> (AOGOC, 1997, p. 3)

*Key message*

> Commercial programmes help make the Olympic Movement what it is today. These initiatives provide much needed expertise, products, technology and financial support to the IOC, the National Olympic Committees, the Athletes, and the Olympic Games Organising Committees.
>
> (AOGOC, 1997, p.3)

*96*

## THE OLYMPICS AND THE MASS MEDIA

1   Explain why the Olympic Games are so attractive to the media.
2   What makes the Olympics a media event?
3   Examine the coverage of English/British performances at the 2004 Athens Olympic Games provided by a tabloid and a broadsheet newspaper.
4   Write a short essay of up to 1500 words on the media impact on the Olympics.

## CHAPTER SEVEN

# OLYMPIC MARKETING

**Chapter aims:**

- to analyse the nature, structure and organisation of the Olympic marketing
- to examine the concept of Olympic marketing in the light of the Olympic ideal.

After studying this chapter, you should be able to explain:

- what marketing means in Olympic terms
- the evolution of Olympic marketing and the key forces for shaping its recent structure
- the contribution of Olympic marketing to financial stability of the Olympic Movement
- some of the threats posed by commercialisation to the integrity of the Olympic Movement.

This chapter on Olympic marketing is an exploratory journey into the history and contemporary nature of the complex mechanism that is responsible both for the promotion of the Olympic idea and for raising revenue for the Olympic family, while keeping the right balance between sport and business. The chapter also sets out to analyse the nature of Olympic marketing and its role in asserting the mission of the Olympic Movement.

The first section examines the evolution of the Olympic marketing concept whilst the second discusses the key factors responsible for shaping modern Olympic

marketing. The third section unveils the structure of Olympic marketing, and finally, the main Olympic marketing programmes are explained.

Additional information, video clips and useful Internet links on the book's website complement the text. No marketing background is required to follow the narrative and to comprehend the key concepts. However, additional reading will be needed to build up a sound understanding of the fundamental issues covered in this chapter.

## WHAT IS OLYMPIC MARKETING?

Olympic marketing is globally and territorially co-ordinated and executed by the International Olympic Committee (IOC) programme of activities.

The aim of the IOC is to promote the Olympic Games and to enhance the financial stability of the Olympic Movement. Olympic marketing is not a new idea and has a long history dating back to Ancient Greece and to the first modern Olympics of 1896. The commercial association of the Much Wenlock Olympic Games (1850) organised by Dr W.P. Brookes was one of the most influential factors in shaping the vision of the founder of the modern Olympics, Baron Pierre de Coubertin.

> ## STUDY ACTIVITY 7.1
>
> Look at the chronology of Olympic marketing on the book's website and try to identify the key social, economic and political factors in the evolution of the modern marketing concept.

However, Olympic marketing emerged only recently as a co-ordinated global activity, triggered by two principal concerns – political and economic.

Until the beginning of the 1980s only a handful of National Olympic Committees (NOCs) had financial independence from their governments. Furthermore, the Olympic Movement was heavily dependent on the revenue generated by television rights, which accounted for more than 90 per cent of its total revenue – and 85 per cent of this came from US broadcasters.

The IOC Congress first addressed this issue in Baden-Baden in 1981 and in an attempt to redress the situation a New Sources of Financing Commission was created in 1983. In 1997 this Commission changed its mandate to focus on the future, and was renamed the Marketing Commission under the leadership of then IOC vice president Richard Pound.

The recommendations of the Marketing Commission (now chaired by Gerhard Heiberg) proved successful and income from new sources generated nearly US$15 billion. As a result the proportion of income from TV rights fell to 50 per cent with fees from US broadcasters accounting for less than 25 per cent of total revenue.

**IN BRIEF**

## OLYMPIC MARKETING – FUNDAMENTAL OBJECTIVES

- To ensure independent financial stability of the Olympic Movement and thereby assist in the worldwide development of Olympism
- To create a long-term marketing programme, rather than recreating the structure for each Olympics
- To ensure equitable revenue distribution throughout the Olympic Movement, and to provide financial support to emerging nations
- To ensure that the whole world can experience the Olympic Games via free-to-air television
- To curtail uncontrolled commercialisation and protect the inherent equity of the Olympic ideal
- To enlist marketing partners to promote Olympism and Olympic ideals.

### A marketing framework

The classical interpretation of marketing, which revolves around the notion of transaction, provides us with an important framework for understanding its function in an Olympic setting.

This suggests that marketing occurs any time one social actor (individual or organisation) tries to exchange something (goods, services or ideas) of value with another social actor.

In contrast to business marketing, which usually targets one group, the IOC, as a non-profit-making organisation, is involved with two major markets:

- *contributors* (or commercial partners in Olympic terms) who provide cash or services to the organisation
- *clients* – the recipients of its money and services.

The clients include members of the Olympic Family: National Olympic Committees (NOCs), International Federations (IFs), Organising Committees of the Olympic Games (OCOG) and athletes.

In the context of the Olympic Movement, this framework has four significant implications:

- the IOC associates with business or commercial enterprises for the mutual benefits of both parties
- this association (exchange) is not altruistic but commercial in nature – the commercial enterprise contributes something to the Olympic Movement and gets something in return
- IOC marketing programmes should cater equally for contributors to the Olympic Movement and for its clients
- as the IOC is a non-profit-making organisation (promoting Olympism) it possesses only ideas (imagery of the Games) and not tangible goods or services.

The above implications urge us to consider the notion of 'Olympism' as being subject to transaction, and a source of revenue for the Olympic Family. It would be useful therefore to widen our analysis and to examine some key environmental factors.

## FACTORS SHAPING MODERN OLYMPIC MARKETING

Four key factors require further consideration in order to clarify the concept of Olympic marketing:

1 organisational
2 economic
3 cultural
4 political

## Organisational

The IOC is the sole owner of the most expensive cultural commodity in the world – the Olympic Games. The cost of Sydney 2000 exceeded $1.7 billion.

Unlike a typical business the IOC has an unusual role in the production and marketing of the Games. This is because the preparation of its stars – the athletes – is the responsibility of their clubs, national associations and governments.

The responsibility for staging the Games lies with the host city and country although TV rights and sponsorship money cover a substantial part of their budgets. Staging the Games also involves a minimum of ten years' hard work by public and private agencies and thousands of volunteers.

Another untypical feature of the Olympic family 'business' is that the athletes, NOCs, IFs and OCOGs are producers and consumers of their own product. Therefore, achieving the key outcomes of marketing – customer satisfaction and organisational success – is contingent upon disposal of income. This is evidenced by regular constitutional squabbles within the IOC about the distribution of its wealth.

---

### STUDY ACTIVITY 7.2

Look at Tables 7a and 7b and Tables 9a and 9b on the book's website. How would you distribute the marketing revenue amongst International Federations?

---

The mission of the Olympic Movement is to aspire for a better world by encouraging equal physical education and opportunities, excellence, international understanding and fair play. Although it is non-commercial, this mission requires huge human and material resources within a uniform marketing concept. Table 7.1 shows the subtle difference between 'Olympic' and 'product' marketing. We may differentiate between three types of sports marketing (Mullin, 1983):

- to promote the interest of fans
- to promote participation in sport
- to promote consumer products via sport.

*Table 7.1* Comparison of commercial and Olympic marketing objectives

| Product marketing | Olympic marketing |
|---|---|
| Stimulate brand loyalty | Popularise Olympic cause |
| Change buying habits | Change physical activity habits |
| Increase product use | Increase rate of sport participation |
| Communicate product features | Communicate principles of Olympism |
| Improve product image | Improve public attitude of the Olympics |
| Inform public of new product | Inform public of new Olympics |
| Remind public to buy again | Remind public to watch and experience |

Source: after Bovee and Arens, 1989

Clearly Olympic marketing relates directly to the interest and participation of fans in sport (both intangible) and by doing that it is linked indirectly to the marketing of consumer goods.

Having outlined the nature of the 'Olympic idea' from a marketing point of view, it is equally important to examine the economic environment in which this idea becomes the subject of economic transactions.

## Economic

Olympic marketing is a global practice involving multi-national companies and is part of the current trend towards economic globalisation. This trend involves a new division of labour, an enhanced role of finance, increased capital mobility and a flow of intangible products/ideas (from software to images) rather than commodities.

This type of economic growth becomes possible because the cost of reproducing an idea is essentially zero and any returns it produces increase indefinitely with the scope of the market. In this respect the comments of former IOC vice president Richard Pound (quoted in Whannel, 1992) indicate that the Olympic idea is a significant subject for business or commercial transaction:

> When the only thing you have to sell are the aspiration of the youth and five rings, then misappropriation of intellectual property becomes a very serious matter.

Intellectual property protection is a massive issue recognised by both national and international laws. Opportunities to trade and profit from an association with the indicia of the Olympic brand (i.e. the five rings, the torch and flame and the word 'Olympic') were first regulated internationally by the Nairobi Treaty on the protection of the Olympic symbol (1981). The universal application of this law is, however, somewhat problematic as currently only twenty-six countries have ratified the convention.

In Australia, there are two detailed and strict statutory regimes in the form of the Olympic Insignia Protection Act (1987), and the Sydney 2000 Games Indicia and Images Protection Act (1996). Similar to these is the British Olympic Symbols (Protection) Act (1995).

In the words of John Moore (1996), marketing director of the Sydney 2000 OCOG, The Olympic brand is 'a rich and complex living synthesis of human endeavour, sport and multi-culturalism' and has some areas for development and fine-tuning that will allow its phenomenal growth to continue. He sees this growth in expanding consumer opportunities and promoting the brand beyond museums, for example in retail venues (Olympic stores). An example of similar activities is 'Talk Olympics', a service offered by the British Olympic Association which provides motivational speakers (former and current Olympic athletes) to interested parties (e.g. to schools, professional meetings, as after-dinner speakers) for a charge (Plate 7.1).

Plate 7.1 Talk Olympic (British Olympic Association)

## STUDY ACTIVITY 7.3

Study the Olympic Symbols Act (1995) on the book's website and draw up a list of 'cans' and 'cannots' for British businesses wishing to be associated with Olympic symbols.

## STUDY ACTIVITY 7.4

Read the article on the Olympic brand on the website and discuss the extent to which Olympism and all that it stands for can be referred to as a 'brand'.

Along with commercialisation come certain threats to the Olympic ideal concerning the behaviour and practices of athletes, officials, businesses and broadcasters. Some behaviour has been contrary to the fundamental Olympic principles and one of the 'marketing objectives' stated above is to prevent that from happening. In this respect, in 2000 the IOC expelled six of its members for inappropriate conduct in connection with the 2002 Winter Olympics at Salt Lake City.

Another threat facing the IOC is the misappropriation of the Olympic symbols – a practice often referred to as 'ambush marketing'. This occurs when a commercial company tries to establish or imply an association with the Olympic Games without paying royalties. The IOC Marketing Commission takes this issue very seriously and takes action to curtail all practices that threaten to tarnish the integrity of the Olympic ideal.

During the 1996 Atlanta Games, Nike ran an advertising campaign on billboards featuring slogans such as 'You don't win Silver – You lose Gold' and 'If you are not here to win – you are a tourist'. Another example was that of the Swiss broadcaster that tried to superimpose advertising over sporting images of the Games. Neither of these companies was an official Olympic sponsor.

In order to protect the brand value of the Olympic image and the rights of the global sponsors at the Salt Lake City Winter Olympic Games, ten organisations, including all NOC and IFs, the FBI, US Customs, local police and Sports Marketing Surveys joined together in a co-ordinated effort against ambush marketing. In the words of Michael Payne, IOC former marketing director:

Ambush marketing is not clever marketing – it is cheating. And who wants to be a cheat?

(IOC, 2001)

IOC marketing policy takes a proactive stance in trying to ensure the appreciation and support of commercial and media partners in the pursuit of its mission. Two examples illustrate this approach.

- In 1997 the IOC invited members of the sporting goods industry to establish an Olympic Marketing Code to encourage these companies to play fair. The outcome of this was that the industry leaders – Nike, Adidas, Reebok, Mizuno and Asics – have all signed an agreement committing their advertising to be in line with Olympic ideals.
- Every broadcaster who signs with the IOC is contractually obliged not only to transmit the Games, but to promote the Olympic Movement, 365 days a year. This includes public service announcements as well as year-round Olympic and pre-Games programming.

## Cultural

This element is essential for understanding the way in which Olympic marketing works. It is best characterised by the notion of 'commodification' – a process by which objects and people become organised as 'things' to be exchanged in a market.

Commodification reduces the value of any act or object to only its monetary exchange value, ignoring historical, artistic, or relational added values.

(Real, 1996, p. 44)

This process is a consequence of the emergence of a consumer-based economy complementing the productive structure of capitalism. It nurtures a mercantile culture keen to trade and profit whenever the opportunity presents itself and imposes exchange principles into daily life.

Olympic examples are numerous – from corporate logos to memorabilia – and includes claims such as those of the Express Mail Service (EMS) – an Olympic sponsor – that their three and a half million postal employees are part of the Olympic Movement.

The argument here is that consumer values differ from the basic principles and values of Olympism. Nonetheless, the Olympic Games are considered to be the major sporting event and consequently the Olympic rings are amongst the most easily and readily recognised symbols in the world.

**IN BRIEF**

## RESEARCH RESULTS ON THE POWER OF THE OLYMPIC SYMBOL

Tables 7c, 7d, 7e on the book's website represent the results of two Olympic marketing research studies (1995 and 1996) carried out in thirteen countries: Australia, Brazil, China, Germany, India, Jamaica, Japan, Malaysia, Nigeria, South Africa, Spain, the United Kingdom, and the United States. The principal message they convey is that the Olympic Games hold an unrivalled position as the world's top sporting event and that they stand for uniqueness and excellence.

### Political

Over the years the Olympic Movement has experienced various political interventions by governments and movements. The most prominent of these were the boycotts of the Moscow (1980) and the Los Angeles (1984) Games led by the US and Soviet administrations respectively.

Prior to 1984 governments around the world, whilst being sensitive to the opportunities presented by the staging of an Olympic Games, were reluctant to support them financially. The massive losses incurred by the host cities of the Munich (1972) and Montreal (1976) Olympics had evoked hostility rather than enthusiasm on the part of many public administrations.

Many governments were also forced to cut public spending including much of what might have been earmarked for sport.

Consequently the IOC found itself in a difficult situation with no bidding cities for the 1984 Olympiad. The Los Angeles notion of a Games financed wholly by private enterprise was viewed with considerable trepidation.

It was not surprising that there were no bidding cities for the 1984 Games. The Moscow Olympic Games were the last to enjoy substantial government financial support despite the stipulation of the Olympic Charter that National Olympic Committees should be politically independent from their national governments. In actual fact, in the 1980s not more than 5 out of the then 150 NOCs had any independent sources of revenue.

Taken together, the four key environments created the preconditions and the kind of thinking needed for the emergence of Olympic marketing.

## OLYMPIC MARKETING ORGANISATION AND SOURCES OF REVENUE

The underlying philosophy of Olympic marketing is to enhance the enduring and valuable image of the Olympic Movement. The overall direction of the Olympic marketing policy and the management of various programmes is the responsibility of the IOC, its Executive Board, and its Marketing Department, founded in 1989.

Their work is assisted by the following specialist agencies:

- Meridian Management S.A. (co-ordinates the management of The Olympic Partners (TOP) programme, Games marketing operations, and acts as NOCs marketing liaison)
- Olympic Television Archive Bureau (OTAB) (co-ordinates the management of the Olympic Movement's historical moving image archive and special broadcasting programming. OTAB is managed by TWI, the world's largest sports television producer)
- Olympic Photo Archive Bureau (OPAB) (manages the historical photo archive of the Olympic Movement and develops special Olympic photographic projects. OPAB is managed by All Sport, the world's largest sports photographic library)
- Sponsor Research International (executes the IOC global research)
- Sports Marketing Surveys (executes the IOC broadcasting data analysis).

The principal sources of Olympic marketing revenue include:

- television rights
- sponsorship
- licensing

- coins
- tickets.

**IN BRIEF**

## INCOME FROM TELEVISION

Since 1960, television revenues have replaced Olympic ticket sales as the principal source of income from the Games. The following data give television income as a proportion of total income for Olympics that took place between 1960 and 2000:

1960 – $1 of every $400
1972 – $1 of every $50
1980 – $1 of every $15
1984 – $1 of every $2
1996 – $1 of every $3
2000 – $1 of every $2.5

### Television rights

The IOC in conjunction with the Organising Committee for the Olympic Games (OCOG) allocates television rights to the Olympic Games. For more details on the IOC television policy see Chapter 6.

Avery Brundage, who presided over the IOC between 1952 and 1972, identified television as a viable source of revenue and as a means of promoting Olympism as early as 1954.

The first fees in return for TV rights were established by the IOC in preparation for the 1960 Summer and Winter Olympics in Tokyo and Innsbruck for the sums of US$150,000 and US$20,000 respectively. These amounts reached the unprecedented levels of US$1.482 billion in Athens 2004 and US$832 million in Turin 2006.

Income from television rights has allowed the IOC to allocate a record US$161 million to 26 international sports federations whose sports are on the Summer Olympics programme and more than US$92 million to 7 international sports federations whose sports are on the Winter Olympics programme. See Table 7.2 for an overview of TV revenue and its distribution (see also Tables 7a and 7b on the book's website).

*Table 7.2* Global TV revenue for Olympics, 1980–2008

| Summer Games | | Revenue (million US$) | Winter Games | | Revenue (million US$) |
|---|---|---|---|---|---|
| 1980 | Moscow | 101 | 1980 | Lake Placid | 21 |
| 1984 | Los Angeles | 287 | 1984 | Sarajevo | 103 |
| 1988 | Seoul | 403 | 1988 | Calgary | 325 |
| 1992 | Barcelona | 636 | 1992 | Albertville | 292 |
| 1996 | Atlanta | 895 | 1994 | Lillehammer | 353 |
| 2000 | Sydney | 1318 | 2002 | Salt Lake City | 748 |
| 2004 | Athens | 1482 | 2006 | Turin | 832 |
| 2008 | Beijing | 1697 | | | |

Source: IOC *Olympic Marketing Fact File* No. 45, 1999, 2000

## Sponsorship

The second major source of Olympic marketing revenue is sponsorship, which accounts for approximately 40 per cent of the overall marketing programme.

All sponsorship programmes are co-ordinated by the IOC and operate on three levels. Their aim is to ensure independent financial stability, continual support for, and an equitable revenue distribution throughout the Olympic Family.

The three levels of sponsorship are:

- *international* – with a world-wide programme known as TOP (The Olympic Partners)
- *host country* – with the local programmes of the OCOG
- *national* – with the NOC programmes.

More information about these programmes is available on the book's website.

The commercial partners participating in various programmes provide not only cash but also vital technical support, expertise and service for the IOC, NOCs and OCOGs (known as value in kind – VIK). Other Olympic marketing programmes include IOC suppliers, IOC licensing and Olympic Philately and Coins. The evolution of the TOP programme is shown in Table 7.3.

The Olympic Suppliers programme is another category of commercial activity that offers less than the TOP programme in marketing rights and opportunities.

*Table 7.3* Stages of evolution of the TOP programme

| | TOP I 1988 Calgary/Seoul | TOP II 1992 Albertville/ Barcelona | TOP III 1994 Lillehammer 1996 Atlanta | TOP IV 1998 Nagano 2000 Sydney | TOP V 2001 Salt Lake 2004 Athens |
|---|---|---|---|---|---|
| No. of companies | 9 | 12 | 10 | 11 | 11 |
| No. of countries | 159 | 169 | 197 | 200 | 200 |
| Total revenue (million $US) | 95 | 175 | 350 | 550 | 600 |

Source: *Olympic Marketing Fact File*, Nos. 60, 65, 1999, 2000

## Licensing

The IOC Licensing programme is an agreement between the IOC, NOC or the OCOG and commercial companies for the right to use either the appropriate national or Games emblem on their merchandise.

This usually includes commemorative items such as T-shirts, pins and baseball caps. In return, these companies pay a royalty fee of between 10 and 15 per cent. Commercial companies also use Olympic athletes to endorse their products, as in the case of the Sydney swimming gold medallist Ian Thorpe (Plate 7.2).

## Coins

The Olympic Coin programme (commemorative coins) is as old as the Games themselves. Huot (1996, p. 39) writes:

> Today the value of a coin is determined by its face value which, for the most part, has little to do with its intrinsic value. This difference between intrinsic and face value, referred to as seignorage, is a very important source of revenue for governments of all nations.

The first government to use an Olympic coin (a 500-Markaa silver coin) to commemorate a modern Olympic Games was that of Finland in 1951. It is reckoned that the 605,000 coins issued over two years produced a US$1 million profit for the Finnish mint, part of which was used to cover the cost of staging the Games.

Plate 7.2 The face of Australian athlete Ian Thorpe is used for product endorsement

Since 1951 this successful innovation has seen more than 350 million Olympic coins sold globally, raising more than US$1.1 billion for the issuing authorities and the Olympic Family. In 1984 the revenue from TV rights was exceeded by the US$73.5 million raised for the Los Angeles OCOG and the US Olympic Committee.

## Tickets

Ticketing is another major source of revenue for Olympic Organising Committees. Out of 7.6 million tickets available for the 2000 Sydney Games, 6.7 million (a record 92.4 per cent) were sold, generating US$551 million.

This figure represents 19 per cent of the total revenue from the Games, with the opening and closing ceremonies and the athletics, triathlon and gymnastics events being sold out.

The ticketing revenue for the 2002 Salt Lake City Games was US$183 million. More than 1.365 million (83 per cent of all) tickets were sold, with skiing and ice hockey being the most popular sports among spectators.

## MARKETING THE OLYMPIC BRAND

The Olympic image can be compared to a commercial brand. It represents core values that are communicated to the people of the world. The Olympic Games is unique because:

- its underlying philosophy is to celebrate humanity – a celebration of culture, art, education and participation
- it is the biggest multi-sport event in the world
- it attracts a global television audience which reached 3.7 billion people for Sydney 2000 and 2.1 billion for Salt Lake City 2002.

The 'Olympic Image' comprises four complementary messages:

- hope
- dreams and inspiration
- friendship and fair play
- joy in the effort.

This unique image has not only had to be established, and must now be maintained. Past experiences have shown that a harmonious and colourful image embracing the Games and the host city environment is vital for their success.

A tough lesson was learned in Atlanta (1996) where lack of co-operation from the Atlanta City authorities led to an unauthorised street bazaar that contrasted sharply with the hoped-for image of the Games as a catalyst for change.

In 1998 the IOC introduced the Olympic Games Identification Project (OGIP), the sole purpose of which is to ensure continuity and quality in the exposure of Olympic imagery from one Olympiad to the next. The driving force behind this project is a commitment to the development of consistent brand experiences for the Olympic broadcast audience, the athlete and the spectator.

## THE OLYMPIC IMAGE

*Hope*: The Olympic Games offer hope for a better world, using sport for all without discrimination as an example and a lesson.

*Dreams and inspiration*: The Olympic Games provide inspiration to achieve personal dreams through the lessons of the athletes' striving, sacrifice and determination.

*Friendship and fair play*: The Olympic Games provide tangible examples of how humanity can overcome political, economic, religious and racial prejudices through the values inherent in sport.

*Joy in the effort*: The Olympic Games celebrate the universal joy of doing one's best, regardless of the outcome.

(Source: IOC, 2001)

## STUDY ACTIVITY 7.5

The video *Through the Eye of the Beholder* shows the IOC approach to Olympic imagery. Can you identify the key elements used for the creation of a singular feeling during the Olympics? Watch the video on the book's website.

### The Olympic Games Identification Project

Three particular elements of the OGIP deserve mention.

The first is the 'Celebrate Humanity' global campaign launched in Sydney 2000, which includes television, radio and print executions run throughout the world before and during the Games. Various audio-visual presentations tell remarkable stories of Olympic athletes' dedication, friendship, strength of character and effort.

For example, the creative message of the 2002 Salt Lake City Winter Olympics was 'Light the Fire Within' and was complemented by the ideas of contrast, culture and courage, representing the landscape and cultural history of Utah and the global heritage of the Olympic Games.

## STUDY ACTIVITY 7.6

Watch the six video clips of 'Celebrate Humanity' on the book's website. Can you relate some of these messages to your personal experience?

The second element of the OGIP, which is consistent with the IOC's image identification efforts, is the expansion of consumer opportunities.

The Sydney Olympic Licensing Programme resulted in the development of more than 3000 different product lines that were sold in more than 2000 retail outlets across Australia. The first Olympic Stores were opened and an average of 45,000 customers per day visited the superstore in Sydney Olympic Park. By day 9 of the Games the Superstore had surpassed its budget of US$7 million (Plate 7.3).

The third element of the OGIP – the growth and popularity of the Olympic spectacle – has led to bigger, better and more professionally organised Games. Along with this growth, however, have come increased levels of complexity and risk.

To improve the efficiency of the Games, and to ensure that the knowledge and expertise developed during previous Olympiads is not wasted, the IOC

Plate 7.3  The Olympic Store, Sydney

introduced the Transfer of Knowledge Programme in February 2002. This was done to help ensure that host cities do not have to 're-invent the wheel' every four years and helps to facilitate the transfer of information, support and knowledge services between the IOC, bid cities, host cities and Games organising committees. This programme is run by the Olympic Games Knowledge Service Company, which assists various stakeholders of the Olympic Family to conceive, bid for, scope, plan and operate the Games.

Over the past 20 years Olympic marketing has managed to secure the financial stability of the Olympic Games and of members of the Olympic Family. It is responsible for the optimistic prospects up to the year 2008, with the TV rights and TOP programme already in place.

The future, however, will demand that all 200 National Olympic Committees around the world develop a clear marketing orientation and become managers of the Olympic image as well as fund-raisers. This may pose some great challenges to the whole Olympic Family.

## OLYMPIC MARKETING

1    What are the key marketing objectives of the IOC?
2    Discuss the effect of organisational, economic, cultural and political factors on shaping the notion of modern marketing.
3    Elaborate on the dangers inherent in marketing the Olympic Games.
4    Discuss the compatibility between marketing and sponsorship and the Olympic ideal.
5    Explain the meaning of the commercialisation of the Olympic Games. What in your view would be a viable strategy for protecting the athletes and their governing bodies (NOCs) from commercial exploitation?
6    Consider whether or not you believe that the cultures of some nations or other groupings of people should be studied more carefully than others by the business community when associating their products with the Olympic symbols.
7    In what sense can you discuss the Olympics as a brand?

## CHAPTER EIGHT

# ECONOMIC AND ENVIRONMENTAL IMPACTS OF THE OLYMPIC GAMES

## Chapter aims:

- to discuss the Olympic Games as a strategy for social, economic and environmental change
- to examine the economic impact of the Olympic Games
- to analyse the environmental impact of the Olympic Games.

After studying this chapter, you should be able to explain:

- the role of the Olympic Games (and sport in general) in city and country strategies for asserting their place on the global cultural and economic map
- various approaches for assessing the economic impact of sporting events
- a range of environmental issues concerning the organisation of the Olympic Games
- the standards in setting short- and long-term economic and environmental objectives established by previous Olympics.

## INTRODUCTION

Since their first edition in 1896, all organisers of the Olympic Games have been aware of the spin-offs generated by such an undertaking. However, it was not until the mid-1980s that the issue of the economic importance of sport became a part of the agenda of sport managers, entrepreneurs and politicians.

The first study of the economic impact of sport in the UK was undertaken in 1985, and served as a model for a Council of Europe co-ordinated nine-nation study in 1989. The results of both studies surprised governments across Europe and showed that, on average, sport contributed 1.5 per cent to the countries' gross domestic product (GDP), raising its status to that of a significant economic factor.

As far as it can be ascertained, the first in-depth study of the economic and social impacts of an Olympic Games was conducted by Ritchie and Smith (1991) on the 1988 Calgary Winter Olympics. The issue of the environmental impact gained recognition in a similar vein and since the mid-1990s environmental protection has become the third dimension of the Olympic Movement alongside sport and culture.

> The International Olympic Committee (IOC) in its capacity as coor-dinator of the Olympic Movement, has resolutely committed itself to extending the range of its activities in the field of the environment and making the environment the third dimension of Olympism, after sport and culture. It sees to it that the Olympic Games are held in conditions which demonstrate a responsible concern for environmen-tal issues and works to promote a policy of consciousness-rising among the members of the Olympic Movement in order that all sports events may take environmental considerations into account in a responsible way.
>
> (http://www.olympic.org.uk/organisation/missions/environment-uk.asp)

## A STRATEGY FOR SOCIAL CHANGE

The revival of the Olympic Games by Pierre de Coubertin was based on the belief that organised sport can be an agent of physical and cultural change. The notion of social democracy and equality was an essential part of this change and was substantiated by the principle of rotating the locations of the Games every four years, thus enabling more countries to benefit.

Since, among other things, Olympism stands for physical and health education and equal opportunities, staging the Olympic Games inevitably urges organisers to address this issue and to introduce strategies aiming to raise public awareness and provide better conditions, ensuring that education in and through physical activity can take place.

The entertainment value of the Olympics adds another important element to the social change. This is because they contribute to enhancing national identity and pride, and mobilise social support for state projects which otherwise would not have materialised.

As a result of post-industrial developments at the end of the twentieth century, cities are experiencing the need to re-define their image by developing policies aiming to compensate for reduced public expenditures, and equally to bring in more inward and foreign investments. Hallmark sporting events, and the Olympics in particular, are seen as catalysts for such economic growth, because of their potential to generate business activities, such as job creation or tourism, and to contribute to the feel-good factor.

The Olympics also play an essential role in urban regeneration by transforming the physical environment, including renewing and building facilities, parks, recreational areas or transport infrastructure. This justifies their inclusion as a strategy in urban policies, and specifically as a means of enhancing a city's landscape and physical appearance. Cities are vying to host major sporting events, and since 1984 there have been between seven and eleven bidding cities for the Olympics.

There were nine world-renowned cities, including London, in the race for the 2012 Olympic Games, shortlisted by the IOC in July 2004 to the cities of London, Madrid, Moscow, New York and Paris. The benefits associated with an Olympic bid concern not only the host city but all contenders. The Manchester 1996 and 2000 Olympic bids illustrate the point. Among various tangible and intangible effects was a governmental subsidy of £50 million to the city for the construction of a new indoor stadium for cycling and other sports.

## ECONOMIC IMPACT OF THE OLYMPICS

The economic and environmental impacts of the Olympic Games are many and vary from city to city because of factors such as specific aims, scale and geopolitical and economic conditions of the host city and country. Examining the economic impact of the Olympic Games poses several methodological questions, which need to be taken into consideration if we are to produce a coherent account.

### Measuring impact

Collins and Jackson (1998) identified two basic methods for measuring the impact – 'cost–benefit analysis' and 'planning and balance sheet' – and pointed out the strengths and limitations of each. They also highlighted the misapplication of economic impact studies because of the use of inappropriate multipliers of sales or employment, omitting cost, and including spending by visitors who would normally be in the city anyway. Similarly, Preuss (2001) advocated a complex input–output model, but pointed out that multiplier is fine to demonstrate the economic effects of the Games in general.

---


**IN BRIEF**

## MULTIPLIERS

Multiplier analysis converts the total amount of additional expenditure in the host city to a net amount of income retained within the city after allowing for 'leakages' from the local economy. For example, the total amount of money spent in a hotel will not necessarily all be re-circulated within a given city. Some of the money will be spent on wages, food suppliers, beverage suppliers, etc., the recipients of which may well be outside the city. Thus the multiplier is a device that converts total additional expenditure into the amount of local income retained within the local economy.

(Gratton and Taylor, 2000, p. 181)

---

D. Howard and J. Crampton's definition (quoted in Dubi, 1996, pp. 89–90) of economic impact as 'the net economic change in a host community that results from spending attributed to a sports event or facility' brings more clarity to the discussion.

It suggests that we pay attention to quantifiable data such as overall demand connected with an event, regional income, employment and investment.

Dubi (1996) developed a simplified model for calculating the impact of the Olympics. It is based on the size of direct and created demand, in which the greater the demand, the bigger the impact (Table 8.1). It follows the logic that the overall demand results from the direct and indirect expenditure made in

120

*Table 8.1* Calculating the impact of the Olympics: direct and created demand

| Direct demand | Created demand |
| --- | --- |
| Investment by the state (sports, town planning or other) | Public investment created |
| Private investments (sports, town planning or other) | Private investment created |
| Public consumption (publicity, cultural activities, protocol) | Public consumption created |
| Private consumption (visitors, sponsors, OCOG expenses) | Private consumption created |
| **Gross total expenditure** | **Created impact** |
| Leaks (expenditure by firms outside the region) | |
| **Net total expenditure** | |
| Disturbance effects (tourists kept away by the event) Internal expenditure (expenditure by residents) Direct impact (net direct injection) | |

order to organise the Olympics. This includes infrastructure and operation-related costs necessary for holding the Games: to satisfy this demand, it is necessary to invest. The result is demand created by the initial expenditure.

## Positive and negative effects

Based on this model Dubi calculated the overall impact of the Olympic Games in Los Angeles, Seoul and Barcelona, shown in Table 8.2. The value of the multi-

*Table 8.2* Overall impact of the Olympic Games from 1984 to 1992

| Criterion | 1984 Los Angeles | 1988 Seoul | 1992 Barcelona |
| --- | --- | --- | --- |
| Multiplier (k) | 3 | 2.99 | 2.66 |
| Net direct injection (US$) | 792 million | 3.1 billion | 9.8 billion |
| Created impact (US$) | 1584 billion | 6.2 billion | 16.2 billion |
| Total impact (US$) | 2376 billion | 9.3 billion | 26 billion |

Source: Dubi, 1996

Table 8.3 Economic impact of the 1992 Barcelona Olympics

| | | Operating expenses† | | | | Other effects | |
|---|---|---|---|---|---|---|---|
| Investment* | (%) | Expenditure | (%) | Income | (%) | Positive | Negative |
| City Olympic facilities/villages | 33.6 | Technology | 5 | Tickets | 6 | Unemployment down from 128,000 in 1986 to 78,000 in 1993 | Rentals increased by 339% 1986–92 |
| Olympic facilities elsewhere | 9.1 | Sites | 25 | Accomm. | 2 | | |
| Other sports facilities | 3.9 | Media | 10 | Sponsors | 22 | Hotel beds grew by 38% 1990–92 | 48% of population 'apathetic' about developments |
| Cultural facilities | 2.1 | Organisation | 14 | Licences | 4 | | |
| Roads | 33.1 | Promotion/ advertising | 9 | Lotteries, coins, stamps | 20 | | |
| Airport | 3.5 | Security | 3 | Services | 33 | New beaches attract 2.5 million users | |
| Public transport | 1.5 | Housing/ transport | 18 | State transfers | 10 | | |
| Hotels | 5.1 | Test events/ Paralympics | 8 | Asset sales | 3 | New sports facilities jointly managed by clubs, federations, or companies | |
| Communications/other services | 4.5 | Ceremonies | 5 | | | | |

Source: Collins and Jackson, 1998
Notes: * Allocations of a total of US$5.4 billion
       † Allocations of a total of US$1.08 billion

plier reflects the size of the city. The larger the city, the less will be the leakages from the local economy, and the higher the value of the multiplier.

The economic impacts shown in Table 8.2 were achieved as a result of different approaches to the organisation of the Games. In Los Angeles, staging the Olympics was predominantly a private project with little or no public investments. By contrast, public authorities in Seoul and Barcelona were very active, and the share of their investments was 67.3 and 77.6 per cent respectively. However, investment in sports facilities constituted a relatively small proportion of total investments, reaching 16 per cent in Seoul and 9.1 per cent in Barcelona.

A more detailed breakdown of the 1992 Barcelona Summer Olympic Games is offered by Collins and Jackson (1998) (Table 8.3). This helps us appreciate the areas where the major costs were incurred and the sources of income (Table 8.3). It indicates that the economic impact cannot be all positive, but has a negative aspect as well. One area that has clearly suffered in the past, and will continue to do so, is the increased price of land, housing and rentals in and around the city hosting the Games.

The Sydney 2000 Games were no exception to this trend despite their projected (1994–2004) A$7.3 billion contribution to Australia's gross domestic product, the creation of 150,000 full and part-time jobs and an extra 1.32 million visitors from overseas (Plate 8.1).

Plate 8.1 Japanese tourists visit the Sydney Opera House

The cost of accommodation rocketed, the increase being between three- and eight-fold. In addition to the negative impact of the Games it is also a fact that for a long period (from six to ten years) a host country's major inward investment is inevitably channelled to the Olympic city and its immediate vicinity, thus depriving other areas of much needed improvement. For a summary of the economic impact of the 2000 Sydney and 2002 Salt Lake City Olympic Games, see Chapter 15.

Local Olympic commercial sponsorhip is an example which illustrates both sides of this argument. The money generated through it goes to the National Olympic Committee of the country but is then distributed to fund the preparation of young and elite athletes who live and train in their localities (Plate 8.2).

The 1996 Atlanta Olympic Games raised a significant amount of revenue for the state of Georgia, estimated to have been worth US$5.1 billion. This was broken down as follows:

- $9.3 million (5 per cent) corporate income taxes
- $10.7m (6 per cent) selective sales taxes
- $65.4m (37 per cent) personal taxes
- $91m (52 per cent) sales and use taxes.

Plate 8.2 An example of local sponsorship at the 2000 Sydney Games

This was not the case, however, with the 1994 Winter Olympic Games in Lillehammer, Norway, where the cost of the Games (US$1.17 billion) far outweighed the revenue (US$0.8 billion). This did not, however, detract from the long-term objectives of the organisers, which were to establish the small ski resort of Lillehammer on the world map and to promote the country in the broadest sense.

## Costs to participating countries

An often-overlooked aspect of the economic impact concerns the ever-increasing cost of the Olympic Games to participating countries. Sending more and better-prepared athletes to the Games is an objective of many National Olympic Committees but it comes at a price. At the same time expenditure associated with the participation of a national team for the Games, such as pre-Games competitions and training camps, hospitality and communications, represents a significant part of the investment flow to the local economy.

As an independent sports governing body, the British Olympic Association has the responsibility for sending British athletes to the Games without recourse to government money. This is done by means of an Olympic Appeal, which invites contributions from individuals, companies and activities, and through the Gold Club Sponsor's Programme. This was first launched after the Games in Stockholm in 1912, and between the 1952 Helsinki and 1996 Atlanta Olympics generated a total of £33,139,000.

If we are to calculate the cost of an Olympic medal based on the money generated by each appeal (which is spent on athletes' preparation and participation in the Games) against the number of medals won at the respective Olympics, the cost for medals won in Atlanta would be a staggering £918,000, compared to £6363 for an Olympic medal in Helsinki. Achieving Olympic excellence therefore appears to be a costly business.

---

### STUDY ACTIVITY 8.1

Examine the UK Sport Policy (1999) for staging major sporting events on the book's website. Identify the key economic criteria which sport governing bodies should take into account when planning to host an event.

---

125

## A complex phenomenon

The economic impact of an Olympic Games is a complex phenomenon and is difficult to measure precisely. It is concerned both with the concentration of cash flows from domestic and foreign consumers and investors, and with the opposite financial flows (leakages) to contractors and suppliers. For example, in the case of Sydney, Preuss (2001) identified the following categories of national and world-wide consumer expenditure:

- sponsors
- television
- tickets
- licences
- coins and stamps
- taxes
- IOC mediated revenue
- Olympic Coordinating Authority spending on sport and government investments.

On the outflow side, that is, money not retained in the country, expenditures were made on wages for:

- overseas personnel employed for the Games
- the supply of technology
- athletes' and officials' travel
- other essential services such as communications.

## ENVIRONMENTAL IMPACT OF THE OLYMPIC GAMES

It could be claimed that there is an inherited conflict between sport and nature. Since the renewal of the Olympic Games in 1896 they have grown enormously not only in popularity, but in scale, numbers and cost. Inevitably, striving to stage the 'best ever' Games has led to a massive intervention in nature. Data from authoritative international studies suggest that annual deforestation is equal to the surface area of Great Britain, and warn that pollution of the air and the sea as well as irreversible loss of other natural resources have reached dangerous proportions.

Unfortunately, the Olympic Games also contribute to these negative processes. An alarming recent example was the 1992 Winter Olympic Games in Albertville in the Savoie region of France. The Games were highly regionalised with competition venues located in thirteen Alpine communities spread over 1657 square kilometres. This model of organising the Games necessitated an ambitious construction programme comprising sports facilities, hotels and roads. The accomplishment of these projects resulted in irreversible losses of massive forest areas and disturbance of wildlife, and earned the Albertville Games the label 'environmental disaster'.

## Urban impacts

In a comprehensive study of the urban impact of the Olympic Games from 1896 to 1996, Essex and Chalkley (1998) identified three categories of Olympic city according to the scale of their building and investment projects. Table 8.4 sums up the key findings of the study. Cities in the first category (low impact) are those that sought to keep expenditure to a minimum and did not build, or made only modest investments in new sports facilities.

The second category includes cities where major sports facilities were built but where only modest changes to the city's environment and infrastructure resulted.

*Table 8.4* Urban impact of the Olympic Games, 1896–1996

| Impact | Olympic Games | Projects |
|---|---|---|
| Low | 1896 Athens | Panathenean stadium |
| | 1900 Paris | No new facilities |
| | 1904 St Louis | No new facilities |
| | 1948 London | No new facilities |
| | 1968 Mexico | Modest investment – no new facilities |
| | 1984 Los Angeles | Modest investment in new facilities |
| Focus on sports facilities | 1908 London | White City Stadium (a multi-sport facility) |
| | 1912 Stockholm | New stadium, specialist facilities for separate sports |
| | 1932 Los Angeles | New stadium, Olympic village, facilities for other sports |
| | 1936 Berlin | 100,000 capacity stadium, substantial sports facilities, a sports forum, Olympic village, House of German Sport administrative building |
| | 1952 Helsinki | New stadium, Olympic village |
| | 1956 Melbourne | Olympic Park complex, Olympic village |
| | 1996 Atlanta | Olympic stadium, Aquatic Centre, basketball gym, equestrian venue, hockey stadium |

*Table 8.4* continued

| Impact | Olympic Games | Projects |
|---|---|---|
| Stimulating environmental transformation | 1960 Rome | New sporting infrastructure along a new Olympic Way; modern municipal water supply system; airport facilities |
| | 1964 Tokyo | A new road and network of 22 highways; 2 underground railway lines; facilities |
| | 1972 Munich | 280 hectare derelict site redevelopment; restoration & pedestrianisation of a historic quarter; improved public transport; underground car-parking; shopping centres, hotels, expressways |
| | 1976 Montreal | Olympic park; 20km subway system; new airport, hotels and roads |
| | 1980 Moscow | 12 new sports facilities; new hotels; airport terminal; Olympic TV & radio centre, Olympic communication centre, Novosti Press Agency building |
| | 1988 Seoul | Sports facilities, Olympic village; de-polluting the Han River; 3 subway lines, 47 bus routes; Seoul Arts Centre, National Classical Musical Institute, Chongju Museum; refurbished shrines; garbage/general hygiene improvement |
| | 1992 Barcelona | 15 new sports venues, Olympic village; coastal ring road, new marina; re-structuring sewage system; regeneration of the waterfront facilities; upgrading communications |
| | 2000 Sydney | All designs and renovations based on 'green principles'; new Olympic stadium and village; buildings with solar power and water recycling |

The third category deals with cities where organisers used the Olympics to introduce large-scale urban developments and improvements that went far beyond the necessity of constructing new sporting facilities. For example, the principal types of projects for the 1992 Barcelona Olympics were (Brunet, 1995):

- road/transportation infrastructures
- housing, offices and commercial venues
- telecommunication and services
- hotel facilities
- sports facilities
- environmental infrastructures.

Table 8.4 shows that the environmental impact will differ between Games. What is certain, however, is that any Olympic project is bound to intervene with nature and to produce changes in the environment.

## Sport and nature

The conflict between sport and nature was seriously addressed in the early 1970s. An environmental initiative by the organisers of the 1972 Munich Olympic Games invited all participating National Olympic Committees to plant a shrub from their country in the Olympic park, and coined the slogan *certatio sana in natura sana* (healthy competition in an intact environment). These first ad hoc steps were gradually transformed by the IOC into well-defined strategies and actions aimed at arresting the harmful influence of sport on the environment.

The destructive impact on the natural environment of Albertville in 1992 served as a wake-up call for the IOC, which prior to then did not have an environmental policy. The growing concern for the natural environment brought into play a new way of thinking captured by the notion of 'sustainable development'. Its core idea is to establish a balance between the ever-expanding scale of major sporting events and the conservation of natural resources.

## The IOC takes action

The IOC took part in the United Nations' Conference on Environment and Development in Rio de Janeiro in 1992 and committed the Olympic Movement to the concept of sustainable development (The Global Plan AGENDA 21). Among other policies, the IOC developed a list of environmental requirements concerning the cities bidding to host the Olympic Games. These demand more responsibility and accountability from the Organising Committees of the Olympic Games (OCOG), and bind them to co-operate with respective agencies, to plan and implement environmentally sound projects.

The template for the IOC environmental policy was set up by the Norwegian city of Lillehammer, which hosted the 1994 Winter Olympic Games. At the outset Lillehammer made environmental issues a priority and committed the bid to deliver sustainable Games. This promise was reinforced by the personal involvement of the Norwegian Prime Minister Gro Harlem Brundtland, who at the time was also Chair of the United Nations World Commission on the Environment and Development. The 1994 Lillehammer Winter Olympic Games will go down in history as 'an environmental–political showcase'.

129

## STUDY ACTIVITY 8.2

Consider the Olympic Movement AGENDA 21 policy document on the book's website.

1   Visit your local sport/leisure centre and find out whether the use of energy and water follows the standards set out in paragraph 3.1.6 of the document.
2   Pay a visit to a sport store and enquire how many sports goods have an ISO certification for quality assurance and environmental management as set out in paragraph 3.2.2.

In 1995 the IOC organised the First World Conference on Sport and the Environment in Lausanne, which has since been held every two years. The conference was supported by the United Nations Environment Programme (UNEP) and addressed four major issues:

- governmental responsibility
- duties of the Olympic Movement
- education and the environment
- sports industries' responsibility.

### Environmental initiatives

A practical outcome of the conference was the launch of the 'Eco-wave' movement by the Federation of the European Sporting Goods Industry (FESI). It introduces 14,000 ISO ecological standards for businesses. Another important development was the setting up of the IOC Sport and Environment Commission in 1996.

Environmental initiatives have become a standard requirement for Olympic organisers. In the search of a solution to the conflict between sport and nature, the IOC and other authorities apply various strategies. A good example of agreement between the Organising Committee of the Olympic Games, government, local community and private enterprises was demonstrated in the 1994 Lillehammer Winter Games. Another strategy is the control of environmental harassment in sports areas, enhanced in Germany and to a certain extent for Sydney in 2000. (See the book's website for a more detailed description of these examples.)

IN BRIEF

## ENVIRONMENTAL MEASURES AND RESULTS AT THE ATLANTA OLYMPIC GAMES

*Environmental protection*

- At Lake Lanier (rowing and canoeing) tree cutting and shoreline erosion were prevented by using temporary seats on floating barges.
- The Centennial Olympic Park in downtown Atlanta replaced derelict buildings with a 21-acre urban park, including 650 new trees and plants.
- The US Environmental Protection Agency recorded a 30–50 per cent decrease in air pollution levels for that time of year.

*Resource management*

- A photovoltaic energy system (2856 solar panels, generating 340 kilowatts) covered the roof of the Atlanta Aquatic Centre.
- Appropriate energy-efficient lighting was installed at all competition venues.

*Transportation*

- Around 1.3 million spectators used buses or subway – four times the normal daily average.
- Air quality in the Olympic village was protected by the use of electric trams.

*Waste management*

- Recycling initiatives produced a 50 per cent diversion level during the 16 days of the Games, and a remarkable 82 per cent diversion during the best 8 days.
- More than 10 million cans and bottles, 500,000 wood pallets and 50,000 kilograms of scrap metal were recycled.

131

Following the standards set by Lillehammer, the Sydney OCOG incorporated the concept of environmental sustainability, which according to its Mission Statement aims 'to promote environmental awareness and innovative techniques of environmental protection by both practical example and adherence to an agreed set of principles'. Clearly, the organisers of the Olympic Games are making efforts to enhance their role as a contributing factor in protecting the environment and providing better conditions for sport in the future. In this they are supported by commercial companies sponsoring or supplying services to the Games, which deserved the name 'environmental sponsors' in Nagano 1998.

For 2004 the city of Athens is also taking environmental issues very seriously. Four key elements of the city environmental policy that are being implemented deserve mention.

- The siting of Olympic venues has been in full alignment with the land use and sustainability plan for the metropolitan area of Athens.
- In all Olympic poles (areas with Olympic venues), the post-Olympic use excluded the construction of hotels, offices, private houses, casinos and night clubs/restaurants. Such provision was included in special legislation on the Olympic Games (Law 2730/99 on the design and integrated development of areas hosting Olympic constructions). This decision was taken in full knowledge that self-financing of the projects would not be feasible.
- In all Olympic poles the number of construction permits granted during and following the Games was kept very low. For instance, the percentage of the total permits granted for the Olympic Village was 24 per cent, for the beach volleyball facilities 3 per cent, the rowing centre 1 per cent and the sailing centre 10 per cent.
- All temporary constructions for the Olympic Games will be removed at the latest six months following the completion of the Games (included in Law 2819/2000 on the establishment of a private company for the Olympic Village, protection of Olympic symbols, and other provisions.

As the overview of the economic and environmental impact of the Olympic Games demonstrates, it can be interpreted as a measure of the evolution of the Olympic Movement. The growth of the Games has increased their potential for economic gains and regeneration of host cities and countries. Equally, however, this growth has brought in many economic and environmental risks, which present a challenge to present and future organisers.

A well-substantiated analysis of the economic and environmental legacy of the Olympic Games would have to account both for the benefits associated with the project and for the disadvantages it may incur to certain groups and the environment.

**REVIEW QUESTIONS**

## ECONOMIC AND ENVIRONMENTAL IMPACTS OF THE OLYMPICS

1   Explain the main criteria for measuring the economic impact of the Olympic Games. Give examples.
2   Discuss the Barcelona 1992 Olympic Games as a strategy for urban and economic regeneration.
3   Consider the IOC Environmental Guidelines for Olympic host cities and examine their implications for the organisation of a local sporting event.
4   Two students develop an environmental argument that is in favour or against London 2012 Olympic bid respectively. How would you argue your case?
5   Evaluate the economic and environmental impact of a sporting event (e.g. Wimbledon, or an international or county tournament): this should be a group assignment in the form of a case study.

## CHAPTER NINE

# ORGANISING THE OLYMPIC GAMES

**Chapter aims:**

- to analyse political, economic and social considerations for putting forward an Olympic bid
- to identify strategic aspects concerning the scale and operations of the Olympic Games
- to discuss various models of organisation of the Olympics.

After studying this chapter, you should be able to explain:

- the nature of the Olympic project from an organisational perspective
- the complexity of the biggest sporting event, the Olympic Games
- various stages and procedures for selecting the host city of the Games
- the relations between Games organisations and the interests of different parties involved.

## INTRODUCTION

According to the Olympic Charter, the Summer Olympic Games are called the Games of the Olympiad and form a separate cycle from the Olympic Winter Games. An Olympiad is a four-year period celebrated by the Olympic Games. The Games of the XXVII Olympiad were held in Sydney in 2000, and those of the XXVIII Olympiad in Athens in 2004. The four-year interval is believed to continue a tradition of the ancient Games and contributes to the attractiveness or appeal of the Games.

The first Olympic Games of the modern era were held in Athens (Greece) in 1896, and the first Olympic Winter Games in Chamonix (France) in 1924. Until 1992 the Summer and Winter Games ran in parallel in the same year, but then they split and started to follow a different cycle. Barcelona (Spain) and Albertville (France) were the host cities of the 1992 Summer and Winter Olympic Games respectively.

Chapters 1 and 3 refer to the Olympic idea possessing both a doctrinal and practical manifestation. The Olympic philosophy and principles represent the doctrinal or the conceptual part of Olympism. The Olympic Games are the practical manifestation of those principles and serve many important purposes:

- to celebrate human endeavours, epitomised in the performances of the best athletes in the world
- to bring nations together in a peaceful competition
- to promote sport
- to encourage young people to participate.

These broad aims clearly define the Olympic Games as more than a sporting competition. As they aspire to achieve wider social change in the world, their organisation would require more than the technology needed to stage a sporting event.

## ORGANISING THE GAMES – FROM SYMBOLISM TO PRAGMATISM

When Pierre de Coubertin and his associates renewed the Olympic Games they were fully aware of the efforts and resources needed for such a massive undertaking. It had been decided that the site of the Games would rotate, thus enabling more countries and people to experience and share the responsibility of staging them.

Although the host cities of the first four Olympic Games were voted for by the IOC, they were nominated rather than selected because of their symbolic significance. Apparently, Athens 1896 was awarded due its historic contribution, Paris 1900 as a tribute to de Coubertin's role, St Louis 1904 in appreciation of the New World, and London 1908 for the sporting tradition it had given to the world.

The Games of 1896, 1900 and 1904 were poorly organised, and the latter two turned out to be failures. Reduced to a mere appendage to the World Exhibition and the Louisiana Purchase Exhibition respectively, the 1904 Games lasted for several months, were poorly attended, and some athletes did not even realise they were competing at the Olympics. However, all this changed as London (1908) and Stockholm (1912) paved the way to a more rational approach, greater public commitment and careful planning.

The last Olympic Games to be organised on an ad hoc basis with no bidding and selection process was the post-Second World War 'Games of Austerity' in London in 1948. With barely two years' notice, the then British Prime Minister Attlee, in a cryptic letter, ordered the chairman of the organising committee, Viscount Portal, to 'run the Games and make a profit'. London did so after a gap of 12 years (the 1940 and 1944 Games were not held because of the Second World War), and produced the first comprehensive Official Olympic Report.

## STUDY ACTIVITY 9.1

Consider the Official Report of the 1948 London Olympics, available on the book's website. Examine the organisational structure and the cost of the Games. Compare it with the forecasted budget of the London 2012 bid (see Chapter 15).

Since then hosting the Olympic Games has become subject to ever-increasing scrutiny and careful planning. A marked change in the organisation of the Games occurred in 1984. The city of Los Angeles pioneered the so-called 'capitalistic Games' which were privately run. The financial success of the 1984 Games sent a clear message to the International Olympic Committee, governments and private sector that a similar model was feasible. The social, political and economic benefits of hosting the Games are proving very attractive. One only has to consider

## STUDY ACTIVITY 9.2

Study chapters 3 and 13 of the *Official Report of the 1984 Los Angeles Games* available on the book's website. Analyse the management concept of the Games (chapter 3) and the concept of the role of government relations (chapter 13, vol. 2). Compare these with the Barcelona 1992 approach.

the line-up for the 2012 Games, which includes world capitals such as London, Paris, Moscow and New York.

## A mammoth enterprise

In the past 100 years or so the organisational concept of the Olympic Games has evolved from a rather modest undertaking concerned predominantly with the logistical operations of sporting competitions, to a mammoth enterprise involving at least six years of meticulous planning. As a result of this development, two important trends have emerged.

First, the continuous growth of the Olympic Games has led to corresponding increases in their complexity, participation, cost and risk. Table 9.1 illustrates this trend. In the words of Ron Delmont, Director of Logistics, Salt Lake 2002 Organising Committee: 'We try to manage the chaos, essentially'.

Second, as a consequence of the first trend, the number of stakeholders has also increased dramatically. A stakeholder in Olympic terms is any individual or group that has a genuine interest in the Olympic Movement, and that may be affected by decisions of its supreme authority, the International Olympic Committee (IOC). The key stakeholders of the Olympic Movement include the athletes, National Olympic Committees (NOCs), International Federations (IFs), broadcasters, media, governments, sponsors and spectators.

*Table 9.1* Growth of the Olympic Games, 1984–2002

|  | Summer Games | Winter Games |
|---|---|---|
| Sports | 17 to 28 (+121%) | 4 to 7 (+75%) |
| Athletes | 4092 to 10,651 (+160%) | 699 to 2,399 (+243%) |
| Women participants | 385 to 4,069 (+957%) | 77 to 886 (+1051%) |
| Events | 136 to 300 (+121%) | 22 to 78 (+255%) |
| NOCs | 59 to 199 (+237%) | 28 to 77 (+175%) |

Source: McLatchey, 2003

The interplay between these two trends has produced an irresolvable organisational dilemma. This concerns all organisers of Olympic Games as they have to ensure the right balance between the requirements of the stakeholders (e.g. altruistic versus commercial objectives), the available resources (which are always limited), and the physical capacities of the host city to stage the Games (the IOC requirement for 'unity of place'). For example, the inclusion of a single athlete in a Games costs its Organising Committee an extra US$30,000 in the cost of services such as accommodation, food, security, workforce and transport. The cost of an additional press representative would be US$15,000.

## THE TEAM BEHIND THE GAMES

It took a logistics staff of 500 people to pull off the Winter Games in Salt Lake City 2002. The Director of Logistics has to carry a dozen security passes on his belt to gain entry into the warehouse and other Olympic venues. The staff included:

- material handlers – 160
- drivers – 40
- temporary logistics crew – 200
- support staff – 100
- volunteers – countless.

The warehouse – a 300,000 square-foot distribution centre – housed almost every item used in the Games including 33,000 uniforms for volunteers, and dealt with tracking and packing 328,000 pieces of clothing, burning software into 5500 PCs and storing 4000 TV sets.

### WHAT ARE THE OLYMPIC GAMES?

From an organisational point of view, the summer Olympic Games can be viewed as twenty-eight different world championships (seven for Winter Olympics) held in one city at the same time. This is indicative of the amount of work and resources needed to stage an event of this magnitude. But as we will see, the Olympic Games are much more than that. What makes them so special and different from the world's other major sporting occasions?

Shone's (2001) classification of the main characteristics of special events helps us to understand the nature of the Olympics. He identified eight characteristics.

1   *Uniqueness*: each Games is different despite being repeated every four years.
2   *Perishability*: the Games last for only 17 days but the key issue is how the facilities and services can be used beyond that point.
3   *Intangibility*: we cannot touch or possess the Olympics. However, they can still be 'experienced' and organisers ensure that we take away something tangible in the form of a T-shirt, a badge or a souvenir.
4   *Ritual and ceremony*: one of the truly distinguishing features of the Olympic Games is the spectacular opening and closing ceremonies and other rituals (Plate 9.1).
5   *Ambience and service*: this is a crucial element of the Games. Its success depends largely on the participation of the host city and the services provided to the members of the Olympic Family.
6   *Personal interactions*: unlike a manufacturing process where the producer and the customer do not usually meet, personal interaction between organisers and participants is a critical aspect of the Games. This includes regular inter-action with all International Federations and National Olympic Committees, and daily meetings with Chefs de Mission during the Games.

Plate 9.1   The welcome ceremony at the Sydney Olympic Village

7    *Labour intensity*: the Olympic Games present a massive logistical operation involving years of detailed planning and co-ordination. They would not be possible without the help of paid professionals as well as a huge army of volunteers (some 45,000 in Sydney 2000).
8    *Fixed time scale*: the Games operate within a time scale fixed some six years earlier. The Athens Games opened on 16 August 2004 and closed on 31 August. No changes are possible to this time scale.

## ASPECTS OF THE 2000 SYDNEY OLYMPICS

- 38 competition sites
- multiple venues for some sports
- 75 training venues
- 300 events
- 90,000 square metres of international broadcast centre
- 50,000 square metres of main press centre
- 50,000 meals per day served at Athletes' Village
- 20,000 fixed phones.

What makes the Olympics special, however, goes beyond those eight characteristics. Over the years the Olympic Games have become a transformational project concerned with three main intertwined processes:

- political
- social
- economic.

Politically, Olympic bids have been employed as a means of forging social consensus and for mobilising nation-wide support for the Games. This is particularly important in an age of widening social division and inequalities in most modern societies. The Sydney 2000 slogan 'Share the Spirit' illustrates the point.

Socially, the Games produce a marked change in people's leisure experience. This stems from the functional transformation of the host city landscape. Increasingly, the identity of the host city has been turned into a product designed to generate 'cultural capital' and to be recognised as a place for mass consumption attractive for both tourists and businesses. Another important facet of this social process is the use of the Games to change people's behaviour. For example, the only way to ensure an effective transport system that would guarantee access to Olympic venues in adverse winter conditions during the 2002 Salt Lake City Winter Olympics was to persuade the general public to change their travel habits. This was achieved by a massive public relations campaign 'Know Before You Go'.

Economically, the Games serves as a catalyst for inward and outward investments responsible for increasing economic wealth and standard of living. These investments lead in turn to a lasting legacy in the form of facilities and services but also pose a challenge to the host city, as in order to produce this level of social and economic development it has to think years ahead in terms of investment and jobs.

The organisation of the Olympic Games is therefore a complex undertaking, which can be fully comprehended if it accounts for the eight characteristics of special events and the wider political, social and economic processes involved. Failure to realise that may produce disastrous consequences as in Atlanta in 1996.

IN BRIEF

## THE 'KNOW BEFORE YOU GO' CAMPAIGN

1  *Educating travellers.* Utah Department of Transport (UDOT) implemented an extensive four-part plan to educate travellers during the Olympics.
2  *Disseminating travel information.* The campaign included distribution of a 36-page Olympic Transportation Guide, a website with real-time information on travel routes, and a radio station, with traffic and weather updates every 10 minutes.
3  *Outreach to long-haul trucking.* UDOT distributed four fliers to national long-haul trucking companies and individual truckers at all ports of entry about when and where events would be held. These were followed by emailed news releases during the Games.
4  *Public transport.* UDOT extended the operating hours and capacity of buses and light rail.

5   *Educating businesses and employees.* UDOT implemented a business game plan, notifying companies of how they could help minimise traffic during peak hours. More than 200 businesses were visited prior to the Olympics giving them presentations to enable each company to tailor-make its own transportation plan.

(Source: Matbis, 2003)

## WHAT DOES IT TAKE TO HOST THE OLYMPIC GAMES?

### Bidding

The Olympic Games of 2004 began on 15 August 1996 for the host city of Athens. This was the submission deadline for candidate cities. The IOC took the actual decision in September 1997. It takes at least eight years to put forward a bid and organise the Games. The IOC charter stipulates that all candidate cities must reply to a very comprehensive questionnaire, and present detailed arguments in favour of their bid. This must have municipal, social and commercial support and be backed by governmental guarantees.

A decision to bid for the Olympics is therefore made not by a single sport or public organisation but by the city's political authorities in alliance with commercial partners and its government. The co-operation between various agencies in putting forward a bid does not necessarily entail democratic procedures in consulting the public opinion, or a complete evaluation of the social and economic implications.

For Sydney 2000 the public participation in the bidding process was reduced to opinion polls. As Cochrane *et al.* (1996) argue, in the Manchester bids for the 1996 and 2000 Olympics, the local government-based decision-making and bureaucratic politics were essentially replaced by a dynamic business leadership.

The case of the 1994 Lillehammer Winter Olympic Games also illustrates the point. When it was first launched in 1982, the original idea behind the project was to use the event to stimulate economic activity in the region, and to 'go back to basics' by organising more 'modest' Games. Accordingly, the Games' budget and proposed venues and installations reflected these goals. However, they all had to be seriously reconsidered after 15 September 1988 when the IOC Session in Seoul awarded the Games to Lillehammer, whose bid was presented personally by the Norwegian Prime Minister.

The emphasis of the Olympic project had changed from regional to national with the aim of putting Norway on the world map, and using the Games as a showcase for Norwegian culture and industry. This was accompanied by struggles between competing local, regional and national political and economic interests and the initial budget of NOK 1.8 billion voted by the parliament had to be altered to NOK 7 billion (US$1 billion). Additionally, the concept of the 'compact games' was partly abandoned as alternative venues were proposed and the construction, running and arrangement costs rose by 23, 70.2 and 36.3 per cent respectively.

It could be argued that Lillehammer should not be viewed as an isolated case as cities vying to host an Olympics do have a tendency to deliberately underestimate the cost of the project. The budget of the 2000 Sydney bid rose by some 300 per cent twelve months before the Games – after all, it would have been politically unwise to flag up the real figures earlier, for fear of putting off the IOC, sponsors, politicians and the general population.

Because of the potential benefits for the host city and country, the bidding process urges candidates to go to extreme ends to secure the privilege of staging the Games. The means used to persuade the IOC members' vote range from traditional lobbying, to preparing a secret profile of each member and approaching the key figures personally. Other 'psychological' tricks include changing the IOC members' hotel pillow-cases the night before the vote for ones with the name of the city's main sponsor imprinted on them, in order to imprint it on their minds, too (see Simson and Jennings, 1992).

## The selection process

The selection process for the host city of the Olympic Games has been reviewed several times by the IOC in order to ensure an objective evaluation of the bids and to arrest excessive expenditures made by cities for lavish hospitality and eventual manipulation of the outcome.

It would be interesting to consider what factors affect the IOC members' decision in the selection of the host city of the Games. The Olympic Charter requires all cities to answer a comprehensive questionnaire covering 23 subject areas from athletes' accommodation to waste management. Only members of the Evaluation Commission (not individual IOC members) are allowed to visit bid cities. Therefore, when casting their vote they rely on three sources of information:

- answers to the IOC questionnaire
- the Evaluation Commission Report
- city presentations to the IOC Session.

In a rare study of this issue Persson (2002) revealed some interesting findings concerning the choice of Salt Lake City as host of the 2002 Winter Olympic Games. The IOC members rated as very important the following five bid components:

(i) Olympic Village (37 grades)
(ii) transportation (34)
(iii) sports/arenas (31)
(iv) finances (30)
(v) IOC members' visits to the bid cities.

The person identified as the most influential in marketing the bid was the Bid Committee Chairman and President (84 per cent of the respondents). As for the most important channels for affecting the outcome of the vote, 'the visits of the IOC members to the bid cities' and 'the final presentation' were considered the strongest.

**IN BRIEF**

## SELECTION PROCESS FOR THE 2004 OLYMPIC GAMES

Candidate cities:

- Athens
- Buenos Aires
- Cape Town
- Istanbul
- Lille
- Rio de Janeiro
- Rome
- San Juan Seville
- Stockholm
- St Petersburg

Stages in selection process:

1   Candidate cities submit their candidature files to the IOC by 15 August 1996.
2   IOC Evaluation Commission visits candidate cities, 15 September to 10 December 1996.
3   IOC Evaluation Commission publishes its report by February 1997.
4   IOC Selection College meets to select the finalist candidate cities, 6–7 March 1997.
5   IOC Members visit finalist candidate cities, April to August 1997.
6   Election of the host city for the Games of the XXVIII Olympiad at the 106th IOC Session in Lausanne, 5 September 1997.

## ORGANISATION OF THE OLYMPIC GAMES

### The role of Organising Committees

The Olympic Games are awarded to the National Olympic Committee (NOC) of the country in which they will be held. The NOC, in partnership with municipal authorities, government agencies and commercial businesses, then forms the Organising Committee of the Olympic Games (OCOG), which will be responsible for running the Games. Usually, the OCOG is made up of the key members and agencies involved in the initial bid. However, whilst an Olympic bid is still very much a local affair, if successful, it automatically becomes an issue of national and international prominence. The leading figures of several successful bids (e.g. Lillehammer 1994, Sydney 2000, Athens 2004) had to step down following successful bids and be replaced by more nationally and internationally recognised personalities.

Once selected, the OCOG must develop an adequate organisational structure and provide all the infrastructure and services needed for the Games. These include:

- compliance with the rules and standards established by the 35 International Federations (28 for summer and 7 for winter sports), whose sports are on the Olympic Programme
- ensuring that there will be no social or political unrest during the Games
- providing the physical and logistic infrastructure, equipment and training
- accommodating and catering for the athletes, coaches and staff

145

- providing required facilities (press and broadcasting centres) and services for the mass media
- providing the necessary information (documents, invitations, accreditations, event timetables, signs, results, reports) before, during and after the Games
- organising cultural events such as the youth camp, and art, music and dance events, accompanying the celebration of the Olympiad.

For example, the Sydney OCOG provided free accommodation for 15,000 athletes and team officials and paid for them and their equipment to travel to and from Australia. The Sydney OCOG's organisational structure evolved over time and reflected various levels of hierarchy and specialisation. It was transformed from a centralised structure in the pre-Games period to more functional and independent structure during the Games.

The Sydney OCOG responsibilities in relation to the Games included the organisation of:

- the sports programme, including preparing and operating all venues and facilities for the Games
- the cultural programme
- a marketing programme
- arrangements and availability of the host broadcaster, TV and radio facilities and other information services.

The above considerations pre-suppose to a certain extent the approach and activities of any OCOG. There is, however, another set of issues beyond the remit of the OCOG, but which have great implications for the organisation of the Games: the number of sports, events and athletes in the Olympic programme. Currently there are 28 summer and 7 winter sports on the programme, but a dozen other sports are clamouring for inclusion by the IOC. Any new sport means additional facilities, transport, services, communications and additional costs for the organisers.

Two points deserve mention here. First, the ever-increasing number of sports, events and athletes poses the problem of 'gigantism' which would destroy the original spirit of the Olympics, a notion which until recently was utterly rejected by the IOC. Instead, the growing size of the Olympics was viewed as a reflection of the popularity of modern sport. However, the IOC Session in Mexico City (2003) made several proposals aimed at addressing this issue. These included identifying a number of sports that may have to be removed from the Games programme.

The second point concerns the rather slim chances of a typical city, and particularly those in industrially less developed countries, hosting the Olympics.

The Olympic Movement has a membership of 200 nations but the Summer Olympics (including the Games in Athens 2004) have been organised by only 17 countries. Of these, one country, the USA, has hosted five Games, and another five countries have hosted two.

The Winter Olympics represent an even more worrying perspective. Cities from only seven countries have had the privilege of staging the event and two of them – France and the USA – have hosted four Games each.

---

**STUDY ACTIVITY 9.3**

Identify three sports from the programme of the Summer Olympic Games and trace their participation in three Olympics. Can you envisage the organisational implications for the host city as a result of the changing number of athletes, officials and equipment? The programmes of the Summer and Winter Olympic Games are available on the book's website (Tables 9a and 9b).

---

As the Games have grown, various organisational models have developed. The first Games in Athens was tiny compared to the centennial edition in Atlanta (see Table 9.2). Also relevant are budgets and staff structures. The 1912 Stockholm Games were in many ways the prototype of today's Olympics, with specialist facilities, organisation, marketing and a budget of US$681,000. However, they were run almost entirely by volunteers.

In contrast, today's OCOGs are massive enterprises with highly professional staff. The 1992 Barcelona Games employed 89,723 people, of whom 5965 were OCOG personnel, 23,467 were employed by service enterprises and 21,116 were security staff.

In Atlanta 4000 staff were employed by the organising committee with a budget of US$1,721 billion, whilst the Lillehammer OCOG (1990–1994) budget was US$2 million.

The Games are not of course run only by professionals, and OCOGs invest huge sums in training armies of volunteers (34,548 in Barcelona and 25,000 in Salt Lake City). Figures 9.1 and 9.2 show expenditure for the 1996 Atlanta and 1912 Stockholm Olympic Games, respectively.

147

*Table 9.2* Comparison between 1896 Athens and 1996 Atlanta Olympic Games

|  | *1896 Athens* | *1996 Atlanta* |
|---|---|---|
| *Games comparison* |  |  |
| No. of days | 5 | 17 |
| No. of sports | 9 | 26 |
| No. of events | 32 | 271 |
| No. of countries | 13 | 200 |
| No. of athletes | 311 | 10,000 |
| Tickets available | 60,000 | 11 million |
|  |  |  |
| *Funding sources (%)* |  |  |
| Private donation | 67 | – |
| Sponsorship | – | 32 |
| Television | – | 34 |
| Tickets | 11 | 26 |
| Licensing, retail, other | – | 8 |
| Programme, advertising, stamps | 22 | – |

Source: IOC *Marketing Matters*, No. 9, 1996

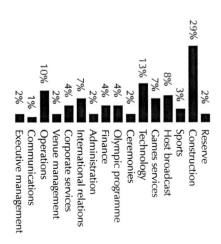

**Figure 9.1** Expenditure by programme area: 1996 Atlanta Olympic Games

Source: AOCOG, 1997, vol. 1, p. 209

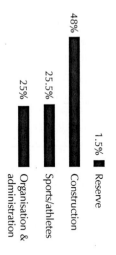

**Figure 9.2** Expenditure by programme area: 1912 Stockholm Olympic Games

Source: SOC, 1913, pp. 43–49

## Organisational models

An analysis of the history of the Olympic Games suggests that, generally, there are three different models under which they have been organised:

- state-led
- private initiative
- partnership.

The state-driven model of organisation of the Games, in which the governmental contribution represented some 80 per cent of total cost, dominated until 1984. The most illuminating example was the Moscow Games of 1980, where the then Soviet 'superstate' took responsibility for most of the construction, running and administrative costs by imposing the financial burden on its taxpayers.

As the previous Olympics in Munich in 1972 and Montreal in 1976 had been financial disasters, there were not many cities willing to host the Games. There was a need for a new model, which emerged in the form of the first privately financed Games in Los Angeles in 1984. This was run by a 'non-profit' corporation made up of the US Olympic Committee and a business syndicate.

Thanks to its entrepreneurial approach, which did not include the use of taxpayers' money but did involve new sponsorship and TV rights concepts, this supposedly non-profit organisation ended up with a profit of $150 million.

Other 'new' commercial arrangements allowed the Los Angeles OCOG to extract a further $117 million for 'service facilities'. The destiny of this money remained unclear, but it was certainly not made available to the Olympic Movement.

The example set in Los Angeles was effectively repeated in Atlanta in 1996 but left a great deal to be desired for both participants and spectators, with very little in new infrastructure and improvements. This probably explains why IOC President Samaranch referred to these Games as 'a qualified success' and not 'the best Games ever' during the closing ceremony.

## LESSONS FROM THE ORGANISATION OF THE 1996 ATLANTA OLYMPIC GAMES

It is now widely acknowledged by all Olympic stakeholders that the 1996 Games in Atlanta were poorly organised. In their analysis of the Games, Ratnatunga and Muthaly (2000) identified three main categories of issues where failures were most acutely felt.

- *Logistical issues*: these relate to traffic planning, street closure, garbage disposal, etc., during the period of the Games.
- *Business issues*: these include forecasting demand, strategic planning, product and brand positioning, relationship marketing, cost control, asset investment, equipment leasing, granting of credit, collection of debts, inventory control, etc., in periods of concentrated demand.
- *Infrastructure issues*: these include licensing, permits, employee supply and training and crisis management (e.g. handling of the bombing incident). Many of these issues relate to government and quasi-government support of small business initiatives.

The third model of organising the Games represents a partnership between the public and private sector, and reflects the shift from a government and purely private to a governance approach.

The best example of this model was demonstrated in Barcelona in 1992. The Games were run by HOLSA, a company of which 51 per cent was owned by the federal government and 49 per cent by the city and involved many commercial partners as investors and sponsors.

This approach resulted in significant investments in public projects and urban improvements. Similar practices in both Seoul in 1988 and Sydney in 2000 have provided evidence of its successful application. For example, government expenditures for the 2000 (Summer) and 2002 (Winter) Olympics reached more than US$1 billion and US$700 million respectively (see Chapter 10 for more details).

Any analysis of the three models of Olympic organisation, however, must account for the different political ideologies and beliefs of the state in which they are rooted. The principal issues at stake concern the levels of public expenditure and personal taxation that are proposed in order for an Olympic project to materialise.

The IOC has also long been aware of the organisational challenges posed by the growth of the Games. In 2002 the IOC, in conjunction with the Sydney OCOG, launched an initiative aimed at tackling four key problems pertinent to the management of Games:

- (i) 're-inventing the wheel' every four years
- (ii) establishing specific service levels
- (iii) controlling growth in participation
- (iv) increasing efficiency and reducing waste.

The overriding purpose of what has become known as the Transfer of Knowledge Programme is to formalise the transfer of expertise from one Olympic Games organiser to the next.

A special company, Olympic Games Knowledge Services (OGKS) (www.ogks. com), was set up with a mandate to provide information, support and knowledge services to the IOC, Olympic Games candidate cities and Organising Committees. More specifically, the OGKS provides assistance in preparing the bids, in conceiving, planning and operating the Games. This initiative represents a major development in introducing greater uniformity and efficiency in the organisation of future Olympic Games by providing a comprehensive service to all bidding and host cities.

REVIEW QUESTIONS

## ORGANISING THE OLYMPIC GAMES

1   Explain the role of municipal authorities, National Olympic Committees and central government in putting together a bid for the Olympics.
2   Discuss the advantages and disadvantages for the host city of the three models for organising the Olympic Games.
3   Use the materials provided in Chapter 15 concerning the London bid for the 2012 Olympic Games to identify and elaborate on the key actors and the interests they were trying to promote.

4    Compare the organisational approaches of two host cities of the Winter
     Olympic Games. Refer to the Games Official Reports available on the
     book's website.
5    Study the British Olympic Association (BOA) Athletes' Commission
     2000 Report and identify key organisational problems experienced
     by athletes during the Games. This is available on the BOA website
     <www.olympics.org.uk>.

152

## CHAPTER TEN

# OLYMPIC POLITICS

**Chapter aims:**

- to offer an understanding of the political dimensions of the Olympic Movement
- to analyse the key sources of political power of the Olympic Movement
- to elaborate on the forms of political intervention of governments and social groups, and the benefits and threats for the Olympic Movement.

After studying this chapter you should be able to explain:

- the political and structural characteristics of Olympic sport
- the sources of political power of the Olympic Movement
- relationships between national and international policy and the Olympic Movement
- the nature of political transformations in the Olympic Movement
- various forms of political intervention in Olympic sport.

## INTRODUCTION

Since the resurrection of the modern Olympic Games in 1896 politics has always been present in one form or another, and has had in some respects profound effects on sport structures, functions and relations, both nationally and internationally.

Debates about the relations between politics and Olympics are often confined to some of the manifestations of political discord among states, such as the

153

boycotts. Although similar analyses are very instructive, they nonetheless can provide only a limited picture of the relationship under investigation.

In the words of Lord Killanin, IOC President 1972–1980:

> Ninety-five percent of my problems as president of the IOC involved national and international politics.
>
> (quoted in Senn, 1999)

The original motivation for the ancient Olympic Games was the religious celebrations of traditional cults. The religious traditions and the political and military neutrality of Olympic sites, such as the city-state of Elis (chosen as the site of the Games), were the underlying factors of ancient Olympic unity and integrity. Although this model of political neutrality was eroded, and eventually in AD 393 the Games were outlawed by the Roman Emperor Theodosius, it was later used as a base from which the myth of sport's political autonomy sprang.

Subsequently, throughout most of its just over 100-year history, the International Olympic Committee (IOC) has claimed that the worlds of sport and politics should stay apart and that the Olympic Games should not be used by nation-states for political gains.

---

**STUDY ACTIVITY 10.1**

Consider the question of whether sports and politics should stay apart. What arguments would you put forward to support your position? Try to formulate your view now before reading the rest of this chapter.

---

### THE POLITICAL DIMENSION OF THE OLYMPIC MOVEMENT

As early as 1908 Pierre de Coubertin expressed concern about the misuse of the Olympic project for political aims when he said of the London Olympics: 'The Games have become an affair of states'. The Olympic Charter expresses prohibition on any form of political dependence of members of the Olympic Family or the promotion of nationalism, and provides a constitutional framework based on this attitude. It was well epitomised by Avery Brundage's eloquent statement 'sport has nothing to do with politics' (Brundage was president of the IOC from 1952 to 1972).

In reality, Olympics and politics have always been closely intertwined. Issues concerning states' presentation, flags, assertion of national identity, recognition and boycotts of political regimes, and promotion of social and economic values have accompanied the modern Games since their first edition in 1896. Eventually, this was acknowledged clearly by J.A. Samaranch (IOC President 1980–2001) who advocated a more pragmatic approach towards Olympics and politics:

> The Olympic Movement is an integral part of society and therefore has a duty to come to terms with the public authorities.

Table 10.1 shows the relationship between major political conflicts and the Olympic Games.

The Olympic ideal makes six key claims (see Chapter 1) and seeks to promote:

1   mass participation in sport
2   personal excellence
3   fair play
4   equality
5   international understanding
6   education for the youth of the world.

These claims represent social values to which various governments and social groups may or may not subscribe. Thus, promoting equality in sport or indeed education for everyone become political issues because they involve rational

*Table 10.1* Political conflicts and the Olympic Games

| Olympic Games | | Conflict | Repercussions |
|---|---|---|---|
| 1956 | Melbourne | Invasion of Hungary | Boycott |
| | | Invasion of Suez Canal | Boycott |
| 1968 | Mexico | Repression of student protests | Black Power salute |
| | | US race problems | |
| 1972 | Munich | Arab–Israeli conflict | Israeli held as hostages |
| 1976 | Montreal | Apartheid in South Africa | Boycott |
| 1980 | Moscow | Invasion of Afghanistan | Boycott |
| 1984 | Los Angeles | Security problems | Boycott |
| 1988 | Seoul | Two Koreas | Boycott |
| 2000 | Sydney | Indigenous political issues | Aborigine protests |
| 2003 | March | America-led war on Iraq | IOC suspends the Iraqi NOC |

judgement, calculation and choices made by public authorities about how to prioritise resources and expenditure outcomes.

A local authority's decision whether or not to provide subsidised swimming is inherently political because it involves a choice about the distribution of resources on the basis of two competing values – community well-being (encouraging participation through equal access) and individual freedom (offering access for those who can pay the market price).

An obvious manifestation of the political dimension of Olympism centres on IOC decisions about the inclusion of sports on the Olympic programme. The introduction of a single sport (such as triathlon in the 2000 Sydney Games) automatically implies better prospects for development of that sport both nationally and internationally.

Benefits include heightened public awareness and increased commercial potential due to global television exposure, improved financial health of the sport's governing body due to the allocations of marketing revenue (global/national sponsorship and TV rights) generated, and greater public spending on grass-roots developments and infrastructure.

Indeed, the Olympic Games have always been organised with the support and participation of governments and enjoyed the co-operation of political parties across the spectrum. The increased importance of the Games assisted critically by the success of the mass media in transmitting events instantaneously to a global audience has proved tempting for all political systems as a testing ground for the nation. As J. Hoberman (1984, p. 17) puts it:

> German Nazis, Italian Fascists, Soviet and Cuban Communists, Chinese Maoists, western capitalist democrats, Latin American juntas – all have played this game and believed in it.

### Political interventions

The history of the Olympic Games contains ample evidence of political interventions and manipulations (see Table 10.2).

More recently, the political appeal is perhaps best illustrated in the way the bids for hosting the Games are presented. It is not often that the highest ranking political and public figures (including members of royal families, prime ministers and other key officials) gather for non-political events but this has occurred during

156

*Table 10.2* Political interventions and manipulations in the Olympic Games

| Olympic Games | Political interventions |
| --- | --- |
| **1896 Athens** | De Coubertin attempts to bar Germany from the first Olympics. Crown Prince Constantin of Greece escorted victorious countryman, marathoner Spiridon Louis across the finish line in a display of national triumph. |
| **1904 St Louis** | Originally scheduled for Chicago but moved to St Louis due to the intervention of President Roosevelt and the US Government who wanted the Games as part of the Louisiana Purchase Exhibition. |
| **1908 London** | American delegation refused to dip their flag in honour of King Edward. |
| **1936 Berlin** | The Games used as a Nazi propaganda tool. Whilst aware of the looming war, the British Government supported the Games because it wanted to improve strategic relations with Germany. |
| **1948 London** | Germany, Japan and Bulgaria not invited because of their role in the Second World War The question of the two Germanies? |
| **(1951–1978)** | The question of the two Chinas (recognition of Taiwanese NOC as China). |
| **1956 Melbourne** | Spain, Switzerland and the Netherlands withdrew in protest at the Soviet invasion of Hungary; Egypt, Lebanon and Iraq boycotted to protest the Anglo-French seizure of the Suez Canal. |
| **1968 Mexico** | American athletes Tommie Smith and John Carlos and the 'black power salute'.<br><br>South Africa barred from participation because of racial policies |
| **1972 Munich** | Palestinian terrorists killed 9 Israeli athletes and demanded the release of 200 prisoners. |
| **1976 Montreal** | African countries boycotted and demanded New Zealand's expulsion due to its rugby team's tour to South Africa. |
| **1980 Moscow** | America and 63 other countries boycotted the Games because of the Soviet invasion of Afghanistan. The British government put enormous pressure on the BOA but was defeated and the national team took part. That same year the government cut spending on sport by £20 million simultaneously with an offer of £50 million to move the Games from Moscow. |
| **1984 Los Angeles** | USSR and 15 communist countries boycotted the Games in retaliation. |
| **1988 Seoul** | Political tension between S. and N. Korea for moving the Games to the North and fear of a repeat communist countries boycott. |
| **1992 Barcelona** | Tension between the IOC and the former Soviet republics of Ukraine and Georgia. Both insisted on appearing as independent states and not as part of the unified team of the Commonwealth of Independent States (CIS). A meeting between Presidents Yeltzin and Samaranch and subsequent intervention by the Russian president proved essential in lessening the crisis. |

*Table 10.2* continued

| Olympic Games | Political interventions |
|---|---|
| **1996 Atlanta** | After Greece was denied the privilege of organising the Centennial Games, (the centenary of its part in the revival of the modern Games in 1896), Atlanta was chosen instead and the Greeks threatened to boycott. This somewhat predetermined the awarding of the Games of 2004. |
| **2000 Sydney** | Native Aborigines staged a series of protests against their government's blatant and long-term lack of concern over indigenous political issues. This partly prompted the organisers to appoint the indigenous athlete Cathy Freeman to light the Olympic flame. Environmentalists also organised a massive campaign against the transformation of the natural Bondi beach into a venue for beach volleyball. |
| **2003** | The invasion of Iraq. The IOC suspends the Iraqi NOC after allegations of involvement in torturing athletes and supporting the brutalities of the regime. Questions over the legitimacy of the IOC decision remain however, as these allegations had been known since 1997 with no prior response from the IOC. |

IOC Sessions for appointing an Olympic host city. Diplomatic and business lobbying is also part of the process.

Two examples illustrate the political dimensions of the Olympics and their relation to national policy in the USA and Great Britain.

Until the 1972 Munich Olympic Games there was no legislation to specify the structure of American Olympic sport. At the Games, American athletes suffered a series of failures and were defeated by their Soviet counterparts who for the first time obtained more Olympic medals than American athletes. Particularly humiliating for national prestige were the defeats by the Soviets in basketball and athletics – two of America's favourite sports.

These results were given prominence because of the coverage by ABC television, and this served as justification for public policy-makers to intervene. As a result President Nixon and his government became personally involved and passed a legislation (The Amateur Sports Act, 1979), which radically transformed the structure of sport in the USA. This entrusted the US Olympic Committee with the authority of a central sports organisation (previously held by the National Collegiate Athletic Association and the Amateur Athletics Union) responsible for policy-making and implementation in Olympic matters.

Britain has always been conscious of the significance of Olympic sport in enhancing its image as a world leader and in asserting a strong national identity. A team of 710 athletes took part in London's Olympic Games in 1908. Their participation was understandably hailed as victorious when they won 145 medals, followed by the US team with a modest 41 medals.

The situation was reversed in Stockholm four years later when the UK team came home with 41 medals after Sweden (65 medals) and the USA (62 medals): finishing third in the medal table was considered a British defeat. The effect of this 'defeat' was so dramatic that in 1913 a nation-wide appeal was launched to raise £100,000 (a huge amount of money at that time) to fund the preparation of the 1916 Olympic team. The King supported the appeal, and *The Times* took the lead in promoting it.

Ninety years on, the appeal is still a private undertaking but the government role has changed and much public money is now invested in sports excellence. This is evidenced in a recent government policy document *The Value of Sport* (Sport England, 1999, pp. 10–11) where the international value of sport is ranked before its social, economic and environmental value. The document also promotes the view that:

> sport has the ability to project a positive image of a nation and this can provide significant diplomatic and economic spin offs, . . . successful sports people are part of our country's history and folklore. The sense of pride and the positive 'boost' that people feel when our teams and individuals achieve international success cannot be quantified but they are real . . . seven in 10 adults (68%) think it important for Lottery money to be spent helping the country to achieve sporting success.

---

## STUDY ACTIVITY 10.2

Study the document *The Value of Sport* (Sport England, 1999, pp.10–11) available at <http://www.sportengland.org/resources/pdfs/publicat_pdfs/bestval.pdf>. Identify the social, economic and political justification for the British government's involvement in Olympic sport and the structural changes that this intervention has brought about.

### The IOC and politics

At the international level of politics it is important to consider the IOC over 50 years of co-operation with the United Nations (UN) and UNESCO. The highest recognition of this partnership was the proclamation from the UN general assembly of 1994 as the International Year of Sport and the Olympic Ideal.

Political recognition of the contribution of sport for the betterment of the modern world was given by the 185 Member States of the UN when agreeing to consider, at the level of Ministers of Youth and Sport, national policies 'For the building of a peaceful and better world through sport and the Olympic ideal'.

The changing political attitude of the IOC is supported by the presence of many influential political figures among its ranks, including heads of state, prime ministers, ambassadors and members of royal families. Meetings of the IOC former and current presidents with heads of states around the world are an almost daily occurrence. Table 10.3 shows the highest political positions held by IOC members. The IOC members enjoy a unique status as representatives of the Committee in their countries. However, it would be difficult to imagine that they would have acted only as prescribed by the Olympic ideal and would not seek to assert the national values and interests they represent.

The discussion about politics and the Olympic Movement has some parallels with the broader issues of compatibility between political projects and political and structural characteristics of sport.

As suggested, the Olympic ideal represents a political project, in the sense that to aspire to equal opportunities and participation in sport and to achieve international understanding and world peace require top level political decisions and actions.

Clearly, the good will of athletes and sport officials alone would not suffice if the backing of the political community were not to be secured.

### POLITICAL CHARACTERISTICS OF OLYMPIC SPORT

A materialist view of politics, to use Harold Laswell's (1936) popular phrase, suggests that it is about 'Who gets what, when, how'.

Real politics therefore is about the haggle over the distribution of resources. A similar approach sees sport as being heavily dependent on this reality. Whilst to

Table 10.3 Political offices held by IOC members in countries of which they are citizens

| Presidents | Members of Parliament | | Prime Ministers | Cabinet Ministers |
|---|---|---|---|---|
| D. Stanchov, Bulgaria 1906–08 | Britain | 1906–09 | R. Willebrand, Finland 1908–20 | Finance: 5 |
| A. Guintan, Argentina 1907–10 | | 1927–33 | T. Lewald, Germany 1920 | Public Affairs: 4 |
| M. Alviar, Argentina 1922–32 | Bulgaria | 1952–87 | J. Rangell, Finland 1941–44 | Defence: 4 |
| M. Fuentes, Guatemala 1958–63 | Egypt | 1960–93 | M. Msali, Tunis 1965 | Foreign Affairs: 3 |
| R. Ractobe, Madagascar 1959 | Finland | 1948–76 | P. Charusatiar, Thailand 1971–74 | Health: 2 |
| | France | 1908–09 | D. Chullasapia, Thailand 1974–89 | Information: 2 |
| | | 1951–92 | | Food: 2 |
| | | 1970–95 | | Agriculture: 2 |
| | Hungary | 1905–27 | | Youth & Sport: 2 |
| | | 1909–46 | | Culture: 1 |
| | Indonesia | 1977–89 | | Internal Affairs: 1 |
| | Italy | 1894–89 | | |
| | | 1909–13 | | |
| | | 1913–39 | | |
| | Japan | 1909–38 | | |
| | Luxembourg | 1910–29 | | |
| | Madagascar | 1968–71 | | |
| | Malaysia | 1978– | | |
| | Pakistan | 1949–56 | | |
| | Poland | 1961–98 | | |
| | Portugal | 1946–56 | | |
| | Sudan | 1968–89 | | |
| | Sweden | 1965–95 | | |
| | Taiwan | 1970–88 | | |
| | Tunis | 1965– | | |
| | Turkey | 1908–30 | | |
| | | 1930–33 | | |
| | | 1933–52 | | |
| | Yugoslavia | 1960–87 | | |

ignore the importance of material conditions for the development of sport would be naive, it would be equally wrong to dismiss the significance of sport as a cultural phenomenon in its own right. As one of the most popular human activities, modern sport has the capacity to be a symbolic system used for the creation of meaning, to serve as a source for socialisation and identity assertion and to mobilise mass support for various political regimes.

Politics and sports therefore appear to be mutually constructive. One has only to think about the World Cup of 2002, when a pub landlord in England successfully challenged a century-old law concerning opening hours and the serving of alcohol before 11.00am. As a result, English supporters gained the right to watch the national squad games early in the morning, whilst younger supporters saw thousands of schools across the country alter their daily timetables in order to avoid the prospect of empty classrooms during England matches.

The political characteristics of sport can be interpreted on two levels – national and international. At the level of nation-state, sport exhibits a capacity to perform political functions in a number of important areas. Bramley *et al*. (1993) identified six useful categories used by states to legitimise sports policies.

1   Political and organisational aspects of sports behaviour:

  - nation-building and enhancing national prestige
  - forging social integration
  - protection and promotion of citizenship.

2   Economic significance of sport:

  - creating jobs and business activities
  - economic generation of inner city areas.

3   Socio-cultural goals of government policy:

  - enhancing people's ability to make sense of a variety of symbolic systems, such as sport
  - increasing people's participation in these activities.

4   Time-spatial characteristics of sport:

  - staggering of holidays
  - scheduling sporting events.

5   Physical aspects of sport:

  - contributiing to people's health and recreation of work-force
  - creating awareness of environmental issues.

6   Trans-national character of sport:

  - staging/participating in mega-events such as the Olympic Games and World Cup
  - developing economic and political relations.

*Table 10.4* Barcelona 1992: goals of the various institutional agents

| Agents | Goals | |
|---|---|---|
| | *Substantial* | *Procedural* |
| Central government | '1992' project | Control |
| Regional government | Catalanization of the Games | Participation |
| City of Barcelona | Urban change | Autonomy |

Source: Botella, 1995

It should be noted that all politicians do not perceive these criteria in the same way. For some nationalistic groups the universal appeal of the Games is seen as a threat. Central governments, on the other hand, would aspire to portray an image of the host country as being more open to the world.

Table 10.4 illustrates different political interests of three key institutions involved in the organisation of the 1992 Barcelona Games.

---

**STUDY ACTIVITY 10.3**

Study the UK Sport publication *United Kingdom's Sporting Preferences* (2001) available at <http://www.uksport.gov.uk/template.asp?id=245> and examine the attitudes of various socio-economic groups (p. 8) and home countries (p. 17) towards Olympic success. Can you explain the differences?

---

At international level sport also has the capacity to perform political functions (for example, boycotts) without the risk attendant upon other modes of political actions, such as breaking diplomatic ties or a war. According to Spotts (1994), political actions at the Olympics can be designated into five categories.

1   *To attain prestige*: when South Korea was chosen to host the 1988 Olympics, North Korea became concerned with the prestige South Korea would garner and urged Cuba to speak to the IOC on its behalf to have the Games moved to the North.
2   *To effect non-recognition of nations*: a classic example was the 1976 Montreal Olympics when the People's Republic of China threatened to boycott the Games if the Republic of China (Taiwan) was allowed to participate.

3   *To institute propaganda*: the most extreme method – terrorism – was performed by the Arab group 'Black September' at the 1972 Games.
4   *To protest*: at the 1968 Mexico Games two African-American athletes refused to face the American flag and raised their fists in the Black Power salute; another notorious example was the 1936 Nazi Olympics.
5   *To combat human rights violation*: disqualification from the Games (1968–1992) of South Africa and Rhodesia for practising apartheid in sport.

The structural characteristics of international sport are less appealing to government leaders because of the independence of the IOC, the International Federations (IFs) and the National Olympic Committees (NOCs). The IOC members, according to the Olympic Charter, are not representatives of their states to the Olympic body; rather they are ambassadors of the Olympic ideal to their homelands.

The exclusive right of National Olympic Committees to decide all Olympic-related questions is recognised by law not only in countries with long democratic traditions, such as the USA, but also in transitional democracies such as Bulgaria.

To better comprehend the unique position of the IOC in a global political context it will be instructive to see this organisation not merely as an international but as a trans-national body. Huntington (1981) contrasted the trans-national organisations with international organisations and suggested three important characteristics, shown in Table 10.5. As can be seen from Table 10.5, the emphasis is clearly on the access a trans-national organisation requires to nations as opposed to accord required by the international organisation.

An Olympic athlete possesses enormous symbolic power and politicians are well aware of this (Plate 10.1). As John Lucas (1992, p. 64) notes:

*Table 10.5* Comparison between international and trans-national organisations

| International organisation | Trans-national organisation |
|---|---|
| (i) Requires identification and creation of a common interest among national groups | (i) Has its own interest which is inherent in the organisation and its functions, which may or may not be closely related to the interests of national groups |
| (ii) Designed to facilitate the achievement of a common interest among many national units | |
| (iii) Requires accord among nations | (ii) Designed to facilitate the pursuit of a single interest within many national units |
| | (iii) Requires access to nations |

Plate 10.1 An athlete's joy (Sport England)

> Living three lives at the same time – that of a private person, a national
> figure, and a member of an international elite – renders the Olympian's
> actions especially significant.

The Olympic Games represents great opportunities through the medium of global
television to attract world attention, which is particularly appealing to newly
emerging and less developed nations.

Furthermore, this specific political status of the IOC is transformed into an
economic advantage as the IOC TOP marketing programme demonstrates (see
Chapter 7). It offers the multinational companies involved in it an almost instant
and exclusive access to the market of 200 countries around the world.

For example, one of the TOP global partners is John Hancock, an American
insurance company, which operates only in a small number of counties. But what
happens if an insurance company from Iceland approaches the NOC of the
country and offers to sponsor the Olympic team? It will be turned down. This is
because John Hancock has the exclusive rights to be associated with all NOCs and
their Olympic teams around the world in this particular product category.

In an Olympic context, the concept of exclusive rights clearly implies political and economic power. The increased popularity and economic power of the IOC also means a greater bargaining power in political negotiations. An illustration of the political influence of the IOC is that now every TV rights holder is contractually obligated not only to broadcast the Games, but also to promote the Olympic ideal throughout the year.

Similarly, the IOC has established an ethical code of conduct with the world association of the sports goods producers (including big names such as Nike, Adidas and Reebok) to observe the moral values of sport. Therefore, the above characteristics of the structural elements of international sport make the Olympics less vulnerable to political manipulations.

**IN BRIEF**

## SPORT AND POLITICS

Sport and politics are mutually constructive. The Olympic ideal is inherently political because it involves political judgements, calculations and choices by public authorities about how to prioritise resources and expenditure.

As a cultural phenomenon sport has the capacity to be a symbolic system used for the creation of meaning, to serve as a source for socialisation and identity assertion and to mobilise mass support for various political regimes. Political characteristics of Olympic sport are exhibited both nationally and internationally.

### THE OLYMPIC MOVEMENT AND POLITICAL TRANSFORMATIONS

Over the past century the positioning of the IOC as an influential trans-national organisation reflected the global political re-mapping of the world, and can be divided into five successive stages.

1   *1894–1915*: the setting up of the International Olympic Movement with 22 member countries from Western Europe and Anglo-Saxon populated regions overseas (e.g. USA and Canada); Japan, which joined in 1912, was the only outside country.

2   *1915–1945*: further expansion as south and central European countries are included. Apart from the USSR (which joined in 1951) the whole of Europe

became involved and clearly dominated the Olympic Movement. Five important centres of power were established:

- Greece was inevitably seen as the mythical centre because of its role in the re-creation of the Olympic Games
- France was considered as the symbolic centre as host to the IOC headquarters
- Switzerland was seen as the technical centre
- Germany's use of the Games' image for propaganda purposes raised it to the ideological centre of power
- Great Britain was the fifth centre of power because of its prominent role in the development of modern sport.

Latin American countries also entered the Movement.

3  *1945–1970*: a period of decolonisation and political emancipation in Africa and Asia. Developing countries and the last big European nations (USSR and Germany) entered and returned to the Olympic Movement.
4  *1970–1989*: this period saw the process of political independence for countries of former colonial empires, bringing 44 small countries into the Olympic Movement.
5  *1989–present day*: the post-communist period in Europe. Following the collapse of the USSR, Czechoslovakia and Yugoslavia, a group of 21 newly independent states emerged and joined the Olympic Movement, which at the beginning of the twenty-first century includes 200 NOCs, making it the most popular international movement in the world.

Within these five stages there were many political struggles and military conflicts that posed great threats for the integrity of the Olympic Family and impacted on the IOC constitution and policies. At present the IOC, in line with its Olympic Charter, and in co-operation with a number of governments and international bodies, has developed distinct policies in several key areas, which include:

- a world anti-doping policy (2003)
- environmental policy (Lillehammer 1994 and Sydney 2000 being the first truly environmentally friendly Games; today no Olympic bid stands a chance if major environmental concerns are not seriously addressed)
- media policy
- marketing policy
- Olympic Solidarity for the developing countries
- security policy

- 'Transfer of Knowledge' policy aimed at preserving and promoting the legacy of the Olympic Games.

These diverse policies also required considerable political skills on the part of the IOC leadership to guide the Movement in times of success, unrest and crises.

---

## STUDY ACTIVITY 10.4

Read the article 'The Olympic Movement as an example of the inter-dependence of sport and politics' by Paul Stauffer (1999) available at <http://www.geocities.com/olympic_seminar7/papers/stauffer.htm>.

Develop a list of structural changes of the Olympic Movement, discussed during Olympic Congresses concerning the relationship between sport and politics.

---

**REVIEW QUESTIONS**

## OLYMPIC QUESTIONS

1 Using your library resources, and the Internet in particular, compile an annotated bibliography on the topic of Olympic politics.
2 Identify and discuss one form of political intervention in Olympic sport both at national and international level.
3 Examine the IOC policy with regard to disintegration of the USSR and its participation at the Olympic Games in Barcelona 1992.

## CHAPTER ELEVEN

# ETHICS OF SPORT AND OLYMPISM

- to introduce the concept of 'fair play' as a central value in sport and Olympism
- to explore conceptual and ethical aspects of the moral issues of cheating, violence and doping
- to model an analytical and critical approach to ethical issues.

After studying this chapter you should be able to:

- explain the nature of fair and unfair practices, and to give examples
- engage in critical analysis of ethical claims
- construct arguments in support of your case.

## OLYMPISM

Chapter 1 referred to Olympism as an ethical commitment to competitive sporting activity under universal principles and conditions of mutual respect, fairness, justice and equality, with a view to creating lasting personal friendships and international relationships of peace, toleration and mutual understanding.

## SPORT AND FAIR PLAY

Initially, we need to identify certain characteristics of 'sport', that may suggest appropriate ethical indicators:

- sports are *contests*, requiring an unspoken 'contract to contest'
- sports are *institutionalised*, suggesting 'lawful authority'
- there is an *obligation to abide by the rules*, requiring 'fairness'
- *due respect* is owed to opponents as co-facilitators.

---

### STUDY ACTIVITY 11.1

(a) The above definition of sport is simply a starting point; but, on reflection, do you think it is an adequate definition?

(b) Consult the European Fair Play Movement website at
<http://www.fairplayeur.com/index.html>
and its nine declarations on various aspects of fair play at
<http://www.fairplayeur.com/declarations/declarations.html>

How would you define fair play? What kind of personal qualities are suggested?

---

A factor in the development of modern sport has been the internationalisation of competition and the globalisation of spectatorship on the back of spectacular progress in the global travel and communication industries. This has required:

- ever-greater rule clarity in order to avoid cross-cultural misunderstanding, and to resolve variant interpretations, construals and 'custom and practice'
- ever-greater controls involving increased surveillance and rule enforcement
- the ensuring of fairness and lack of arbitrariness, for the 'meaning' and 'significance' of the event are threatened by 'arbitrary' decisions.

The purpose (or role) of rules and of 'fair play', then, seem to be fundamental to the enterprise of sport. 'Fair play' refers to a complex set of features that emerge from principled engagement in competitive sporting activity.

1   It is primarily a virtue of rule-adherence, which is a duty upon all contestants to abide by the rules of the competition, since, by their participation, they are deemed to have entered into a 'contract to contest'.
2   It may also include a commitment to contesting in such a spirit as may lead to good actions over and above those strictly required by rules ('supererogatory' actions).
3   It also sometimes refers to a general attitude towards sport (and even life itself) involving respect for others, modesty in victory, serenity in defeat and generosity aimed at creating warm and lasting human relations (see Borotra, 1983, p. 84).

## CHEATING – A MORAL PROBLEM?

A major difficulty in requiring a principled approach to games playing lies in the area of cheating and rule-infraction.

McIntosh (1979) notes that one form of cheating involves 'breaking a rule with the intention to deceive'. (Compare this with the immoral practice of lying, which is telling untruths with the intention to deceive.) He also draws our attention to the fact that 'the intention to deceive' is not necessarily wrong in sports, and might even be regarded as good strategy (e.g. selling a dummy, feinting, disguising a shot, executing a 'deceptive' change of pace, etc.).

This problem has also been noticed more recently by Jeu *et al.* (1994, p. 216), who remark that the internal logic of some sports:

> . . . Consists in deluding the other . . . Who does not approve of the feints of bodies or the dribble of football players who in this way mislead their opponent? How can we conciliate fair play with trickery . . .?

McIntosh (1979) suggests two criteria for distinguishing morally acceptable forms of deception from deception which counts as cheating:

- that the deception is only momentarily secret (i.e. the result of the deception makes the means obvious)
- the means are acceptable to other participants (even if they had not thought of that means and wished they had).

But neither criterion will suffice because:

- this would make robbery acceptable, if it were achieved by momentary means of deception
- it also smuggles in a moral criterion, for surely a *sine qua non* of 'a means acceptable to all participants' is that it is morally acceptable (in which case we remain in need of a criterion to distinguish morally acceptable means).

The problem presented by McIntosh is resolved if we remind ourselves of his starting-point: 'one form of cheating involves breaking a rule with the intention to deceive'. This makes it clear that deception is permissible in sport when it is employed as a tactic *that does not break a rule*. What makes such deception morally acceptable is simply that, under the contract to contest, I have agreed to abide by the rules. Indeed, since I have also agreed to contest (i.e. do my best to win) there might even be an obligation to deceive – or attempt to deceive if I'm any good at it. Deception involving rule infraction is morally unacceptable not because it is deception but because it is rule infraction.

To reinforce this point, we may return to McIntosh's two criteria: 'deception involving rule infraction is morally unacceptable even when the means are only momentarily secret' . . . 'even if those means were acceptable to other participants'.

However, the 'deceptions' involved in feinting, etc., are not morally relevant deceptions. Not only are such deceptions permitted by the rules of the contest, but (as McIntosh observes) they are also encouraged. What he fails to acknowledge is that what makes them morally irrelevant is that they are precisely the kind of skills which the rules constitutive of the activity call into play.

Jeu et al. (1994) regard sport as 'paradoxical' because it is a practice within which deception and fair play can co-exist. However, it might be reasonably pointed out that the foregoing discussion decisively demonstrates that there is no such paradox. Fair play outlaws only those deceptions that are against the rules. It clearly allows deceptions that are within the rules. There is nothing paradoxical about that.

## DECEPTION, CHEATING AND UNFAIR ADVANTAGE

Notice that the intentional breaking of a rule in order to gain an advantage is not necessarily 'cheating' as long as the offender doesn't try to 'get away with it'. Sometimes a player may be content to break a rule and accept the consequences, having calculated that this would be to the advantage of himself or his team. For example, he might give away a free kick but in doing so prevents an almost certain goal being scored. However, if he tries to avoid the punishment by deception, or by pretending that he did not commit the offence, then this is cheating.

Rules are always to some extent 'arbitrary' in that they might have been different, and they can be changed at any time. Rules, also 'freeze' social reality to some degree, in order that the agreed conditions of the contest can be identified.

'We will play with this kind of ball, on this size court, with this kind of racquet, under this kind of scoring system': all these things could have been different, and we can argue about how they might be changed for the good of the game, or the good of the players. But, as long as they are the rules, we must abide by them if we are to play the game.

172

Imagine that there is a new golf ball, or a javelin, that flies further. Can it be used? Of course, it can be used in training – but before it can be used in competition it must conform to the rules governing the equipment in that particular sport. If not, it cannot be used – unless the rules are changed.

Often there are interesting disputes. Should spikes or studs be allowed? If so, what kind and for which event? Helmets, headguards, gloves, fibreglass vaulting poles, swimming costumes of a certain material – all have been the subject of controversy. How many substitutes can we use, how many horses can we bring, what kind of surface shall we use?

The point is that the rules are the rules – at least for the time that they are in force – and anyone who seeks to evade the rules in order to gain an advantage is cheating. He or she unfairly seeks conditions for the contest that have not been agreed and that exclude other competitors. He (or she) is seeking to evade the 'contract to contest'.

The same applies to anyone who deceptively breaks other kinds of rules for advantage. For example, anyone using banned techniques or substances typically does so secretively in order to enhance performance and gain an advantage over others. Otherwise it is difficult to see why such deception might be practised. Issues associated with doping in sport are examined in some detail in Chapter 12, but whatever the complexities of the matter, what is primarily wrong with this is that it is cheating, pure and simple.

Certainly, there are many arguments that consider that doping should not be against the rules. But it is. It may be that our current rules are irrational, or express the values of a bygone age, and should be changed. All we are saying here is that, in the absence of any agreed rule change, the dopers are simply cheating. They use deception in order to evade the conditions of contest (rules) to gain unfair advantage.


## EQUALITY

One reason why this is so important is that evading the existing rules by deception infringes arguably the most important ingredient of the sports contest: equality of conditions. Two distinctions are often made to avoid confusion when talking about equality.

Firstly, we should distinguish between formal and actual equality. There might well be no legal barrier to women becoming members of the International Olympic

Committee (IOC), but there are actually very few who are members. In this case, men and women have formal but not actual equality in regard to membership and representation on the IOC.

Secondly, we should distinguish between equality of opportunity and equality of treatment. Whilst it is true that, once on the playing field, everyone is treated equally, it is quite another matter whether everyone has an equal opportunity to make the team, or the competition, in the first place.

Now let us consider some examples.

## Gender

No women competed in the first modern Olympics. De Coubertin thought that the only role for women was in presenting wreaths to the winners. Since then some progress has been made. Sport has followed, and sometimes led, gender equity reforms. Many events that previously excluded women are now open to them, and there is a steady increase in the numbers of female events and participants at successive Olympic Games.

There are those who claim that women have, in most respects, formal equality with men, but the fact remains that, for whatever reason, they still do not have actual equality. There are still more men's events and more male competitors.

This may have something to do with inequality of opportunity in the wider cultural life of many societies, where girls still do not have equal access to resources for physical education and sport. However, women now compete in greater numbers than ever before, and in general the status of women's sport does seem to be improving world-wide.

A major question remains, however, as to the role of sport in the promotion of gender equity. In one sense sport may be seen as a means towards the emancipation and equal status of women, as they begin to participate in the same sports as men, under equally resourced conditions and with equal public regard. In another sense sport may be seen as contributing to the perpetuation of existing inequalities by reinforcing or 'naturalising' the view that women are different and inferior.

## Race

The 1936 'Nazi Olympics' in Berlin is often cited as the most obvious example of discriminatory racial policies in sport, with Jews excluded from the German team.

Yet those same Games are also often cited as an example of the overcoming of prejudice, given the success of Jesse Owens, a black athlete who won four gold medals in track and field events and the sportsmanship shown to him by Lutz Long, a German long-jumper, who publicly befriended him.

### STUDY ACTIVITY 11.2

Find the transcript of a talk given by Jesse Owens at the International Olympic Academy in 1969 at <http://www.ioa.leeds.ac.uk> and read what he says about Lutz Long, and about sporting attitudes.

Plate 11.1 Signatures of Sydney Olympic athletes

A different argument on sport and racial equality is sometimes heard – which says, for example, that black athletes in Western societies are used as gladiators and are sidetracked from exploring other avenues to social success because of such stereotyping.

The theory is that, seduced by the image of the successful black athlete into putting their effort into sport at the expense of education or vocation, they are subtly denied equal access to educational and social goods. This is indeed a danger for all those seeking athletic success, which is why Olympism emphasises the all-round harmonious development of the individual.

We should also consider the IOC response to the apartheid regime of racial segregation in South Africa. The IOC refused to recognise South Africa from 1970 to 1991 and excluded it from Olympic competition during that period.

It is important to remember that it was not politicians who banned South Africa from international competition but the world community of sports people. At a time when politicians could not agree on the manner or level of economic sanctions against South Africa – indeed sport had sometimes to defend itself quite strongly against political attack over its stand (especially in countries such as Britain) – the Olympic community was united over apartheid.

Although sport reflects some of the wider issues and tensions associated with race and is not immune from political manipulation, the above is an example of an international sports body taking a firm initiative towards racial equality, in line with its stated ethical principles.

> The social and political phenomenon of apartheid cannot be reconciled
> with the Olympic ideal and is a source of concern for the whole world.
> (J. A. Samaranch, 1988, quoted in Mbaye, 1995, p.11)

## Social class

In the past there has been discrimination on the grounds of social status or social class, sometimes cloaked in the guise of regulations relating to amateurism. For example, in Olympic equestrian events, no armed services personnel below the rank of officer were allowed to compete. Nowadays this sort of formal inequality seems ludicrous and totally unacceptable but a considerable degree of this kind of actual inequality, both within societies and between societies, still remains.

In Britain, some sports are quite clearly seen as being class-based. Horse-riding, yachting and ski-ing, for example, require the level of resources that few average families could provide. In any sport, however, unless there are facilities and support provided by society, it is inevitable that those from wealthier backgrounds will have better equipment, more training time, more and better coaching, and so on.

The question is: What should we be expecting the Olympic Movement to do about this? As an absolute minimum Olympism must express its strong opposition to formal inequalities and should support government commitment to provision of good basic physical education in schools and colleges and to 'Sport for All' programmes and provision. If access to basic sporting provision is not available, this will obviously inhibit 'take-up' of serious sporting activity.

Of course, it is unreasonable to expect Olympism, or sports organisations generally, to solve all social problems. But on the other hand we must be prepared to stand up for Olympic principles, and if that means fighting for a world within which all have an opportunity to compete equally, then we should do so.

## VIOLENCE AND AGGRESSION

The 'problem of violence' in sport is another paradox because (some claim) aggression is a quality required in sport, especially at the highest levels; and so it should not be surprising if sport attracts aggressive people, or if sport actually produces aggression. The results of violence, however, are widely condemned. How can this apparent circle be squared?

---

### STUDY ACTIVITY 11.3

Before you read on, try to spot the confusion in the above paragraph. Then ask yourself: Is the problem of violence paradoxical?'

---

You will have noticed that the two ideas, aggression and violence, were run side-by-side in the last paragraph. This illustrates the fact that they are often confused. So our first task must be to clarify what is at issue here, so that we can see just what is a threat, and why. In standard sports psychology texts the concept of violence is usually raised in the context of studies of aggression.

## Assertion

Some see the biological organism as active and positive, and see 'aggression' as a basic biological drive, a pre-condition of existence, human flourishing or excellence. However, this is also simply referred to as 'assertiveness' or 'self-assertion' because there is no suggestion of a necessary forcefulness. Rather, there is the sense of affirming or insisting upon one's rights; protecting or vindicating oneself; maintaining or defending a cause.

## Aggression

Aggression, however, is forceful. Some recognise defensive as well as offensive aggression, but both are served by force.

Aggression is:

- vigorous (gaining advantage by force)
- offensive (battling for the ball)
- proactive (striking first).

Such features may or may not be morally objectionable – dependent upon context – in everyday life, but all are often within the rules of team sports.

## Violence

Just as it is possible to be assertive without being aggressive, it is quite possible to be aggressive without being violent. A player can be both forceful and vigorous without seeking to hurt or harm anyone. Violence, however, is centrally to do with intentional hurt or injury to others, as well as attempts to harm, recklessness as to harm, and negligence. Since such injury is very often seen as illegitimate, legitimacy has often been seen as an important ethical issue in sport. Accordingly, violence in a sport might be seen as 'attempted or actual harm to others, where this is against the rules'.

Sometimes, violence may be justifiable (in war, or revolution, or terrorism; or in boxing, where 'violence' within bounds is legitimate). *Illegitimate violence* must be characterised as the attempt to harm by the use of illegitimate force.

There is a particular moral problem involving what might be called *gratuitous violence*: when violence exceeds what is necessary for its success.

### Justification – the ethics of violence

Violence involves the pursuit of interests in situations where legitimate forms of activity have failed, or seem likely to fail. But it does this in such a way as to fundamentally overturn the expectations on which a game proceeds (rules, fair play, etc.).

Violence is used in order to:

- gain an advantage
- intimidate
- force withdrawal
- enforce a contest on abilities not specified in the game's constitutive rules
- challenge the referee's claim to a monopoly on the use of sanctions.

However, there are some possible justifications of a resort to violence (although some in this list might better be seen as defences or mitigations, rather than justifications):

- non-intentional ('I went for the ball')
- non-premeditated (spur of the moment, automatic response)
- self-defence ('he was coming for me')
- pre-emptive self-defence
- defence of others
- duress ('my coach insisted that I do that [. . .] my job was on the line')
- preventing an offence
- provocation (retaliation)
- lack of an adequate authority (the referee 'lost it')
- rules are unclear, and it's legitimate to push them to the limit
- it's not a moral issue, because game rules aren't moral rules
- it works (achieves the end)
- custom and practice ('that's what's expected of a professional')
- consent ('everyone knows the risks').

### What's wrong with offering violence?

If violence is 'against the rules', then objections to violence in sport are based on the following questions:

1   What is wrong with rule-breaking (in general)?

- failing to uphold the laws and conventions of the sport
- failing to maintain the institution (breaking the rules of the practice).

2   What is (in addition) especially wrong with violence?

- intending to harm
- failing to accord proper respect to opponents.

That is to say, some forms of violence conflict with the requirements of sport. Violence stands in the way of a proper equality of opportunity to contest, and it fails to respect the rules of the contest.

Thus far it has been suggested that assertion and aggression are not wholly bad, but it is now necessary to intimate a much stronger thesis: that aggression and violence in sport present opportunities for moral education and moral development.

### OLYMPISM AND SPORT ETHICS

When playing sport we exercise our potential for aggression, and we may be tempted by the attractions of violence in pursuit of our aims. In the educational setting, games function as laboratories for value experiments. Students are put in the position of having to act, repeatedly, sometimes in haste, under pressure or provocation, either to prevent something or to achieve something, under a structure of rules. The settled dispositions which it is claimed emerge from such a crucible of value-related behaviour are those which were consciously cultivated through games in the public schools in the nineteenth century.

The impetus and opportunity for 'values education' here is tremendous. The questions are: How do we come to terms with our own behaviour and dispositions, motivations and propensities? Is there a route from the potentially risky confrontations that sometimes occur in sport to the development of a self with greater moral resolution? And, more generally, is there a possibility for peace and the non-violent conduct of human affairs?

Nissiotis says (1983, pp. 106–108):

> . . . this is the ethical challenge that faces humanity: how to harness the creative and motivating forces of aggression into the service of humanity.
>
> Sport in Olympic practice is one of the most powerful events transforming aggressiveness to competition as emulation. Sports life moves on the demarcation line between aggressiveness and violence. It is a risky affair . . . Citius-Altius-Fortius is a dangerous enterprise on the threshold of power as aggression, violence and domination. But this is, precisely, the immense value of Olympic sports: they challenge people to react, to pass the test of power . . .

It is both an attractive and intriguing idea that the competitive sports situation challenges individuals to develop and use their power and aggressiveness; but not, finally, to use this power to control and subjugate the other. May we see more assertive and aggressive people and fewer violent ones, and may sport be an agent of moral change.

The Olympic tradition presents a view of sport which sees it as necessarily tied to the idea of fair play and without which its educative potential is destroyed. Olympic ethics are therefore firmly set against cheating, violence and doping.

## MULTICULTURALISM AND INTERNATIONAL UNDERSTANDING

There are other aspects of Olympic values that we have not yet considered. We refer of course to those values relating to a concern for 'all sports for all people' – mutual respect, international understanding and multiculturalism (de Coubertin, 1934b).

Let us consider this in terms of both theory and practice. There is a close relationship between ethics and structures, in as much as structures encapsulate and express values. It is possible to 'read off' working values from practices and structures, and compare them with professed values.

Conversely, the test of the sincerity with which professed values are held is whether or not they are represented in working practices. What the Olympic

Movement means by its values should be written into its practices, and its sincerity may be interrogated through the reality of those practices.


## The Olympic programme

Let us apply this test to the Olympic programme, i.e. those sports that are favoured by their official status as Olympic sports.

The main principles on which the selection of Olympic sports is based are popularity and universality: the existence of the sport in an organised form in a sufficient number of countries and continents. However, it also affirmed that one of the missions of the Olympic Movement is to contribute to the development of sport in all its forms.

There is something of a contradiction here: the present criteria, though reasonable, tend to produce a list of sports that have already attained world popularity, which means, in effect, those that reflect the earlier cultural hegemony of the West (see Landry, 1984).

Most sports on the Olympic programme were codified in Western Europe towards the end of the nineteenth century, during the period of imperialism. 'Our' sports were exported around the globe, and now dominate Olympic and world sport.

This has the effect of reducing the popularity and influence of traditional and regional sports in favour of those on the Olympic programme.

The underdevelopment of those sports is therefore produced by Olympic criteria, i.e. their underdevelopment is not simply a condition of a society, but rather a condition that is produced by development elsewhere. Resources are diverted away from traditional sports in order to promote Olympic sports. Eichberg (1984) has described this as 'the non-recognition of non-Western sports', corresponding to neo-colonisation.

But, if we really believe in 'all sports for all people', or the values of multiculturalism, why don't we try to think of ways in which we can de-centre Western practices within Olympic ideology, and recognise significant sporting forms and practices from around the world?

There are many simple ways of doing this. The most radical suggestion might be to entirely re-think the Olympic programme of sports and events.

ethics of sport and olympism

A simple provocative suggestion might involve the implementation of a compensatory policy, according to which (for example) eight sports are deleted from the Olympic Summer Games programme, and two popular sports from each non-European continent are included in the official programme.

This would help to promote regional sports which have hitherto received little exposure (the Indian sport of kabbadi is one example), and it would be a practical way of affirming a commitment to multiculturalism – an exemplar of the way in which Olympic values might be enshrined in its structures.

---

**STUDY ACTIVITY 11.5**

1   If you had to delete 8 sports from the 28 on the Olympic Summer Games programme, which would you choose and why?
2   Did you use an 'Olympic' reason, or principle? If not, think again, and delete sports for a particular 'Olympic' reason (for example, someone might suggest boxing, because it is 'violent' or equestrian events, because they are socially elitist; or football, because the International Football Federation (FIFA) reserves its most excellent players for its own World Cup, etc.).

---

## THE OLYMPIC MOVEMENT AND INTERNATIONAL UNDERSTANDING

We should draw attention here to the emerging relationship between the Olympic Movement and the United Nations, two global organisations facing similar problems in regard to universality and particularity. The general difficulty in both cases is how they are to operate at a global (universal) level whilst such apparently intractable differences exist at the particular (local) level.

Some seek to resolve such difficulties by speaking of sport as a universal language, but this may under-represent the case. It is not simply sport, but Olympism itself that seeks to be universal in its values: mutual recognition and respect, tolerance, solidarity, equity, anti-discrimination, peace, multiculturalism, etc. These are a quite specific set of values, which are at once a set of universal general principles, but which also require differential interpretation in different cultures, i.e. stated in general terms whilst interpreted in the particular.

This search for a universal representation at the interpersonal and political level of our common humanity seems to be the essence of the optimism and hope of Olympism and other forms of humanism and internationalism, including United Nations organisations and Human Rights movements.

In the face of recent events in Europe and the Middle East this may seem a fond hope and a naive optimism; but there is a place for those who continue to argue for and work towards a future of promise, and there is still a strong case for sport as an efficient means of doing so.

Sport has made an enormous contribution to modern society over the past 100 years or so, and those who ally themselves with the philosophy of Olympism argue that it has been the most coherent systematisation of the ethical and political values underlying the practice of sport to have emerged thus far.

## ETHICS OF SPORT AND OLYMPISM

1   Write a critical account of the role of fair play in sport, giving examples.
2   Critically assess the arguments against deception in sport, and explain how it relates to cheating.
3   Are violent sports immoral? Use examples of Olympic sports, e.g. judo, football, boxing, etc.
4   Multiculturalism is a recent addition to the language of Olympic values. Explain how it might be seen as a contemporary re-working of long-established Olympic ideals.

# CHAPTER 12

# DRUGS AND THE OLYMPIC GAMES

## Chapter aims:

- to analyse critically the arguments against doping in sport
- to broaden the analysis so as to explore the concept of sport and its ethical Olympic ideals.

After studying this chapter, you should be able to explain:

- a range of arguments that have been used to criticise/excuse doping
- the relationship between arguments about doping and wider issues in the ethics of sport
- your own assessment of these arguments and your position on the ethics of doping.

## INTRODUCTION

There are five parts to this chapter. The first is negative, since it is the intention to show how some popular arguments against doping do not work. The second part looks, conversely, at arguments against a ban on doping. The third highlights a positive feature of the debate, which is not often noticed and which has serious consequences. The fourth presents a thought experiment in order to reveal those foundational values of sport threatened by doping practice. Finally, the fifth considers the notion of the fair advantage.

Currently, an athlete is held responsible ('strictly liable') for whatever substances are found in his or her body. Such a strict liability provision rules out any defence of ignorance or lack of intention to cheat. 'I didn't know it was any different from the British product', insisted Iain Baxter, the first British skier ever to win an Olympic medal. But his American 'Vicks' nasal spray did contain a tiny quantity of a banned substance and so he lost his 2002 bronze medal. British sprinter Dwain Chambers denies knowingly having taken a 'designer steroid' but was still banned from the Olympic Games for life in 2004 after testing positive for THG.

On the advice of team doctors the Romanian gymnast Andreea Raducan innocently took one dose of cold medicine, which contained the banned stimulant pseudoephidrine. Her denial of any intention to cheat was publicly accepted by Jacques Rogge, President of the International Olympic Committee, who nevertheless said, 'The rules are the rules' and stripped her of her Sydney 2000 gold medal.

There are interesting and important issues associated with such cases, but what follows concentrates on the obvious case of intentional doping.

## *IF* DOPING IS WRONG, *WHY* IS IT WRONG?

One difficulty for those who favour a total ban on certain kinds of drugs in sport is persuading others of their undesirability. Apparently, many athletes continue to use doping substances and techniques, and some of them must surely believe that a ban is not justifiable.

In order to persuade them otherwise, good reasons are required; and it is not that easy to come up with reasons that are decisive. Let us look at some of the more common arguments against the use of drugs and see whether they are persuasive, especially when each reason is applied to areas other than doping.

---

### STUDY ACTIVITY 12.1

So the question is: *if* doping is wrong, *why* is it wrong? Take a few moments to answer this question yourself, before we explore some answers.

---

### Drugs enhance performance

Do they? Certainly, some are supposed to enhance performance directly, and certainly some athletes believe it. But this may simply be a result of lack of adequate drugs education. Dr Richard Nicholson (1987) of the Institute of Medical Ethics says:

> It is likely that few sportsmen would use drugs if they were aware of their general ineffectiveness.

Anyway, so what? Expensive 'moonbikes' and fibreglass poles also enhance performance.

In the case of the US cycling squad in the 1984 Los Angeles Olympics, their moonbikes almost certainly made medallists out of inferior performers. If drugs make athletic competitions into contests between pharmacological laboratories, then expensive equipment makes them into contests between technological systems (or even national economies) – but then, that's allowed!

### (Some) drugs allow athletes to train harder

But, if they do, is that so important? Living next door to the swimming pool, or having access to the best facilities, might also allow you to train harder, but that's allowed. Anyway, what's wrong with taking steps to train harder? Isn't this what athletes try to do all the time with the aid of sports medicine? The sooner an athlete can recover from training, or from an injury, the sooner he can train again beneficially.

During competition, the sports medic's job is to help the athlete to recover from injury, or to compete despite injury. Sports medics might use (approved) drugs routinely for this purpose, so it cannot be this aspect of drug use that makes it wrong to take them.

### Drugs are unnatural

That may very well be the case, but approved drugs are as unnatural as prohibited ones – aren't they?

Just what is important about the word 'unnatural'? It's unnatural to pump iron so as to develop huge muscles, but that's allowed.

What is more natural than testosterone? It may even be that in order to be world class performers, athletes have to be born 'unnatural' (or at least be genetically unusual, in statistical terms), or have to develop profoundly unnatural characteristics or skills.

### The use of drugs by some forces others to use them

No, it doesn't! But, even if it does, so does six hours spent training in the pool every day. All top class swimmers know the hours put in by their rivals and must match that in order to compete. Does that make it immoral? If drugs are immoral on this ground, then so are intensive training levels.

### They are harmful

Are they? The evidence so far is extremely patchy. There are some reports of damage due to steroids, but Nicholson (1987) says:

> after more than 30 years of their use there is no convincing evidence of any major health hazards to healthy males.

One problem, of course, is that as long as drugs are prohibited they cannot be taken safely under medical supervision, and so this itself might be a source of harm (i.e. taking the wrong dose, or without medical monitoring). Even aspirin, if taken wrongly, can be very dangerous.

But even if they are harmful, so what? Many sports are hazardous and this seems to be part of what gives them their appeal. Some people seek security by taking out mortgages with insurance policies, paying for superannuated pensions, buying cars with safety features, and so on, and then they go hang-gliding at weekends!

The injury rate in certain sports is horrific, but arguments that point this out are dismissed as irrelevant by sports aficionados. Even if drugs are harmful it still needs to be shown why this kind of harm should be of particular concern, whilst other (even greater) harms go unremarked, or are even glorified.

### They are illegal

Is this true? There are many substances used by athletes that it is not actually illegal to use or possess, especially if they are medically prescribed.

Snooker players (to move the spotlight away from athletics for a change) have used alcohol, tranquillisers, betablockers, marijuana and cocaine. Only some of these are illegal (and only then in certain countries) but is it the illegality of the drug that makes it wrong to use it? Surely if these substances all perform roughly the same function (or perceived function) for the player, they are all equally wrong in that respect, regardless of whether or not they are legal?

This is an extension of the 'legalise cannabis' argument. Why make it illegal to get high on cannabis, whilst there's no sanction against drinking? Alcohol is a killer, but it is legal.

Similarly, sports bodies worry about the harmful effects of drugs, but sometimes collude with tobacco companies in pushing their dope to youngsters through the 'healthy associations' their products are allowed to make with sport.

Tobacco is a killer, but far more fuss is made over the relatively harmless steroid with the odd highly publicised horror-story serving to divert attention from possibly more important issues.

Sugar is also a potential killer, but confectionary firms entice schoolchildren to buy sugary snacks in exchange for sports equipment tokens. If we really cared about harms, then we would take up different attitudes towards the unhealthy effects of these substances, especially in relation to sport.

---

**IN BRIEF**

## WHAT IS WRONG WITH DOPING?

Is it that it:

- ▪ enhances performance?
- ▪ allows athletes to train harder?
- ▪ forces other to take dope?
- ▪ is harmful?
- ▪ is unnatural?
- ▪ is illegal?

---

## THE DANGERS OF INTRODUCING A BAN

So, the usual arguments against doping are not decisive. In addition, we should also note that it's one thing to argue that something is wrong but quite another to argue that it should be banned.

We may think it unfortunate that intelligent people should decide to smoke or drink themselves to death, but we don't do much about it. Since the failure of 'prohibition' in the USA early in the twentieth century, very few people think that we might try a wholesale ban on smoking or drinking. However, the anti-doping lobby seeks not only to argue that doping is wrong, but also that it should be banned.

Another way of approaching this matter in general terms is to ask not what is wrong with doping, but rather what are the dangers of introducing a ban.

## Loss of medical benefits

What of the person who has a genuine medical reason for employing a particular drug but which also contravenes some rule? Is that person to be denied the medical assistance that alone would give him the equality of competition with others who are not afflicted with his complaint? Why should 'deserving cases' be denied the medical benefits of drugs?

One problem is the difficulty in deciding just what is a genuine medical benefit. At the 1984 Los Angeles Olympics, team doctors from the USA and Switzerland provided documentation declaring that their entire modern pentathlon teams needed betablockers for medical reasons (betablockers regulate heart rate and help with certain medical conditions). This is hard to countenance, since modern pentathletes are not known to be particularly prone to heart problems. However, it is difficult to see how all such abuse could be eliminated.

Another problem remains: even if there is a genuine medical reason for the use of a particular drug, does this legitimise its use in sport?

Rex Williams, the snooker player, has admitted that during his competitive career he used betablockers for health reasons. It is still an open question as to whether this legitimate health usage should have disqualified him from competition for, regardless of any health arguments, the use of this medication may still, as a by-product, have given him an advantage over others who did not have a medical reason to use the drug. However, if his contemporary, Bill Werbeniuk, was permitted to use ten pints of lager to solve his medical difficulty, what's wrong with betablockers?

So, was it fair to allow Williams to compete, since he was using the drug? Conversely, would it have been unfair to ban him since he could not have competed on equal terms without medication?

It would also seem that there might be a conflict between what a sports committee decides is permissible in competition and what a doctor would want to prescribe for purely medical reasons. It is not clear how such matters are to be resolved and this particular danger (the loss of medical benefits for those who have a legitimate medical need for a certain treatment in order to compete equally) is magnified in the case of Paralympic athletes, many of whom require drugs on a daily basis.

## Parentalism

As already mentioned, even if it is true that drugs are harmful to the athlete, it does not follow that we have the right to prevent him or her from taking them. To try to do so would be an intrusion into the performer's own decision-making processes.

If the performer decided to start (or continue) to take drugs under medical supervision for the benefits they were seen to be offering, and if the performer was also well aware of the possible dangers of such use, what argument would justify interfering with such a decision?

Again, we may think it unfortunate that people smoke or drink, but we would think it unbearably parentalistic to interfere with their freedom to do so. Why then, should we think that we can interfere in athletes' decisions?

One suggestion is that parentalism is justified in order to prevent harm to the athletes themselves – but we have already seen the weakness of that position. Another suggestion is that parentalism is justified because of the coercive harm caused by imitative doping – but again, we have already seen the weakness of that position too.

Why should sports chiefs believe that they should have more 'parental' power over competitors in their sports than governments have over their subjects?

## Infringement of liberties

Any ban would require enforcement, which entails the introduction of the apparatus, procedures and timetables of testing.

Such an infringement of personal liberties would draw criticism from civil rights groups in other sectors of society. For example, the suggestion in the 1990s that AIDS might be combated by compulsory blood tests was met with total condemnation in both the UK and the USA and, although we can see the need for governments to quarantine their citizens in case of a threat of a major epidemic (such as the SARS outbreak in 2003), we can also see the potential danger here for the unnecessary infringement of the human rights of individuals.

Another rights issue involves the invasion of privacy. This is an inevitable consequence (for example) of the routine procedures of urine analysis, which is now required even for children.

Is it justifiable to require children to expose themselves to the gaze of testing officials so as to ensure the identity of a sample?

So, somehow we have to assess and balance the benefits and disadvantages of a ban, and it is not at all clear just what the outcome of such deliberations might be.

---

### STUDY ACTIVITY 12.2

Consider a recent doping case, where an athlete is accused of breaking the rules. Now, just what are the issues in this particular case? Do you think the athlete in question has done wrong? (In 2004 such cases included those of Alain Baxter, Rio Ferdinand, Dwain Chambers and Greg Rusedski.)

---

## THE ETHICAL BASIS OF THE IDEA OF SPORT

There is, however, a positive feature of the debate about performance-enhancing drugs. The drugs debate has forced everyone to think in ethical terms, and to appeal to ethical principles.

However, if we take these appeals seriously and follow them through, there are some interesting consequences.

Continue to assume that drug-taking in sport is wrong and ask again the question: Why is it wrong? The answers given above were all framed in terms of some ethical principle that is claimed to be central to our idea of sport, and which drug-taking allegedly violates.

Let us re-visit some of the arguments presented in the first part of this chapter and see where the underlying principles lead us.

## The 'natural' athlete – the track versus the laboratory

Some say that what is wrong with drug-taking is that it removes competition from the track to the laboratory.

However, if we are to be consistent we should note that the development of sports science in general promotes competition between physiology, psychology and biomechanics laboratories as support services for training.

If we're so worried about removing the competition from the track to the laboratory, then maybe we should look again at the ethical status of sports sciences more generally. This is not normally regarded as a corollary of the 'natural athlete' argument, but consistency requires that we should reconsider the whole issue of 'natural' sport.

For example, why not return to sprints in bare feet on grass, instead of athletes performing in personally crafted shoes on special surfaces – both designed to maximise traction and therefore enhance performance levels?

## Unfair advantage or inequality of opportunity

Others say that what is wrong with drug-taking is that it confers an unfair advantage.

Notice that no-one can (sincerely) make this objection to drug-taking unless he or she is sincere in their commitment to sport as embodying fairness, and to disallowing unfair advantages as being against the very idea of sport.

However, many of those holding such objections against drug-taking seem perfectly prepared to allow various kinds of very obviously unfair advantages. For example:

- only certain countries are able to generate and enjoy the fruits of developments in sports science
- only certain countries are able to possess the knowledge and technology required for the production of specialised technical equipment.

Is this fair? The company that produced the so-called 'moonbikes' of the 1984 Los Angeles Olympics later shamelessly marketed them under the slogan 'The Unfair Advantage'.

Let's widen the issue. It seems to be an undeniable fact that international competition is grossly unfair because some countries have the resources to enhance the performance of their athletes (legally or otherwise) whilst others clearly do not.

Those performers nurtured within advanced systems might take time to consider the extent to which their performances are a function not just of their individual sporting ability but also of the social/political/economic context in which they have been nurtured. Have not their performances been enhanced? Are not their advantages unfair?

Consistency requires that we re-visit the whole idea of disadvantage and also that of inequality. For example, why are more 'ethnic' sports not included in the Olympic programme, rather than the continuing present Western hegemonic domination?

Kabbadi, a sport popular on the Indian sub-continent, is based on the game form of 'tag', which is known in most societies in the world. It requires minimal facilities and no equipment. Why should we Westerners not have to learn such sports and compete on those terms, rather than collude in the disappearance of indigenous sport forms in favour of our own curriculum?

Anyone who relies on 'unfair advantage' arguments in the case of doping must also re-visit and reconsider such arguments in other contexts.

## Rule-breaking, or cheating

There is a considerable body of opinion that drug-taking is wrong simply because it is against the rules of competition.

However, pace-making is also against the rules of the International Association of Athletics Federation (IAAF), although it is allowed in order to facilitate record-breaking attempts in the commercial promotion of media spectacles. No-one is disqualified!

Athletes can in fact earn large fees for performing this 'service'. If officials so readily flout their own rules then they are poorly placed when athletes do the same, or when critics demand better justification for the rules that presently exist.

In a world where the values of sport are sometimes forgotten under the pressures of medal-winning and the marketplace, it ill behoves those responsible to turn a moralistic eye on athletes.

194

Why should athletes take any notice of the moral exhortation of those who have profited from the commercialisation of sport when they see the true values lived and expressed by those around them?

## Conclusion

The drugs debate has made everyone stand on ethical principle. But think how sport might develop (what it might become) if those principles were not merely used opportunistically over the drugs issue but rather were acted upon consistently in the interests of truly fair competition and equality of opportunity.

There is an opportunity here to open up debate again about the ethical basis of sport, so that our sports practice (and the sports science and training theory that support it) becomes rooted in firm principles that encapsulate what we think sport should be.

---

### STUDY ACTIVITY 12.3

You are an athlete and you have a bad cold for which you would like to take some medicine. How would you protect yourself from the possibility of inadvertently taking a banned substance? Consult the World Anti-Doping Agency website for advice and help <http://www.wada-ama.org/en/tl.asp?=29644>. Go to 'Education' and find links to: 'Athlete Guide', 'Athlete Passport', 'Doping Quiz', and 'Full list of banned procedures and substances'.

---

## A THOUGHT EXPERIMENT

### The harmless enhancer

Imagine that there has been the successful production of a pill whose entirely natural ingredients are derived from herbs to be found only in a remote part of Taiwan and which are so far unknown to Western medical science.

The ingredients of this pill have been used in traditional medicine for 3000 years without harmful effects, but new (and secret) applications have revealed hitherto unsuspected (and remarkable) performance-enhancing effects in the sporting context. Are there any reasons why such a pill should not be used?

This imaginary scenario 'takes out' a certain kind of medical critic, whose complaints are mainly related to harms, whether they are actual or supposed, demonstrable or alleged.

But this scenario also requires us to imagine a substance which is:

- proven to have no harmful effects
- a proven performance-enhancer.

So it asks us to consider the question: What, if anything, could be wrong with taking a harmless enhancer?

### The undetectable enhancer

Imagine further that such a pill is completely undetectable in use. This imaginary scenario 'takes out' the intrusive and (let's not forget it) enriched pharmacologists – for their role has been both to develop performance-enhancing drugs and also to develop ways of detecting them!

This scenario requires us to imagine a substance which is:

- in principle undetectable in use
- a proven performance-enhancer.

It asks us to consider the question: What, if anything, could be wrong with taking an undetectable enhancer?

### Responses

The answer is that despite the fact that they were harmless and undetectable, it would be wrong to take these enhancers if they were banned, because it is simple rule-breaking. If anyone seeks to evade any rule for advantage, especially when they do it knowingly and secretively, it is the clearest possible case of cheating. And the reason behind this rule lies in the phrase 'for advantage'. Although we strive to achieve all sorts of advantages over our opponents, we ought not to seek advantages that are against the rules.

Sporting competitors prepare and compete on certain more or less precise understandings described by the rules, and any attempt to evade these rules for advantage is cheating. It is an attempt to subvert the very basis upon which alone the activity is possible. It is an attempt to pervert the logical and moral basis of the whole social practice of sport.

This is the greatest harm perpetrated by doping cheats. It is not the alleged medical harm to self or the coercion of others, but the harm to self and others caused by behaviour that threatens the social practice of sport itself.

## THE FAIR ADVANTAGE

One argument considered above is that doping gives an unfair advantage.

Let us assume for the moment (although it may not be true) that doping does give an advantage. It is still an open question whether or not that advantage is an unfair one. It is often thought that any (dis)advantage or inequality is unfair, but this is not true. If you are taller or heavier or richer or faster than someone else then there is inequality, and so someone else may be at a disadvantage. However, it requires a further argument to show that such an inequality or disadvantage is unfair.

Here are some advantages routinely experienced in international sport:

■ being from a country with a large population
■ being from a rich country . . .
■ . . . or a country which 'hyper-commits' to elite sport
■ being an individual with a random genetic advantage
■ being an individual with financial and social support . . .
■ . . . or who 'hyper-commits' to extreme training levels.

These are all advantages usually thought to be 'fair enough'. No-one thinks to impose some kind of limit on the number of medals that can be won by Russia or the USA; no-one is actively thinking of ways to reduce the impact of gross domestic product or excessive government support of particular sports on the success of athletes.

So why doesn't doping count as just another route to advantage that is 'fair enough'? There are perhaps three points to be made.

197

## Reducing unfair advantage

We can and ought to reduce 'unfair' advantages. We could quite easily do much more in this regard than we do at present. For example, if we are troubled about the technological advantages enjoyed by certain countries, we could very easily legislate them away.

Let us suppose, for example, that the sport of cycling tests partly for the cyclist's abilities and partly for the cycle-maker's technical expertise. We are in a position to decide what cycling shall become. Do we want to permit technological expertise to help produce the winner, or do we want to test the cyclists only? If the latter, we simply prescribe the features of the cycle which will be used in Olympic and/or international competition over the next (say) four-year period, so that everyone has a chance to prepare and train with it.

Then we rule against the use of personal cycles in competition, requiring instead all competitors to draw lots for the cycles provided by the competition organisation. These cycles are as nearly as possible identical, thus making the race a test of the cyclists rather than the cycles.

Those who retort that it is impossible to constrain scientific or technological advances are probably right, but we do have the power to harness that creativity to human requirements.

For example, the IOC could adopt an 'Olympic javelin' every four years, which would be the winner of the Quadrennial Olympic Javelin Design Competition. This javelin would be unveiled at the end of one Olympic Games to be used at the next. Scientists would have four years to produce the javelin that best suits the IOC's criteria, which would naturally conform to Olympic principles.

For example, it might be suggested that it should have the following properties:

- it should fly straight and true
- it should be cheap and easy to make
- it should be impossible to throw out of the field into the spectators' area!

The point is that it depends what we want. We can decide just what abilities or advantages sports should test. If, as in motor-racing, we seem to want to allow competitions between manufacturers plus their drivers, then we still might have rules limiting construction possibilities, e.g. engine or valve size, type of tyres, length of 'skirt'. Then, if someone seeks to evade this rule (e.g. by building a skirt 2 centimetres too long) he is cheating, just like the doper in athletics, and, if discovered, is disqualified.

## Sports tests for advantage

But this reveals something important about the nature of sport: namely that what sport does is to test for advantages. It tests for who has:

- the best natural ability for the event
- trained hardest
- thought most intelligently about tactics and strategy
- prepared most carefully
- co-operated most effectively with others involved.

All other things being equal, the one having the most advantages will win.

## Intervention

It also shows us how we can intervene. We should try to design future sport so that it actually does test for those advantages that we think it should be testing for.

This means that we need to develop a way of demonstrating which advantages we consider to be unfair and should therefore be legislated against. Our present argument is therefore about whether or not doping is to be considered one of the more serious or important advantages, or whether it is just one factor among many.

---

**REVIEW QUESTIONS**

## DRUGS AND THE OLYMPIC GAMES

1. Choose two of the arguments presented in the first part of this chapter. Assess whether they offer athletes a persuasive reason for not taking performance-enhancing drugs.
2. Are all advantages unfair advantages? If not, which ones are fair and which are not? Why?
3. What (if anything) is wrong with doping? Is doping an unfair advantage? Are there other reasons why it is wrong?
4. If there were a harmless and undetectable (but illegal) enhancer, why not use it?

## CHAPTER THIRTEEN

# SPORT, ART AND THE OLYMPICS

**Chapter aims:**

■ to consider the nature of both sport and art, and possible relationships between the two
■ to explore the role of the fine arts in ancient and modern Olympic Games
■ To present an argument that shows that sport is not art.

After studying this chapter you should be able to explain:

■ the role of the fine arts in the development of the Olympic Idea
■ the role of the fine arts in the modern Olympic Movement
■ the relationship between sport and art.

## ART AND THE ANCIENT GAMES

We have already alluded to the importance of athletics in Ancient Greek life by illustrating its relationship with religion, morality and art.

The collective worship of Zeus, the sacrifices to Apollo and the other deities of the Greek Pantheon in the sacred area of the Olympic Altis, and the contests in the most splendid games of antiquity, the Olympic Games, reaffirmed the linguistic, religious, moral and social unity of the Greeks. Olympia, with its mystic ceremonies, the suspension of hostilities imposed by the truce and the gathering of thousands of men on its neutral territory, neutralised the political discord and disputes between cities and gave people the conviction that beyond small

200

differences and disputes there was a common historical and social background, there were common habits, common thoughts and a common consciousness that linked the Greek tribes together.

An important chapter in the work achieved by Ancient Olympia in the course of classical Hellenic civilisation, is the cultivation of the unity of the Greek world.

The classical art that adorned the temple of Zeus at Olympia undertook the same civilising mission as that of the institution of the Games. Here artists showed their work and poets recited their epics. Here was a place for art. Praxiteles made a god out of marble, Paeonius gave wings to the marble with his Nike and Phidias interpreted in marble the ideological significance of the games of Olympia.

The Twelve Labours of Hercules were depicted on twelve bas-reliefs on the facades of the temple of Zeus, and Hercules was seen as a model for the Olympic champion as hero.

The Labours of Hercules symbolise the abolition of the old deities of prehistoric worship. Hercules represents the migration of the Dorians, which halted the progress and development of the Cretan-Mycenaean civilisation. Hercules does away with animal symbols, beasts and monsters, all remnants of cults, and comes to predominate in Greece against local totems and gods.

In Nemea he strangled a lion, at Lerna he beheaded the hydra, whilst at Erymanthos he captured a wild boar and at Kerynitis a wild stag with golden antlers and brazen feet. At Stymphalia he killed a flight of rapacious birds and then crossed over to Crete to overcome the bull of Knossos and master the wild horses of Diomedes.

He killed Hippolyte, queen of the Amazons, seized the oxen of Geryon and stole the golden apples of the Hesperides. He also cleansed the stables of Augeas, King of Elis, and completed his labours by carrying off Cerberus from Hades.

In this historic age, therefore, the Labours of Hercules acquired moral symbolism. It is certain that they were placed on the small facades of the temple of Zeus at the height of the classical era and at a time when Olympia was at its greatest and most influential, in order to offer their moral precepts, so rich in meaning, side by side with physical education and training.

The strangling of the lion of Nemea is a symbol of the moral testing of man in subjugating his instinctive passions and overcoming his egoism and arrogance. In

Greek legend the Lernaean hydra symbolises the struggle of light against darkness, the victory over inaction and torpor. The Erymanthian boar represents wild instincts, the birds of Stymphalia evil thoughts and the bull of Knossos primitive sexual impulses, all to be overcome.

With the Twelve Labours of Hercules, adorning the temple of Zeus, the athlete preparing for the games is given moral commands, which he must obey in order to master his passions before launching himself in the Olympic contest. So the athlete, after the mental and physical training planned by the Elian organisers, was ready to enter the sanctuary of Altis and offer sacrifices to the gods.

Physical training and competition in the house of the gods and under the eye of the guardians of morality was designed to produce excellent achievement and all-round personality – identical to the goals espoused by the Muscular Christians of nineteenth-century Britain.

---

## STUDY ACTIVITY 13.1

In ancient times there was a strong link between sport, art and religion. Can you identify any of these elements in modern sport?

---

### ART IN ANCIENT OLYMPIA

First of all it is necessary to recall the role that art played over the centuries in Ancient Olympia:

> The whole ancient history of Hellenism with its countless artistic forms
> and its intellectual life is to be found concentrated at Olympia.
> (Yalouris, 1971, p. 90)

A visit to the museum in Olympia amply confirms that one thousand years of Greek Art is represented there. For a picture of Ancient Olympia we can consult Pausanias: details of many of the works of art in the sanctuary are recorded in his *Description of Greece*, Books V and VI.

From his accounts, together with dates we have of Olympic victories and a knowledge of the style of the various periods of art, we can conclude for example that the statue of Entelidas, winner of the boys' wrestling and pentathlon in 628

202

BC, took the form of an archaic Kouros (a standing figure), and that the statue of Milo by Dameus must have been a later development of that style.

Alongside these works stood figures from the later Classic period by Pythagoras, Phidias and Myron, and other figures that, because of technological developments in bronze casting, assumed more dynamic poses than the Kouroi. Later works include those of Lysippos, reputed to have made some 1500, mostly athletic figures.

We should try to catch a glimpse of the original scene: to picture the hundreds of stone and terracotta statues painted in their vivid colours with the bronze figures being chased and polished into bright metal decorated with contrasting inlays.

But what was the reason for the presence of these works of art?

The figures of the victors were votive and commemorative offerings to the gods. But their ritual effigies also invoked the presence of the gods themselves. Pausanias devoted four chapters to descriptions of the various statues of Zeus. Hera, Aphrodite and Hermes were also represented, as were the legends of Pelops and Heracles. Other works commemorated public figures and historical events.

So Olympia was essentially a cultural centre to which athletics was only one contribution. Moreover, although competition did exist between artists for commissions, and for the honour of having their work placed at Olympia, there was no formal competition for prizes.

## THE CONTRIBUTION OF THE FINE ARTS TO THE MODERN OLYMPIC GAMES

One of the foundations of modern Olympism was defined by Baron Pierre de Coubertin as beauty, derived from the participation of art and intellect. For de Coubertin art had to play an essential role, and he devoted the last chapter of his *Pedagogy Sportive* to the close relationship between art and sport, seeking to define the relationship between the two.

It is generally accepted that de Coubertin was primarily concerned with educational reform, at national and then at international level. The humanitarianism of sport was a means towards that end. By choosing Olympia as his 'dream city' and the Ancient Games as an inspiration for modern sport, he found a way of evoking the principles of Greek Idealism.

This idealism, which Lord Clark (1970, p. 32) has described as 'the most extra-ordinary creation in the whole of history', had been inherited by Europe and its principles had dominated European culture and shaped the form of education there since the Renaissance. The games were to exalt sport but also to subordinate it to the general purpose of life, ranging it amongst those activities that embellish human existence.

> It was not by accident that the writers and artists of old assembled at Olympia around the ancient sports; it was from this incomparable coalescence that the prestige sprang which from so long characterised this institution.
>
> (De Coubertin, 1931, quoted in Masterton, 1973, p. 202)

It was, therefore, for the purpose of establishing art into the Olympic Movement that he called the Advisory Conference on Art, Science and Sport in Paris at the Comédie Française on 23 May 1906. In de Coubertin's own words, the purpose of the meeting was to consider:

> to what extent and in what form the Arts and Letters could take part in the celebration of the modern Olympiads and in general associate themselves with the practice of sports in order to benefit from them and ennoble them.
>
> (De Coubertin, 1906, p. 16)

He went on to state that the association of sport and art should extend to embrace local manifestations of sporting activity and proposed competitions in architecture, sculpture, painting, music and literature for unpublished works directly inspired by the idea of sport to be included in the Games.

The programme upon which he invited views from the meeting was as follows.

*Architecture*

> Conditions and characteristics of the modern gymnasium. Open-air circles and urban circles, swimming pools, stands, riding stables, yachting clubs, fencing clubs, materials, architectural motifs, expenses and estimates.

*Dramatic art*

> Open-air performances. Essential principles – sport on the stage.

## Choreography

Processions, defiles, group and co-ordinated movements, rhythmic dances.

## Decorations

Grandstands and enclosures. Masts, escutcheons, garlands, draperies, sheaves. Night festivals; sports by torchlight.

## Letters

The founding of Olympic literary competitions, conditions of these competitions. Sporting emotion as source of inspiration for the man of letters.

## Music

Orchestras and open-air choirs. Repertoire, rhythms and alternations, fanfares. Conditions of an Olympic musical competition.

## Painting

Individual silhouettes and ensemble views. Possibility and conditions of an Olympic painting competition. Aid afforded to the artist by photography.

## Sculpture

Athletic attitudes and gestures in their relation to art. Interpretation of effort. Objects given as prizes: statuettes and medallions.

De Coubertin was not unaware of the problems likely to be encountered. He expected only a limited participation at first and believed that initially the competitions would draw only those artists who were personally committed to the practice of sports. But clearly his intention was to introduce a cultural aspect to the games with the marriage of muscle and mind that had been evident in Ancient Olympia.

No doubt the changes that had occurred since the 1870s had encouraged him. Impressionist and Post-Impressionist painting had paid some attention to sport. The weekend scenes at Argenteuil, near Paris, where Parisians enjoyed sailing, rowing, canoeing and swimming, were favourite subjects for Manet, Monet, Renoir and Sisley. River scenes continued to attract the Neo-Impressionists and Seurat, their leader, rarely failed to include these sports in his pictures of the Seine.

As the century moved into its last quarter many other artists, attracted by athletic contests of all kinds, recorded popular sporting activities. Tennis, foot races and bicycle racing (which was developing from a recreative pursuit into a competitive sport), were especially favoured. Sport as a subject of painting became so popular that an exhibition entitled Sport in Art was mounted at the Georges Petit Gallery in 1885.

De Coubertin must have been aware of these trends. He was also probably familiar with the work of such Post-Impressionists as Lautrec, whose velodrome pictures included not only the cycle races, from which he designed posters, but also portraits of champions such as Zimmerman, 'Choppy' Warburton, Mickael, Vergen, Bardeu and Fournier. Tristan Bernard, Director of Velodrome Buffalo and Velodrome de la Seine, was reputedly the inventor of the now universal bell signal for the last lap of a race.

De Coubertin hoped that the beauty of sport, which he described so fervently in his poem 'Ode to Sport', would bring about the participation of the great artists of his time, but it was not to be. Started in 1912 the competitions were terminated in 1948.

---

## STUDY ACTIVITY 13.2

Consider the differences between a World Championship (in a particular sport) and the Olympic Games. What effect was de Coubertin trying to create, and how was art to be part of it?

---

### ART COMPETITIONS IN THE MODERN OLYMPIC GAMES, 1912–1948

The 1906 proposals were put into practice at the 1912 Stockholm Games but were discontinued after the London Games in 1948. Since then various attempts have been made to re-introduce them. Some consider their omission to be a violation of the Olympic Charter, but the prevailing opinion is that exhibitions rather than competitions of art (and not necessarily associated with sport) should be held concurrently with the Games.

Some believe the competitions to have been doomed from the beginning, because they were never integrated with the sports in ways such as, for example, awarding works of art as prizes – a suggestion made by de Coubertin at the 1906 meeting. Others believe that, by confining the subject to sport, too narrow a field was offered to contemporary Western artists who were exploring styles influenced by Cubism, Futurism, Expressionism and Abstraction, all forms of art in which the subject was subordinated to artistic treatment.

Impressionism had introduced a new meaning to the nature of art and the twentieth century saw an evolution of forms very different from those of previous centuries. This new art rejected the old styles and the concepts of beauty that had ruled since the Renaissance. It substituted new ideas. It experimented with Oriental and African aesthetic forms. It explored ideas about the nature of light, the relationship of time and space, the structure of matter and energy, the unconscious mind, the dynamics or form, the kinetic and optical effect of colour and structure and even its own nature as an aspect of culture.

Such paintings as *Rugby* by Andre Lhote, *The Footballers* by Albert Gleizes, *The Cardiff Team* and *The Runners* by Robert Dalaunay, *The Wrestlers* by Jacques Villon, and such sculpture as Archipenko's *Boxers* and *The Boxer* by Henri Laurens all illustrate how certain 'Cubist' principles were applied to 'sporting' pictures.

*The Dynamism of a Footballer* and *The Dynamism of a Cyclist* by Umberto Boccioni are the best examples of Futurist art, and attempt to portray the sensation of dynamism and energy. Boccioni and other members of this group produced many pictures and sculptures which sought to represent movement and muscular force.

Even Expressionist art, which proclaimed the direct rendering of emotions and feelings to be its goal, occasionally turned to sport. Max Beckmann painted *Rugby Players*, Kirchner painted *Ice Hockey Players* and Oscar Schlummer used the stadium itself as a stimulus for his own particular style.

Nor was sport excluded from the interpretation of Abstract art. Willi Baumeister was the most prolific in this genre with many examples of abstract sporting pictures such as *The Woman Runner* (1927). Also influential was Nicolas de Stael, whose numerous pictures of football include *Parc des Princes* and *Les Grands Footballeurs*. These demonstrate how the artist employed colour harmonies and dynamics to convey something akin to the energy of the players.

In the 1960s and 1970s some art forms attempted to relate fine art with popular culture. Like the art of Ancient Greece that exalted beautiful athletes on everyday domestic pottery, today's 'Pop' art extols the sportsmen heroes of our time.

STUDY ACTIVITY 13.3

Find out about the basic principles of one modern art movement (e.g. Cubism, Futurism, Expressionism). Think also about the 'modern' character of sport and about why sport might have made a good subject for that art movement.

A common suggestion as to the failure of the Olympic art competitions was that the artists in those days also had to be amateurs. Coupled with this was the belief that the value of a prize-winning entry would increase enormously in value. This, however, is not borne out by the facts.

The painting that won the gold medal in the 1948 Olympics, *The London Amateur Championships (Boxing)* by A. R. Thompson, was sold in the auction of the Hutchinson Collection for 10 guineas. It is not absolutely clear why the possibility of an increase in the value of a work should be a valid reason for excluding these competitions when so many athletic victors subsequently capitalise on their success.

## THE OLYMPIC ART PROGRAMME AFTER 1948

Since the abandonment of the art competitions the policy adopted by host countries has been to arrange cultural programmes that have included exhibitions of fine art. The omission of such an exhibition at Melbourne in 1956 elicited much critical comment – a mistake not made in subsequent Olympiads.

The tendency was, however, to stage exhibitions that demonstrated the art of the host country. But this was not true of the Mexico or Munich programmes where the art was international. In Mexico, orchestras, dance groups, ballet and opera companies came from all over the world and the 'Olympic Way' was decorated with sculpture made by such internationally renowned artists as Alexander Calder.

In Munich, theatrical companies, music groups, artists, dancers and other performers from a multitude of nations performed on the Spielstrasse, and other exhibitions, such as that devoted to the art of Ancient Olympia at the Deutsches Museum, were also arranged. Sport in art was displayed in an out-door display of reproductions and a special book was published for the occasion.

The posters for various events were particularly attractive but special mention must be made of those commissioned for the Games by artists of international fame including Kokoschka, Vasarely, Hartung, Poliakoff, Hockney and Jones.

However, alongside this approbatory art were other exhibitions that were highly critical of the festival. Some young European artists exhibited works that condemned the games from a political and economic standpoint. Konkola and Dicken deprecated the cost of them. Montell commented on the racial problem and especially the attitude of the black athletes in the American team.

Others took a critical view of modern training methods. Pezold's poster, for example, likened the training of an athlete to the life of a pig and Petrick's exhibit, depicting winners on the podium, had some similarity with the cynical aspects of George Grosz's work. There were also pictorial statements by Sorge and Weigand, which focused on the apparently violent and aggressive nature of sport. Ueberfeldt related some athletic events to military training. This art, however, should not be condemned, but welcomed as thought-provoking criticism.

---

## STUDY ACTIVITY 13.4

Despite the demise of 'official' art competitions in the Olympic Games, exhibitions have continued. See <http://abc.net.au/news/olympics/features/art.htm> for a report on Olympic art in Sydney 2000. What role is there for art at the Olympics? For fun, see the Kodak site at <http://www.musarium.com/kodak/olympics/olympichistory/indexbody1.shtml>.

---

## DE COUBERTIN AND THE RELATIONSHIP OF SPORT TO ART

In the last chapter of his *Pedagogy Sportive* (1919, quoted in Durry, 1998, p. 60), where de Coubertin explores the relationship between art and sport, he emphasises:

> the double role they could possibly play: Sport should be seen as a producer of art and as an art opportunity. It produces beauty since it creates the athlete who is a living sculpture. It is an art opportunity through the buildings dedicated to it, the spectacle, the celebrations it generates.

So far we have considered only the second of these ideas: sport as an 'art opportunity'. Part of the meaning here is that sport can be the subject of art works, or inspire the creation of sporting venues, or the artistic expression of ideas and emotions connected with sporting experience or sports events, as in sports festivals.

Part of the idea, as in ancient times, is the educative and morally uplifting potential of architecture, choreography, staging, etc. De Coubertin reports such an effect on himself in Olympia:

> I had come from Athens . . . Next day, from my window, I waited for sunrise and as soon as the first rays had touched the valley, I rushed to the ruins . . . It was a moral architecture whose teachings I had come to pick . . .
>
> (De Coubertin, 1997, p. 225)

The idea of sport as a 'producer of art', however, seems problematical. As expressed above, it seems to suppose that the production of any beautiful thing (such as a fit human body) is the work of an artist. But this would then not distinguish an 'artist' (e.g. a famous painter) from the person who wallpapers a bedroom. An extension of de Coubertin's view might be that art is produced in sport just because some sports are beautiful, or aesthetically pleasing, and this possibly misinterprets the nature of art and aesthetic appreciation, as well as the nature of sport.

Let us consider further the relationship between sport, art and the aesthetic.

## SPORT, ART AND THE AESTHETIC

### The aesthetic

*The aesthetic is a way of perceiving* an object or an activity, a kind of interest that we take in it, a kind of attitude that we take towards it. Sometimes people talk as if the aesthetic refers to an object itself, as if we could talk about 'an aesthetic object'. However, the aesthetic does not refer to the object, but to the kind of attitude that we take towards objects.

*This aesthetic attitude is value-neutral,* since it may be taken towards objects that are both valuable and non-valuable in aesthetic terms. Sometimes people talk of 'an aesthetic object' when what they mean is that it is aesthetically pleasing or aesthetically valuable, but we prefer to leave our judgements open: we may assess the object as beautiful or ugly; graceful or clumsy; unitary or fragmentary; profound or superficial. These are all aesthetic appraisals.

*The aesthetic attitude requires us to consider intrinsic features of the object* – to be interested in the object for its own sake, rather than for the practical purposes it may serve. It is possible to treat a sculpture as an investment, but an interest in such an extrinsic economic function is not an aesthetic interest, which is non-purposive (or non-functional).

*The aesthetic attitude can be taken towards any object whatsoever.* If we look upon the aesthetic as content, or as evaluative, then the range of application is limited. On our account there is no such limitation: we are at liberty to take up an aesthetic attitude towards any object of perception or experience.

To summarise: the aesthetic attitude is a way of perceiving an object that is value-neutral, non-purposive, and can be taken towards any object whatsoever.

---

**STUDY ACTIVITY 13.5**

Can you think of sports that are not easily classified as 'purposive' or 'aesthetic'? What problem does this raise for the arguments being presented?

---

### Art

*Art is defined in terms of the aesthetic*, since art is that which has been created for the purpose of aesthetic appraisal. Works of art are:

- artefacts, i.e. objects purposefully created by human beings
- aesthetic artefacts, i.e. objects created with reference to their intrinsic features, which require us to take up an aesthetic attitude towards them.

However, not all aesthetic artefacts are art objects, since . . .

*Art is also defined in terms of embodied meanings*. A distinctive feature of an art form is that it enables the possibility of the expression of moral, social, political and emotional meanings. In fact, the meanings become embodied within the art form, such that the precise meanings as expressed are inseparable from the artistic 'form' of expression. So, although art is defined in terms of the aesthetic . . .

*The aesthetic and the artistic are to be distinguished*. Remember: anything can be perceived aesthetically, but only some things are art. For example:

- Nature is not art. A sunset may be aesthetically pleasing, but it is not art, since it is not an artefact, i.e. it has not been made by a human being.
- Mere decoration is not art. A pattern in a carpet may well be very skilfully crafted and aesthetically pleasing, and a carpet may be an aesthetic artefact, but if it only has a decorative pattern and does not embody meanings then it is not art.
- Mere beauty is not art. Obviously, beauty is aesthetically pleasing, but a beautiful child is not a work of art.

To summarise: the 'aesthetic' refers to an attitude which can be taken towards any object, whereas the 'artistic' refers to a limited class of objects, i.e. aesthetic artefacts which embody meanings.


## Sport

Now let us *distinguish between purposive sports and aesthetic sports*. Purposive sports are those whose purpose or function can be specified independently of the manner of achieving them. For example, in football, what I do can be explained without reference to how I do it – a goal is scored when the whole of the ball crosses the whole of the line between the posts and under the bar; I can explain this without reference to whether I must kick it or head it, or how I must kick it or head it. How I do it is irrelevant (provided that it is within the rules, of course), so long as I do it.

Aesthetic sports are those whose purpose cannot be specified independently of the manner of achieving it. In order to explain what a Tsukahara is, or a piked somersault, I would need to explain how to do it. In football I can distinguish the means of scoring a goal from the end, but in gymnastics the means are part of the end.

*Purposive sports are not art*. The majority of Olympic events are purposive sports, such as throwing, running, combat or team contests. In these events, the winner will be the one who achieves some end specified by rules, regardless of the manner of the achievement. It does not matter how you run, so long as you come first, and it follows from this that an aesthetic interest is incidental.

Of course it is possible to consider purposive sports from the aesthetic point of view (photographers, painters and sculptors often do so, taking sports as their subject matter), but since it is also possible to consider anything at all from the aesthetic point of view, this shows nothing. The fact that both sport and art can be perceived aesthetically is not significant – it does not make sport a kind of art. If it did it would make everything art, since anything can be perceived aesthetically.

Purposive sports are not art since, although it is possible to take an aesthetic interest in them, they are not aesthetic artefacts.

*Aesthetic sports are not art.* Unlike purposive sports, they *are* aesthetic artefacts, since they are produced for aesthetic appraisal. Gymnastics, diving, trampolining, synchronised swimming and ice dancing, insofar as they are judged according to intrinsic criteria, are events where the winner performs (perhaps the same, or a similar, routine) in the best manner. What is performed cannot be judged apart from how it is performed, and it follows from this that an aesthetic interest is central to the activity.

However, although all art objects are aesthetic artefacts, not all aesthetic artefacts are art objects (just as, although all dogs are animals, not all animals are dogs). Aesthetic sports are not art because they do not enable the possibility of expression of moral, social, political and emotional meanings. By contrast, balletic dance forms (sometimes referred to as 'the art of movement') are characterised by just such a possibility. The difference between dance and trampolining is that dance enables meanings to be embodied and expressed in physical movements regardless of required routines or level of difficulty of movement elements, whereas trampolining (whilst it is aesthetic) does not allow for the expression of a view of life issues.

To summarise: balletic dance is an art form, but aesthetic sports and purposive sports are not. If the above arguments hold, then they show that sport is not art. And, indeed, that would seem to be a corollary of de Coubertin's own views, since he holds that sport is the opportunity for art, or that art might be produced in sport – not that sport is art.

## PURPOSIVE AND AESTHETIC SPORTS

*Purposive sports* are those where:

*What* I do (score a goal) can be specified *independently of how* I do it (head, shoot, back-heel).

> *Aesthetic sports* are those where:
>
> *What* I do (a somersault) is only explained *in terms of how* I do it (turning in the air in a precisely determined manner).

## CULTURE AND CEREMONY?

De Coubertin clearly wanted to bring sport, fine art and other modes of cultural expression together in a great celebratory festival to capture the attention of the world for the important messages that he thought Olympism had for individual development and global society. However, it remains true that the educative potential that exists for a closer relationship between culture, art and sport, especially through the Games, has been under-exploited.

Various reasons have been advanced for the failure of the competitions. Mezo, a medal-winner himself, has suggested that they were never more than 'side issues' and that they received very poor publicity. Certainly, only a very small percentage of the public at large seems to have known about these events.

Even the most highly organised competitions, those of the 1936 Berlin Games which drew a total of 810 exhibits, failed to attract entries from France, Norway and the United Kingdom. The London Games in 1948 included no entries from the United States, Australia or New Zealand, countries which were otherwise important participants.

Another possible reason for the failure of the Olympic art contests to live up to de Coubertin's hopes was that artists were unwilling to accept the principle of competition as applying to art. How are we supposed to judge a Renoir against a Degas, never mind two paintings from entirely different continental traditions?

Against this, we should note that there is a Nobel Prize for literature, a Pulitzer, a Booker, an Oscar, an Emmy, and many international music competitions. But, again conversely, we should also note that many actors, writers and musicians scorn such competitions as populist, degrading and perverting of the nature of artistic endeavour.

The opening and closing ceremonies of the Olympic Games have been occasions which have sought to introduce elements of ritual and ceremony, as well as culture and art. The opening ceremony also provides us with the only modern example of a sporting event held under explicitly ethical conditions: those of the Olympic

Oath. In this way, they may be the best hope we have of evoking the significance of the ancient marriage of religion, art, ethics and sport.

However, not all is lost for the future of Olympic artistic competitions. Durry (1998) draws our attention to the IOC's 'Sport–Culture Forum', which has been 'entrusted with the task of re-establishing international competitions in sport and art and sport and literature'.

Perhaps a way may be found to stimulate fresh activity and interest in these collaborative endeavours.

---

## STUDY ACTIVITY 13.6

Visit the website <www.aafla.com> and search for articles on sport and art. Select 'search' on the 'Home page' and enter "Sport and Art" [the " " are important] Select 'Search the whole site' and then 'search now'. Investigate sources that might help you to consider the relationship between sport and art. Summarise your views in a few short sentences.

---

## REVIEW QUESTIONS

### SPORT, ART AND THE OLYMPICS

1  In what ways have the fine arts contributed to the development of the Olympic Idea?
2  Why do you consider that sport has made a good subject for twentieth century art movements? Explain with reference to the basic principles of at least one modern art movement (e.g. Cubism, Futurism, Expressionism).
3  What is the relationship between sport and art, if any?
4  What was the relationship between sport, art and religion in ancient times?

## CHAPTER 14

# OLYMPIC EDUCATION –
# CELEBRATING THE OLYMPICS

**Chapter aims:**

- to introduce the educational mission of the Olympic Movement
- to demonstrate the role of National Olympic Committees in educational work
- to give examples of possible educational activities.

After studying this chapter you should be able to explain:

- the nature of Olympism as an educational movement
- the possibilities available to National Olympic Committees
- the role of a National Olympic Academy
- possible modes of Olympic education in the school curriculum.

## DE COUBERTIN'S VISION

As we have seen, de Coubertin's drive was instrumental in the establishment of the International Olympic Committee (IOC) in 1894, and in the revival of the Olympic Games in Athens in 1896. However, his vision went far beyond the four-yearly celebration of the Olympic Games. For de Coubertin, whose main aims were educational, the Olympic Games were to be seen as an advertisement of sport to youth, and the athletes participating in the Olympic Games seen as role models for a young generation.

Under de Coubertin's leadership, the IOC called for an Olympic Congress in 1897 in Le Havre, one year after the first Olympic Games in Athens. Its purpose was to discuss the educational aspects of the popularisation of physical exercise and sport and to turn this into a mission.

De Coubertin constantly encouraged the IOC to take its educational role seriously and, through the Olympic Games, to ensure that sport occupied its rightful place in the educational programme in all countries and age groups. In 1925, when de Coubertin passed on the presidency to his successor, Count Henri de Baillet-Latour, in Prague, he continued to work for the maintenance and popularisation of his 'Olympic ideals' until his death in 1937.

## THE INTERNATIONAL OLYMPIC ACADEMY

The realisation of the educational vision of Pierre de Coubertin was the creation of the International Olympic Academy (IOA) in Olympia, just a javelin's throw from the ancient stadium (Plate 14.1). The goals of the IOA, referred to in Article 2 of its charter of operation, are expressed as follows:

> The creation of an international spiritual centre in Ancient Olympia which shall cater for the conservation and spread of the Olympic Spirit,

Plate 14.1 Part of the original buildings of the International Olympic Academy at Ancient Olympia, nestling in the hillside

217

the study and application of pedagogic as well as social principles of the Games and the scientific foundation of the Olympic Ideal comprise the goals of the International Olympic Academy.

(Filaretos, 1987, p. 28)

The activities of the International Olympic Academy also include:

- the annual International Session of the IOA, lasting 15 days, with the participation of young men and women sent by National Olympic Committees
- the annual six-week international post-graduate seminar
- special sessions for organisations related to Olympism, such as National Olympic Committees, international athletics federations, sports-medical associations, sports journalists' unions, referees, coaches and others
- the extension of hospitality to organisations and groups visiting Olympia for educational reasons, such as universities, colleges, athletic associations, etc.

Apart from its own sessions, and the cumulative effect of the activities of its participants, the IOA has been responsible for motivating, supporting and monitoring the development of National Olympic Academies. The centrepiece of IOA activity was to be a yearly International Session for Young Participants, which would be the place from which the Olympic ideals would be renewed and taken out into the world.

The IOA was established in 1961 with 30 students from 24 countries taking part in its first session. This coincided with the completion of the excavation of the ancient stadium at Olympia and its opening to the public. After its session in Athens, the entire IOC travelled to Olympia for the event.

In the early years participants lived and worked in tented accommodation, but the premises now boasts a substantial campus with accommodation for over 200 people, a large lecture hall with multi-translation facility, a library, study rooms, and a wide range of sporting and social facilities.

Many reunions of participants at IOA Sessions have been organised, and more recently this has become a biennial meeting of the IOA Participants Association, which works to maintain contacts and information exchange in the interests of maintaining and furthering world-wide Olympic education activity.

## STUDY ACTIVITY 14.1

Consult the 2003 version of the Olympic Charter at
<http://multimedia.olympic.org/pdf/en report 122.pdf>.

Think about whether you believe that the fundamental principles express
something worthwhile.

## NATIONAL OLYMPIC COMMITTEES

Chapter 1V of the Olympic Charter (IOC, 2003) deals with National Olympic
Committees (NOCs), and states the pre-eminent duties of NOCs with regard to
Olympic education:

> NOCs have a mission to develop and protect the Olympic Movement
> . . . [and to] propagate the fundamental principles of Olympism at
> national level within the framework of sports activity and otherwise
> contribute, among other things, to the diffusion of Olympism in the
> teaching programmes of physical education and sport in schools and
> university establishments . . . [and to] see to the creation of institutions
> which devote themselves to Olympic education.
>
> (IOC, 2003, p. 44)

It is difficult to generalise as each NOC is different but it will be useful to explore
some of the ways in which the task of Olympic education might be approached.

### Aims

The British Olympic Association (BOA), for example, has six 'objects', which we
might take as typical for an NOC:

1 to encourage interest in the Olympic Games and to foster the aims and ideals
   of the Olympic Movement, with particular reference to youth
2 to organise and co-ordinate British participation in the Olympic Games
3 to assist governing bodies of Olympic sports in Britain in the preparation of
   competitors for the Olympic Games

4    to provide a forum for consultation among the governing bodies of Olympic sports and the sports associations and a means of representing their views to others
5    to organise and co-ordinate the celebration of an Olympic Day
6    to subscribe, guarantee or lend money to any association or institution for any purpose calculated to further the objects of the Association or to benefit amateur sport in Britain or for any charitable purpose.

The first object refers in the widest possible way to Olympic education and the next two refer directly to preparation for and participation in the Olympic Games. This reflects the relationship advocated by de Coubertin, who saw the Games not as an end in themselves but as a means for the promotion of a certain view of what sport should be about. Detailed below are some initiatives in Olympic education that an NOC might undertake.

## Creation of a National Olympic Academy

There are more than 100 National Olympic Academies, but this means that over 80 NOCs still do not have one.

A National Olympic Academy seeks to provide educational events and opportunities and offers an annual workshop for students, teachers, journalists, coaches, athletes and administrators. It also seeks to promote activity in the areas discussed below.

## The education system

In Britain we have not (until recently) had to argue for the place of physical education on the school curriculum and are fortunate to have a long tradition of support for a range of sports and other physical activities in schools. However, in countries without such traditions or where development is under threat (as now in Britain), it is the duty of an NOC to argue in support of this.

Most children gain their first experience of organised sport and coaching in school and this is the foundation for good attitudes, habits and practices. In Britain many sports federations employ education officers whose task is to develop their sport by supporting the work of teachers by providing introductory materials, structured teaching advice and often an awards system.

220

Children who have grown up in a spirit of honest competition and fair play have the opportunity to implement and display this on almost a daily basis. School sports days, inter-school and area competitions are also opportunities for the practical demonstration of Olympic values.

Some events are called 'mini-Olympics', stressing their moral as well as their competitive nature. Where such events do not already exist there is a clear opportunity for NOCs and sports federations. One particular model is discussed at the end of this chapter.

A great deal of Olympic education teaching materials have been produced by Olympic Games Organising Committees, but not many countries are able to use the fact that they are hosting a Games as a focus for effort and to generate interest and sponsorship.

The main task is to provide something usable for teachers, and some NOCs have organised the production of an education pack (Plate 14.2).

Plate 14.2 Front cover of the BOA educational package (British Olympic Association)

Fortunately, good information is now available on websites such as those for the International Olympic Academy, the 2000 Sydney Olympic Games and for the 2004 Athens Olympic Games.

IN BRIEF

## THE EDUCATION MISSION OF THE OLYMPIC MOVEMENT

- To foster interest in the Olympic Games and in the aims and ideals of the Olympic Movement, with particular reference to young people.
- To provide for study and application of the educational and social principles of the Olympic Movement.
- To contribute to the diffusion of Olympism in the teaching programmes of physical education and sport in schools and universities.
- To help create institutions which devote themselves to Olympic education (such as the International Olympic Academy in Ancient Olympia and National Olympic Academies).

## STUDY ACTIVITY 14.2

Visit the BOA and IOA websites at <http://www.ioa.org.gr/ind-in.html>.

Find examples of their education activities and materials. How could they be used, for example, in schools?

### Higher education

Since future teachers are a very important resource for future Olympic education, it would not be surprising if NOA annual workshops (and other activities) were targeted especially (but not exclusively) on students of sport and physical education in higher education.

A 'contacts' system is often used in such establishments, whereby one person (usually a permanent member of staff) agrees to liaise with the BOA and to publicise its activities within the student population, especially those students training in physical education.

Contacts may help by:

- recruiting for the British Olympic Academy workshops
- publicising the existence of educational materials and resources available through the BOA
- arranging for the organisation of a local Olympic Day Run.

Perhaps the most important function of these 'contacts' is to press for a substantial element of Olympic education in the courses at their institutions.


## Resources

A major task for NOCs and NOAs is to ensure that educational materials and resources are available to educators. The NOC may also prepare booklets explaining its role and the fundamentals of Olympism, certain historical details, etc.

The IOC provides some copies of the Olympic Charter and publishes the *Olympic Review* and *Olympic Message*, all of which are good material for students. It is hoped that the IOC's Olympic Museum and Study Centre in Lausanne will address and support the work of NOAs, since much excellent material remains difficult to acquire, and that the emerging International Olympic Study and Research Network will function as a rich resource for those seeking to provide educational services.

The International Olympic Academy 'Blue Books', containing the collected proceedings of International Sessions since 1961, are an excellent source of information, debate, commentary, Olympic experiences and scholarship. However, they do not have a wide circulation, and some NOCs do not have a full set. It is hoped that this important material will soon become readily available on websites.


## The arts

Some NOCs organise annual painting, poetry and essay-writing competitions. In Britain the last painting and video competitions involved 17,000 schools. Some NOCs also promote the cultural aspects of sport by holding themed exhibitions of sculpture, photographs, paintings, posters and film at national galleries or museums. Some NOCs appoint an Official Olympic Artist for each Olympiad.

## The media

The establishment and maintenance of good media relations is of primary importance, for media officers of NOCs and sports federations should be well-versed in matters relating not only to the sporting aspect but also to the values of Olympism and Olympic education. The educational mission of the Olympic Movement is to some extent in the hands of media journalists. NOCs have a responsibility to promote Olympic ideals, and to present Olympic education themes to the international media.

## Youth work

Some NOAs have a Young Olympians Club, which might be a correspondence club, a school group or, for some, attendance at youth camps. There is an Olympic Youth Camp at each Games which, sadly, can benefit only a fortunate few, so shorter local camps for Young Olympians can make a big contribution with perhaps talks, visits and sport activity.

## Olympians

Following the IOC initiative of lapel pins (one for former medallists and one for all ex-Olympic athletes), many countries have 'Pin Ceremonies' to formalise their distribution. There are now many national Olympians associations as well as an International Olympians Association.

This exciting initiative provides an excellent opportunity for education. These associations can liaise with former Olympians who wish to help with educational initiatives. Similarly, a National Athletes Commission could help with visits to schools, sports clubs and events, and liaise with NOAs. In return the NOA might hold an annual conference to discuss matters of concern to athletes.

## Olympic solidarity

All NOCs can bid for 'Olympic solidarity' funding to host education and training courses for athletes and coaches. Whether at regional, national or continental level, it is an excellent opportunity for the exchange of technical information and co-operation under Olympic principles and sponsorship. Such courses might be on sports medicine, sports administration, or aspects of coaching. One important feature is that, even where courses are offered through one sports federation,

224

aspects of Olympic education are always included. Perhaps 'solidarity' courses are a model for all Olympic sports?

## Olympic Day celebrations

Although the highly successful Olympic Day Run event comes under the aegis of the IOC's Sport for All Commission, it is also a tremendous opportunity for Olympic education. Some NOCs expand the event into Youth Olympic Days and some have 25 June as a national holiday. Some hold sports festivals and arts events and gain good media coverage for Olympism.

## Heritage

Some countries are fortunate enough to have sites of some aspect of Olympic heritage, and it is the responsibility of educators to preserve this heritage so as to make it available to all. In Britain we have the heritage of the Much Wenlock Olympian Games and the Cotswold 'Olympicks' at Chipping Camden, both of which receive the patronage of the BOA. Some countries take care to preserve the site of a past Olympic Games whilst others honour individual events or champions. Some of these sites house permanent collections which become national sports museums.

## Olympic study and research centre

A 'centre' may be in a particular place (e.g. a library, museum or university department) or it may be an organisation, which brings together a range of expertise. In many countries, such a centre acts as the focus for Olympic-related study and research, and there are attempts to co-ordinate an International Olympic Study and Research Network. In Britain, a Centre for Olympic Studies was opened in 2004 at Loughborough University.

---

### STUDY ACTIVITY 14.3

Visit the website <http://www.blues.uab.es/olympic.studies/>. Think about how an Olympic Study and Research Network might be developed in your own country or district.

---

225

**IOC liaison**

In addition to art competitions, youth camps, Olympic Day celebrations and Olympians' pin ceremonies, there are other ways in which an NOA might support IOC educational initiatives.

An NOA might organise study trips to the IOC Headquarters and the Olympic Museum and Study Centre in Lausanne, or it might seek ways to use official IOC publications and films for educational purposes. It might also keep up to date with what the IOC offers (e.g. the IOC plans a series of cartoon books on the history of the Olympic Games and the Olympic Movement).

**International Olympic Academy liaison**

Efforts by the IOA to provide educational opportunities have previously been mentioned but it seems that there is as yet insufficient 'take-up' of IOA facilities.

Even where Olympic Solidarity support is available, some NOCs still do not send delegates to courses, which is a pity because their input is lost, as is their opportunity to learn with others (Plate 14.3).

Plate 14.3 Students at the Main Olympic Session of the International Olympic Academy, in the tunnel leading to the stadium at Ancient Olympia

The first duty of an NOA is to support the ongoing efforts of the IOA: to keep in contact, to send appropriately qualified and briefed participants to courses, and to utilise the expertise of those who return full of enthusiasm.

The International Olympic Academy Participants' Association (IOAPA) has been vigorous in its support and promotion of the work of former participants since 1988. IOAPA holds a biennial session in Olympia and maintains global communication and sharing of information and ideas.

---

## STUDY ACTIVITY 14.4

Visit <http:www.ioa.leeds.ac.uk>. Read the Olympic experiences of a famous athlete of the past (e.g. Emil Zatopek from the 1966 Proceedings, Jesse Owens from 1969 or Peter Snell from 1971). What qualities of mind and character do you detect?

---

### TOWARDS AN OLYMPIC PEDAGOGY

We should now return to schools in order to re-emphasise the central tenet of Olympism: that sport itself is educative.

If the Olympic conception of the human being (its philosophical anthropology) is accepted, we still stand in need of a theory of Olympic pedagogy. The idea is that the promotion of Olympic values will be seen to be the educative task, and sport will be seen as a means. Each of these values, articulated at a high level of generality, will admit of a wide range of interpretation but they nevertheless provide a framework that can be agreed upon by social groups with very differing commitments. The task is to see how the values of sport and Olympism can be promoted in practice.

Many possibilities have been discussed in the previous section. However, a National Olympic Committee, no matter how great its commitment to its educational aims, must seek to influence the nature of sports provision within its national educational system. It is in schools and colleges that the primary work of physical education (PE) takes place and the provision of courses for teachers and materials for students must be of primary importance: for the information transmission function of education is not the main mode championed by Olympism, which sees engagement in sport itself as its primary medium.

227

We therefore need to think also about how sport is presented to students and represented on the curriculum, since the claim of Olympism is that the medium of sport is itself a large part of the message.

Siedentop (1994, p. 3) has outlined what he calls the 'sport education model':

> . . . a curriculum and instruction model developed for school physical education programs. That may not sound new, (but) sport education is not business as usual. . . . sport education has the potential to revolutionize PE.

He criticises the way in which sport is often presented in PE programmes: simply as a set of techniques or skills to be mastered. Sport education seeks to provide a richer, more authentic and more fully contextualised experience than is typical in PE lessons. Students learn not only how to play sports but also to co-ordinate and manage sport experiences. They also learn individual responsibility and effective group membership skills.

Sport education aims to contribute to a humane sport culture that maximizes participation, under the slogan 'sport in all its forms for all the people' (Siedentop, 1994, p. 4) (this echoes de Coubertin's dictum 'all sports for all people').

Siedentop sees the goals of sport education as seeking to 'educate' students to be players 'in the fullest sense' and to help them develop as competent, literate and enthusiastic sportspeople, which he expands as follows:

> A competent sportsperson has sufficient skills to participate in games satisfactorily, understands and can execute strategies appropriate to the complexity of play, and is a knowledgeable games player.

> A literate sportsperson understands and values the rules, rituals, and traditions of sports and distinguishes between good and bad sport practices, whether in children's or professional sport. A literate sportsperson is both a more able participant and a more discerning consumer, whether fan or spectator.

> An enthusiastic sportsperson participates and behaves in ways that preserve, protect, and enhance the sporting culture, whether it be a local youth sport culture or a national sport culture. As members of sporting groups, such enthusiasts participate in further developing sport at local, national, or international levels. The enthusiastic sportsperson is involved.
>
> (Siedentop, 1994, p. 3)

He sees these aims as elevating physical education from a training or competency focus to a truly educative focus, and elevating the teacher from the status of a skill-developer to that of an educator, contributing to wider values than specific skill-based outcomes.

Siedentop (1994, p. 4) lists the 'objectives of sport education' as the following learning outcomes:

- develop skills and fitness specific to particular sports
- appreciate and be able to execute strategic play in sports
- participate at a level appropriate to their stage of development
- share in the planning and administration of sport experiences
- provide responsible leadership
- appreciate the rituals and conventions that give particular sports their unique meanings
- develop the capacity to make reasoned decisions about sport issues
- develop and apply knowledge about umpiring, refereeing and training
- decide voluntarily to become involved in after-school sport.

An important element (for our purposes here) is Siedentop's (1994, p. 7) critical observation that sport in physical education has typically been de-contextualised:

Skills are taught in isolation rather than as part of the natural context of executing strategy in game-like situations. The rituals, values, and traditions of a sport that give it meaning are seldom even mentioned, let alone taught in ways that students can experience them. Students are not educated in sport.

His claim is that the main culturally salient features of sport are hardly ever reproduced in physical education classes. A more complete and authentic sports education would include the following.

1   *Seasons*. Sport is seasonal, and seasons are long enough to allow for significant experience. A sport season encompasses both practice and competition, and often ends with a culminating event.
2   *Affiliation*. Players are members of teams or clubs and tend to retain membership throughout the season. Much of the meaning derived from participation and much of the personal growth that comes from good sport experiences is intimately related to affiliation.
3   *Formal competition*. Sport seasons are defined by formal competition interspersed with practice sessions and occur in different formats: dual meets,

round robins, league schedules, etc. Schedules are often fixed before the season to allow for appropriate preparation.

4   *Keeping records*. Records come in all forms: batting averages, shots on goal, unforced errors, times, distances, etc. They provide feedback for individuals and teams, help define standards and provide goals for players and teams, and are also an important part of the traditions of a sport.

5   *Culminating event*. It is in the nature of sport to find out who is the best each season. The culminating competition provides goals for players to work towards.

6   *Festivity*. The festive nature of sport enhances its meaning and adds an important social element to the experience.

The student should not merely be initiated into sports practice, but into sport as a part of his/her culture. This allows sport education to contribute to wider curriculum aims, such as:

■   a better understanding of the world
■   a better appreciation and respect for a multicultural world
■   the ability to be both a leader and a co-operative member of a working group
■   the ability to persevere at tasks despite obstacles and setbacks.

However, there is an educational movement that emphasises the role of sport in individual, social and cultural development: Olympism. Siedentop (1994, p. 119) argues that the philosophy of Olympism:

> provides an exciting and relevant concept on which to build a physical education curriculum that contributes to the full education of children and youth.

He also quotes Osterhoudt (1984, p. 354):

> It [Olympism] embodies the illumination, the apotheosis, toward which all sport (and for that matter all human endeavor) authentically disposed tends. The basis of this contention stems from the unmatched, the intrinsic depth and nobility of inspiration that Olympism gains from an idea of human life at its compelling best. No movement having to do with sport has so fully connected itself to the foundations of human life per se as has Olympism; no movement having to do with sport has so fully captured the sense of such an ideal. Olympism has brought sport nearer its fully human possibilities than any other modern event.

Siedentop's (1994, p. 120) claim is that sport education involves children and youth in sport and fitness, in a way that:

> . . . fosters individual responsibility (through specific student roles) and the ability to work effectively within groups (through affiliation with team-mates for the duration of a sport season). The Olympic curriculum is meant to extend this model so that the high values of the Olympic charter and the Olympic creed are made educationally relevant and meaningful in the lives of children and youth. To do so, the Olympic curriculum incorporates peace education, global education, multicultural education, and aesthetic education within the sport education model.

The main goals of the Olympic curriculum (Siedentop, 1994, p. 4) are to:

- develop competent, literate and enthusiastic sportpersons
- develop self-responsibility and perseverance in the pursuit of goals
- work effectively within a group toward common goals
- know and respect cultural and ethnic differences, value diversity, become predisposed to work toward a more peaceful world
- know and respect the value and beauty of the human body in motion, the aesthetic value of working together in competition, and the manner in which art, music and literature are related to and supportive of Olympism.

The Olympic curriculum would make a contribution to the organisation of the school year. It might use national team names (or a 'house' system) as an affiliation format and might appoint a committee to choose appropriate sports. It would aim to integrate its work with academic objectives and would work towards meeting the personal development goals of the curriculum, as well as more general and aesthetic education goals.

The philosophy of Olympism is dedicated to creating a more peaceful world through co-operation and friendly competition in sport, based on the value of fair play and the joy found in purposeful effort. The educational goals of Olympism are central to its overall rationale, including the aims of individual development and the understanding of cultural differences.

Siedentop (1994) claims that such a philosophy coheres well with the goals of sport education, and it can be argued that the sport education model provides what is lacking in the simple provision of educational materials, since it puts the sport experience at the very centre of its rationale and its practice.

231

## STUDY ACTIVITY 14.5

(a) Think about physical education (PE) in schools. What kind of contribution does it make to the overall education of the individual?

(b) Ask yourself whether 'Olympic education' would add a fresh dimension to PE in schools. Visit these websites for help and materials:

<http://blues.uab.es/olympic.studies/educationkits.html>

<http://www.aafla.org.OlympicInformationCenter/OlympicPrimer>

<http://www.ausport.gov.au/factmenu.html>

<http://2002.uen.org>, select 'Olympic Education'.

We have explored ways in which an information-based approach to education could be used to promote the aims of Olympic education. That approach could be complemented and supplemented by focusing carefully on the sport experience itself, thus honouring the central claim of Olympic education: that our aims and values can be achieved through the means of sport.

## CONCLUSION

The overall aim of Olympic education is to return sport itself to the central focus of the PE curriculum – not to the exclusion of other forms of physical activity, which have their own worth – but under a rationale which re-emphasises the role and power of educative sport in individual development across cultural difference.

This is an account of sport in physical education as Olympic education, which re-emphasises the role of sport in the development of Olympic education. It suggests that, in addition to the development of Olympic materials for dissemination to schools and colleges as 'Olympism across the Curriculum', further thought should be given to strategies for the promotion of physical education and sport education as Olympic education.

Actual engagement in appropriate sporting activity should be the first aim of an Olympic curriculum, or it runs the risk of contradicting the (practical) values of Olympism. In particular, ways must be found of allying IOAs and NOAs more closely with school systems and with ministries of education, so that Olympic education might be promoted globally as the standard form of PE.

REVIEW QUESTIONS

## OLYMPIC EDUCATION

1   Find out more about Olympism as an educational ideology, and explain its central values.
2   What is Olympic education, and to what extent has it been successful in your country?
3   To what extent do you see a belief in Olympism as an educational ideology expressed in the actual practices of sportspeople, coaches, administrators and sports journalists?
4   Set out a conception of physical education in schools, including a suggested outline curriculum, which you would endorse as an Olympic conception (see also Chapter 1).

## CHAPTER 15

# CASE STUDIES

## INTRODUCTION

Throughout this book the modern Olympic Games have been discussed as a complex phenomenon that embraces a range of historical, social, political and economic aspects. These analyses have been complemented by a number of exercises and supporting materials available on the book's website.

A major challenge, which any book on the Olympic Movement has to address, is the meaningful interpretation of the ever-increasing amount of literature on the subject. The emergence of new information not only enhances our understanding of Olympism by revealing previously unknown facts, but equally it questions the validity of conceptions deemed to be plausible. Due to the constraints of space it has not been possible to include an in-depth coverage of all the aspects in this book but it is hoped that the reader will have developed a solid understanding of the key issues that surround the phenomenon of the modern Olympics.

The purpose of this chapter is therefore to offer three case studies:

■   the 2000 Sydney Olympic Games
■   the 2002 Salt Lake City Winter Olympic Games
■   London's bid to host the 2012 Olympic Games.

The material is presented in sections, which correspond to the key topics discussed throughout the book. It is believed that the selection of these three case studies will increase our understanding of the complexities involved in putting together and staging an Olympic Games. Additionally, it allows for interesting comparisons between what had been planned before the Games were awarded and what was subsequently achieved. London's bid for the Games of 2012 renders us sensitive to the processes involved in the preparation of an Olympic bid and the key debates that will undoubtedly accompanying this ambitious undertaking.

## THE 2000 SYDNEY OLYMPIC GAMES

### The bid

The aspirations of the city of Sydney to host the Olympic Games dated back to the mid-1960s and represented:

- a mix of the political ambitions of the city's Lord Mayor
- a means of addressing long-standing social and environmental problems
- a favourable international political situation.

These three factors dominated the agenda, and the publicity-seeking Labour Lord Mayor Henry Jansen (also known as 'Headline Harry') wanted to build a major sports complex in the heart of the city. He argued that an Olympic bid would help to tackle social deprivation, encourage economic development and resolve problems with the city's sporting infrastructure.

To rise above the political tension of the Cold War, the International Olympic Committee (IOC) declared in 1965 that any city wishing to host the Games would have to guarantee that no visa restrictions would be imposed on athletes from any country. This proviso was aimed primarily at NATO-aligned countries that had previously refused entry to athletes from the former German Democratic Republic (GDR). This unique political situation presented a window of opportunity for Sydney as no major Western city was in a position to meet this requirement.

The cost of staging the Games was estimated at £15,000,000 of which £7,000,000 was earmarked for the building of St Peter's Stadium. Sydney's bid for the 1972 Olympics did not materialise and ironically it was the very same GDR visa issue that proved the major stumbling block. Eventually the Department of External Affairs adopted a policy of non-recognition in line with that of the Allied Control Authorities (Britain, France and the USA).

Although the proposal failed, it made two important contributions to the city's success some 30 years later. Firstly, it put the Games on the city's 'agenda', and secondly, it promoted the idea of the regeneration of industrial wasteland into a central (Olympic) venue, which was finally implemented in 2000.

The road to Sydney's bid for the Games of 2000 was not easy. The city had to compete with bids from Brisbane (1992), Melbourne (1996) and overcome internal political opposition. This partly explains why when the bid was successful the *Telegraph Mirror*'s headline from 17 November 1990 read 'Sydney Wins the Games Battle'.

The promotion of a city committed to the Olympic ideal was central to the concept of the Sydney Olympic Bid Committee. Three innovations in the bid practices deserve mention here:

- to enhance the multicultural theme 160,000 school children signed petitions in support of the Games; these were sent to all 120 IOC members, each of whom was 'twinned' with a specific school
- the 'bid file' included letters of approval from each international sport federation
- to win IOC members' votes, the bid committee created a lobby team of Australia's most influential political, business, sport and entertainment personalities.

The cost of the bid reached A$28 million and was not without its controversies. Concerns were raised (amongst other topics) about the price of sporting excellence. According to a research report (*Adviser*, 15 December 1998):

> the Australian taxpayer will be dishing out $51.8 million Australian dollars for each medal that will be awarded at the 2000 Games.

It was also admitted by John Coates, the President of the Australian Olympic Committee, that he had offered US$70,000 to Kenya and Uganda to help develop their sports programmes and other perks to two IOC members in exchange for their votes.

## Organising the Games

The 2000 Sydney Olympic Games represented a massive undertaking, which would not have been possible without the joint efforts of the public, private and voluntary sectors.

From the outset the Sydney Organising Committee of the Olympic Games (SOCOG) proclaimed that they would be 'Athletes' Games'. A major theme, which the SOCOG wanted to communicate to all Australians and to the rest of the world, was that of reconciliation. For more than two centuries the indigenous Aborigine people had been a deprived minority group.

The opening ceremony, designed to convey this message and recreate Australia's history alongside key Olympic values, comprised eight elements:

- welcome
- deep sea dreaming
- awakening
- fire
- tin symphony
- nature
- eternity
- arrivals.

'Share the Spirit' became the slogan of the Games.

The 'Sydney model' had the following key elements:

- financially underwritten by the Government of New South Wales (NSW)
- a formal and explicit relationship between the Organising Committee, the NSW Government and the Commonwealth of Australia
- recognition of the inherent limitations of the Organising Committee to mobilise all the resources needed for the Games, no matter how well it manages its core responsibilities
- the establishment of specific-purpose entities (e.g. Olympic Co-ordination Authorities, Olympic Road and Transport Authorities, Olympic Security Command Centre) to perform specific tasks under the banner of one integrated team
- strong state and Commonwealth government co-ordination mechanisms, backed as far as possible by legislation
- a planned and structured approach to urban domain management, including major city celebrations
- preparation and reporting to a Global Olympic Budget (government plus SOCOG)
- a co-ordinated and integrated structure for Games-time operations through the Games Coordination Group chaired by Michael Knight, a NSW Government minister.

Partnership and careful planning were critical for the delivery of the Games, between 15 September and 1 October 2000. For 17 days 10,651 athletes from

237

199 countries competed in 28 sports and 300 events for 928 medals. All venues were completed nine months prior to the Games and an unprecedented 92.4 per cent of all tickets were sold.

IN BRIEF

## GAMES OPERATIONS

- 1.1 million articles of clothing (for Olympic and Paralympic staff)
- 1 million hours of training for the Games workforce (110,000 people)
- 5 million volunteer service hours
- 5 million pieces of furniture
- nearly 300 companies involved in staging the Games
- 7000 TV images broadcast per second
- largest ever single dining facility in athletes' village: 50,000 meals per day and 6000 meals per hour
- transport system: 3500 vehicles working 24 hours a day for 19 days
- 4000 artists: 53 major productions and 50 exhibitions at 45 venues
- the largest television operation ever with over 12,000 network personnel and an international broadcast centre of 70,000 square metres.

(Source: IOC *Marketing Matters*, Issue 18, May 2001, pp. 2–3)

### Viewing the Games

The Sydney Games were the most watched sport event ever, with more than 3.7 billion viewers in a record 220 countries. This represents a 20 per cent increase over the viewing statistics for the 1996 Atlanta Olympic Games.

Nine out of every ten individuals on the planet with access to television watched parts of the Olympic Games and the total coverage of the Games was 29,600 hours, the equivalent of three and a half years of continuous 24-hour-per-day programming.

Figure 15.1 and Table 15.1 show 'viewer hours' by region, TV coverage and the average hours viewing per viewer.

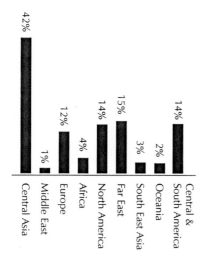

Figure 15.1 Percentage of viewer hours by region: 2000 Sydney Olympic Games

Source: IOC *Marketing Matters*, No. 18, 2001

*Table 15.1* Broadcast coverage and average viewing per viewer per continent

| Continent | Hours of TV | Average hours per viewer | |
|---|---|---|---|
| Africa | | | |
| Egypt | | 6 | |
| Nigeria | | 10+ | |
| N. America | | | |
| USA | 440 | | |
| Canada | 800 | 20 | |
| Asia | | | |
| Japan | | | |
| China | | | |
| Korea | | | |
| Australia | 400+ | 49 | 20 % increase over previous Games |
| Europe | | | |
| Great Britain | 318 | 10 | |
| Switzerland | 730 | 11+ | |
| Scandinavia | | 13 | |
| S. America | 400 | 18 | |

Source: IOC *Marketing Matters*, No. 18, 2001

## Financing the Games

The Olympic Games are a mammoth undertaking, which can only be effected if adequate funding is secured. There were five main sources of revenue for the SOCOG:

- government investments
- collective broadcasting rights
- sponsorship
- tickets
- licences.

Two of the principal marketing sources – broadcasting rights and global sponsorship – had been generated by the IOC and then divided between the SOCOG, which received 72 per cent, with the remaining 28 per cent being distributed throughout the Olympic Movement.

Overall Sydney and the IOC were very successful in generating approximately US$3 billion during the period 1997–2000. All revenue targets were exceeded. The SOCOG local sponsorship programme raised US$492 million. The local marketing programme, which included sponsorship, ticket sales and licensing, generated an unprecedented US$1095 million towards the cost of the Games. Particularly successful was the licensed merchandise generating royalty revenue of approximately US$2.50 for every man, woman and child in Australia. For instance, more than 5 million people visited the Olympic Store in Centrepoint, Sydney.

This result compares favourably to the 1996 Games in Atlanta, which delivered 32 cents for every person in the country. Table 15.2 shows the main sources of funding for the Olympic Games and the main areas of expenditure.

## Legacy of the Games

The 2000 Sydney Olympic Games left many legacies, not all of which could be quantified. Difficulties in quantifying the impact of the Games arise as a result of different methodologies and approaches used for measuring this. For example, the excitement and 'feel-good' factor experienced by many people during the Games could be viewed as a short-term effect. Equally, however, Cathy Freeman's victory may have provided a major inspiration for a generation of new Olympic champions who will be a source of excitement in 10 or 15 years from now.

240

*Table 15.2* The 2000 Sydney Olympic Games: main sources of revenue and expenditure

| Source | A$ millions | % |
|---|---|---|
| Sponsorship – TOP IV | 550 | 20 |
| – Local | 492 | 18 |
| TV rights | 1133 | 40 |
| Ticketing revenue | 551 | 20 |
| Licensing | 52 | 2 |
| **Total Revenue** | **2778.0** | **100** |
| Executive office | 29.6 | 1.4 |
| Communications & community relations | 13.2 | 0.6 |
| Risk management | 19.5 | 1.0 |
| Legal | 12.3 | 0.6 |
| Image, Olympic Arts Festival and special events | 38.6 | 2.0 |
| Technology | 386.4 | 19.0 |
| Transport | 75.4 | 3.7 |
| Security | 41.5 | 2.0 |
| Ceremonies | 68.5 | 3.0 |
| Sport | 133.3 | 7.0 |
| Other | 1154.0 | 57.0 |
| **Total operating expenditure** | **2015.7** | **97.3** |

Source: *Official Report of the XXVII Olympiad*

Note: Selected items only

Most post-Olympic studies tend to be concerned with the economic and environmental impact of the Games. Those of Sydney 2000 clearly demonstrated that the effect of a Games is much wider. This view is well captured by Sandy Hollway (2002), former Chief Executive Officer of the SOCOG. He identified the following areas of impact:

- infrastructure
- economic impact
- showcasing
- an international eye-opener
- pride in the Australian sense of community
- confidence.

Hollway went on to suggest that the Games helped Australians say 'goodbye to cultural cringe'. Other intangible gains for the whole country included an increased internationalism (very important for a geographically remote country) and a massive boost to national confidence.

Tangible benefits of the Olympics include, among others:

- an addition of 6–7 per cent to Australia's gross domestic product
- over 100,000 new jobs
- 1.74 million extra tourists generating over US$3.5 billion in foreign exchange earnings from 1997 to 2004.

For example, during the Games the NSW Government's Olympic Business Programme attracted some 2000 senior business leaders who were directly responsible for export deals and investments worth A$1 billion to Australia.

Expertise is another asset that pays economic dividends. The Australian State Commission states that staging the Games allowed Australian companies to win an estimated 10 per cent of the capital spending projects in Beijing, earning £1.1 billion. Table 15.3 provides an indication of the legacy of Sydney in terms of infrastructure and sports development.

Environmentally, 'the Green Games' (as proclaimed by the SOCOG) set benchmarks for future Organising Committees. For example:

- water recycling saved up to 850 million litres annually
- 400 tonnes of contaminated soil were destroyed on site
- 30,000 tonnes of greenhouse gases and 16 million more sheets of paper were saved than in Atlanta
- 830 hectares of new parkland and open space were created.

*Table 15.3* Legacy contributions of the 2000 Sydney Olympic Games: infrastructure and sport development

| Legacy contribution | A$ million |
| --- | --- |
| Construction, contribution to NSW for aquatic & athletic centres, rail, etc. | 225.3 |
| Construction, contribution to NSW for villages & competition venues | 136.1 |
| SPOC contribution (Paralympic Organising Committee) | 17.8 |
| Athlete legacy paid to Australian Olympic Committee | 88.5 |
| **Total legacy contributions** | **467.7** |

Source: *Official Report of the XXVII Olympiad*

However, despite the economic, emotional and environmental gains, the Games also served to reinforce the west–north class and ethnical divide of Sydney. As Waitt (2001) demonstrates, people living in the more affluent northern suburbs were less affected by the emotional appeal of the Olympics. Waitt's detailed study of citizens' attitudes towards the Games suggests that there was widespread scepticism amongst local residents about the economic benefits which the Games could deliver. Some 67 per cent of the respondents disagreed with the statement that the Olympics would not directly result in an increase in taxes, and 68 per cent also disagreed that the organisations responsible for the preparation of the Games had been economically responsible.

Similarly, there were high levels of environmental concerns: 29 and 52 per cent disagreed that Sydney's water and air quality respectively would not suffer as a result of hosting the Olympics. Although civic opposition to the Games did not take any radical forms and was loosely organised, there were social protests and debates. An illustration of this type of opposition is the activities of the Anti-Olympics Alliance <http://www.cat.org.au/aoa>.


## THE 2002 SALT LAKE CITY WINTER OLYMPIC GAMES

### The bid

When on 16 June 1995, at the end of the IOC 104th Session in Budapest, the President of the IOC, Juan Antonio Samaranch, announced to the world's media 'the winner is Salt Lake City', some 50,000 people watching a giant TV screen in the centre of that city erupted cheering and waving American flags.

The ensuing celebrations marked the end of a 30-year long quest to host the Olympic Games by the city founded in 1847 by the Mormon leader Brigham Young, and which now boasts the youngest population in the United States: an average age of 26 years. The bid was conceived in 1966, but it did not enter the official contest until 1972, when it lost to Sapporo, Japan. It also failed in 1976 and domestic politics prevented the city from representing the USA in a bid for the 1992 Winter Olympic Games.

The 1998 bid campaign brought another disappointment, with Salt Lake City losing to Nagano by only four votes. However, the city's bid committee refused to give up and committed $60 million to its candidature for the Games of 2002. Its major rivals were Quebec (Canada), Ostersund (Sweden) and Sion (Switzerland). Persistence and confidence finally paid off. It was also the first time that a bidding city had been awarded the Games after the first round of balloting.

Sadly, the euphoria was short-lived as three years later, in 1998, Salt Lake City found itself at the centre of the most profound crises of the Olympic Movement in recent times. On 16 December 1998 the *Washington Post* ran a headline: 'Olympic Glory is Fading in Utah. Bribery Allegations Are Just Latest Controversy Concerning 2002 Games'.

A series of ensuing allegations revealed that both the Salt Lake City Bid Committee and the Organising Committee for the Olympic Games (SLOC) were involved in wrongdoings. A large scheme to win the votes of the IOC members was uncovered, which offered several IOC members and their relatives scholarships for American universities, assistance in business deals and other privileges.

As a result, the president and three other high-ranking officials resigned from the Organising Committee. The magnitude of the scandal threatened the very premises of the Olympic Movement. Four independent commissions – by the IOC, the US Olympic Committee, Utah's Board of Ethics and the Federal Bureau of Intelligence (FBI) – were created, not only to establish the facts but to investigate wider structural and ethical issues concerning the IOC and the violations of any federal law.

The outcomes of these investigations and their implications for the future of the Olympic Movement have been far-reaching and can be summarised as follows:

- ten IOC members expelled for inappropriate conduct
- elimination of visits of IOC members to bid cities and vice versa
- introduction of a new bid procedure
- introduction of age limit for IOC members and a maximum eight-year term of office for the IOC president
- opening of the IOC Sessions to the media
- publication of regular reports to enhance the IOC's financial transparency
- creation of four categories of IOC members: athletes, presidents of national organising committees, presidents of international federations, individual members.

### Organising the Games

Salt Lake City is Utah's capital city and the largest urban area (it has a population of 1.5 million) to host the Winter Olympic Games. From an organisational point of view this background offers certain advantages and challenges. From 8 to 24 February 2002 Salt Lake City welcomed 2399 athletes from 77 countries

244

who competed in 78 events in seven sports. All the venues were situated within a 10–60 minute drive from the Olympic Village, and 25,000 volunteers played a critical part in the organisation of the Games.

The overriding philosophy of the Games was captured in the slogan 'Light the Fire Within'. This was complemented by the concepts of 'Contrast', 'Culture' and 'Courage' and was designed to send a unified message to athletes, spectators and viewers around the world, that the best qualities of the Olympic spirit are shared by all of humanity.

The concept of 'Contrast' reflected the diverse landscape of Utah, 'Culture' demonstrated the ethnic diversity of those taking part in the Olympics in addition to the four native tribes of Utah, and 'Courage' represented the enduring spirit of the Olympic athlete. This last concept was reinforced by the resoluteness of the Olympic Movement to overcome the crisis that had tarnished the image of the Olympics.

The 2002 Salt Lake City Games were not only a massive logistic operation but a showcase of the latest technology. The IOC's IT partner SchlumbergerSema provided more than 5300 PCs, 150 industrial-strength servers and 1350 on-site staff to manage this equipment. The telecommunication staff included:

- 120 SLOC personnel
- 865 sponsor operation personnel
- 450 sponsor maintenance technicians
- 485 volunteers delivering 55,000 hours of on-site maintenance support.

It took the SLOC several years to develop, test and manage the system.


## Viewing the Games

The 2002 Salt Lake City Olympics set a new record in global television coverage, with 10,416 hours of action and an estimated 2.1 billion viewers from 160 countries. These figures amount to an average global viewing of 6 hours and 15 minutes per viewer, reaching 18 hours in Japan and 29 hours in the host country the USA. Table 15.4 shows a breakdown of the viewing hours by continent.

It is interesting to note that the US television audience was nearly double that for the 1998 Games in Nagano. In Canada the Olympic broadcasts were watched by 95 per cent of those with access to television, with the men's ice hockey final attracting the highest rating in broadcasting history of 8.6 million viewers. In

*Table 15.4* The 2002 Salt Lake City Games: viewer hours by continent

| Continent | Viewer hours (million) | % |
|---|---|---|
| Europe | 588 | 31 |
| N. America | 210 | 11 |
| Central & S. America | 147 | 7.5 |
| Oceania | 21 | 1 |
| Africa | 2.1 | 0.5 |
| Asia | 924 | 49 |

Source: *Salt Lake 2002 Marketing Report*

Europe, the highest level of viewing hours were registered in Germany with an audience of 11.9 million viewers for the K120 team ski jumping event. In addition, more than 2650 accredited members of the press from 59 countries covered the Games.

The Internet was another major source of information about the Olympics with the SLOC official website attracting 3 million unique visitors per day during the Games, peaking at 5 million on Day 14.

### Financing the Games

There were five principal sources of revenue which provided the budget of the 2002 Salt Lake City Winter Olympic Games. All the marketing programmes co-ordinated by the IOC and SLOC exceeded their targets. The total revenue to SLOC is shown on Table 15.5 whilst Figure 15.2 shows the generation of Olympic marketing revenue.

*Table 15.5* Total Olympic marketing revenue to SLOC

| Source | US$ million |
|---|---|
| Broadcast revenue (co-ordinated by IOC) | 443 |
| TOP V Sponsorship (co-ordinated by IOC) | 131.5 |
| Olympic Partners US Support (co-ordinated by SLOC) | 599 |
| Ticket revenue (co-ordinated by SLOC) | 183 |
| Licensing & coin revenue (co-ordinated by SLOC) | 34 |
| Total | 1390.5 |

Source: *Salt Lake 2002 Marketing Report*

*case studies*

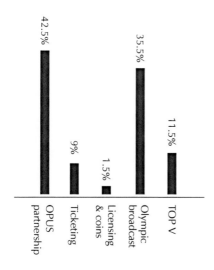

**Figure 15.2** Olympic marketing revenue generation: 2002 Salt Lake City Winter Olympic Games

Source: IOC *Marketing Matters*, No. 18, 2001

An essential part of the SLOC's approach to sponsorship was through an Olympic hospitality programme, which attracted some 52,000 corporate guests of Olympic sponsors to the Games. The commercial implications of Olympic hospitality are discussed in the next section.

## Legacy of the Games

As with the Games in Sydney, the 2002 Salt Lake City Winter Olympic Games left both short- and long-term legacies that cannot be expressed in precise figures or other quantifiable indicators.

For example, the State of Utah implemented a comprehensive Olympic educational programme for each school child and student in the state. Such cultural, emotional and demographic impacts are equally hard to measure.

A summary of the economic and financial impacts from the State of Utah Governor's Office of Planning and Budget are shown in Table 15.6. One of the key benefits concerns Olympic-related jobs, which grew from less than 100 in 1996 to a yearly peak of 12,600 in 2001, and a monthly peak of 25,000 in February 2002. Olympic-related jobs represented 6.2 per cent of employment growth in 1998 and 21.4 per cent in 2001.

An important commercial spin-off from the Games was the Utah Olympic Trade Missions initiative created by the State Government. It is best summarised in the words of the Governor Mike Leavitt in his 2002 State of the State Address:

*Table 15.6* 2002 Salt Lake City Winter Olympic Games: economic, demographic and fiscal impacts from 1996 to 2003

| Impact | Measure |
| --- | --- |
| Output or sales | US$ 4.8 billion |
| Employment | 35,000 jobs for one year of employment |
| Tourism | Increase of 50,000 visitors per day during the Games |
| Population | 17,000 peak increase in Utah during 2001 |
| Net revenue to state & local government | US$76 million |

We will deploy regular trade missions throughout the world to leverage our Olympic networks and to attract venture capital.

By the end of June 2003 trade missions had been undertaken to cities all around the world including Moscow, Mexico City, Athens, Turin, Washington and Chicago, with several visits to southern and northern Asia, London and other places scheduled for the second part of the year.

## THE LONDON BID FOR THE 2012 OLYMPICS

### History

The idea of bringing the Olympic Games back to Britain is not new. Three recent bids to host the Games have been made: by Birmingham for the Games of 1992, and by Manchester for the Games of 1996 and 2000. As all three bids failed, the British Olympic Association (BOA) has been working since 1997 on the viability of a London Olympic bid. The main lesson that emerged was that London was the only UK city with a chance of being selected by the IOC when up against other world cities in a bidding process (Plate 15.1).

The work of the BOA resulted in a 400-page report published in December 2000, which was delivered to Government ministers, the Mayor of the Greater London Authority and opposition spokespersons. The thinking behind the proposal suggests that a successful bid is a combination of favourable 'internal' and 'external' opportunities. Externally, 2012 is seen as a window of opportunity as Europe is expected to be the destination for the Games of that year. Continental

Plate 15.1  'Leap for London' poster (the London 2012 bid)

rotation means that if a European city is awarded the 2012 Games they will not return to that continent until at least 2024.

Internally, there is a rare opportunity to acquire derelict 'brown field' sites in the heart of London's East End which will not be accessible for future Games bids. This would stimulate the regeneration of a whole region of London by bringing other improvements to the rest of the city and beyond. After considerable deliberation the Government announced its support for London's Olympic bid on 3 July 2003.

The words of Craig Reedie, Chairman of the BOA, sum up the bid and what lies ahead:

> We are going out to win. Silver is nowhere in this race. The whole Government has backed the bid. There will be some stiff opposition, but we have a great case and everyone, from the Prime Minister down, will be working hard to make it.

### The Olympic bid process

Following the Salt Lake City scandal of 1999, which led to a serious reshaping of the structure and practices of the Olympic Movement, a whole new host city election procedure had been put in place.

In contrast to past practices, the process is now more professional, transparent and rigid, with IOC members no longer allowed to visit candidate cities. This practice has been replaced by an Evaluation Commission consisting of:

- representatives from the IOC
- representatives from international sports federations
- representatives of National Olympic Committees
- other relevant experts.

This commission is now responsible for the evaluation of a city's bid. It then prepares a report, which is presented to all IOC members. Finally, all candidate cities selected for the final stage of voting make a presentation to the IOC Session, which decides which city will host the Games. Table 15.7 details the election procedure for the host city of the 2012 Olympic Games.

### London Olympic bid as a social, political and economic project

Very few projects can stir such profound reaction from all segments of society as staging the Olympic Games. London's bid for the Games of 2012 is no exception. This is inevitable given the magnitude of the undertaking. Hosting the Games cuts across the interests of various groups and communities – from athletes to politicians, businesses, the media and others who have no affiliation with sport.

Some see the Games as an opportunity to advance social, economic and technological progress, others perceive them as an environmental hazard and as deepening social division.

This explains why opinions vary markedly from headlines such as 'Don't Touch the Olympics with a Bargepole' (*The Sunday Times*, 15 December 2002) or 'We don't need this five-ring circus' (*The Observer*, 19 January 2003) to 'All of the contacts we have had from business confirmed that this will be good a good thing – for London and the UK' (Ian Barlow, Chairman, London Business Board).

An Olympic bid illustrates perfectly the point that the Olympic Games are not merely a sporting event but a catalyst for social, political and economic change.

The BOA proposal provides a consolidated list of UK support for the London 2012 Olympic bid. This includes a wide range of support including major political parties, the Greater London Authority and regional assemblies, to educational

*Table 15.7* Games of the XXX Olympiad 2012: bidding timetable

| Action | Date |
| --- | --- |
| IOC sends circulars to NOCs inviting them to submit the name of an applicant city | Beginning May 2003 |
| NOCs inform the IOC of the name of an applicant city | 15 July 2003 (by letter) |
| Applicant cities reply to IOC questionnaire | 15 January–June 2004 |
| Examination of replies by IOC and experts | 15 January–June 2004 |
| Acceptance of candidate cities by the IOC Executive Board | May–June 2004 |
| Games of the XXIII Olympiad | Athens, 13–29 August 2004 |
| Preparation of candidature files by the candidate cities | May/June – 15 November 2004 |
| Receipt of candidature files by the IOC | 15 November 2004 |
| Analysis of candidature files by the IOC | 15 November 2004 – end January 2005 |
| Visits of the IOC Evaluation Commission to candidate cities | February–March 2005 |
| Evaluation Commission report | Beginning May 2005 |
| Announcement by the IOC Executive Board of candidate cities to be submitted to the IOC session for election | |
| Election of the host city by the IOC session | July 2005 |

Source: IOC, 2002

establishments, leading businesses, all UK sport governing bodies and several opinion polls.

This support, however, does not come unconditionally. Each organisation behind the bid expects to gain certain benefits, which could be monetary, promotional, a form of infrastructure or greater social cohesion. Organisations are determined to make the most of this project. In addition, the bid should accommodate the demands of athletes, media, officials and tourists who will be attending the Games.

## SCALE OF THE LONDON 2012 OLYMPICS

- 11,000 athletes would compete in 300 events over 16 days.
- They would be supported by 5000–6000 coaches and officials, and attended by 4000–5000 members of the Olympic Family.
- Over 7000 sponsors would attend the Games.
- 4000 athletes and 2500 officials would participate in the Paralympics over 12 days – this is equal in size to the Commonwealth Games.
- 20,000 newspaper, radio, television and Internet journalists would cover the events and require state-of-the-art communication facilities.
- Over 9 million tickets would be sold, equal to nearly half a million spectators a day travelling to events in and around London.
- Staging the Games would involve 63,000 operational personnel, of whom 47,000 will be volunteers, many as stewards, marshalls and drivers.

(Source: ARUP, 2002)

All this amounts to a massive logistic undertaking where striking the right balance and pleasing all concerned is very difficult, if not impossible, to achieve.

The key stakeholders of the London bid include representatives from the BOA, the Greater London Authority (GLA) and the Government. The Lower Lee Valley in East London is earmarked as the major geographical site where the Olympic Village, the main stadium and many other facilities will be located. The establishment of four key agencies will ensure the delivery, procurement, co-ordination and management of the Games:

- the London Organising Committee of the Olympic Games (LOCOG) (to be set up in 2005)
- an Olympic Development Agency (in place from 2005)
- an Olympic Transport Agency (in place by 2009)
- an Operational Command Unit within the Metropolitan Police Services (to be set up in 2009).

The key issues concerning the bid include cost, organisation and the Games legacy.

*Table 15.8* Summary of the financial analysis of the London 2012 Olympic bid

| Project | Expenditure (£million) | Income (£million) | Surplus/deficit (£million) |
|---|---|---|---|
| Bidding for the Games | 13 | 7 | −6 |
| Operating account for staging the Games | 779 | 864 | +85 |
| Elite sport development programme | 167 | 0 | −167 |
| Capital cost of infrastructure & facilities | 403 | 0 | −403 |
| Land purchase & residual value (including value of remaining buildings and infrastructure) | 325 | 431 | +106 |
| Cash flow balance | 1687 | 1302 | −385 |
| Provision for risk | 109 | | −109 |
| Cash flow including risk | 1796 | 1302 | −494 |

Source: ARUP, 2002, p. 5

Note: All figures are based on 2002 prices

## Cost of the Games

One of the most sensitive issues concerns the cost and who is going to foot the bill. A summary of the financial analysis of staging the Games in London is provided in Table 15.8. Although ARUP (2002) state that the figures in their analysis are very conservative, past experiences have demonstrated that the actual cost of the Games far surpassed the forecasts made ten years earlier.

Observers express concerns that the cost of the Games will exceed £5 billion and oppose plans for spending taxpayers' money on filling the gaps in the budget.

Politically, this argument is reinforced by the commitment of the current Labour Government to concentrate in its second term on improving schools and hospitals. Further controversy is added by Mayor of London Ken Livingstone's proposal to add £20 per annum to Londoners' Council Tax bills and increase the local business rate for up to seven years.

## Organising the Games

As previously demonstrated, staging an Olympic Games is a massive undertaking which requires meticulous planning and management. London's previous experience in hosting the 1908 and 1948 Games at very short notice will be of little use here because the Olympics have grown markedly in size, complexity and cost.

Interestingly, some of the key issues, such as transport and security, which are under public scrutiny on a daily basis, will also be a central part of any Olympic bid.

Britain's reputation of being able to organise global sporting events has been considerably boosted following the success of the 2002 Commonwealth Games in Manchester; however, sceptical voices are pointing to the failure of the Millennium Dome where millions of pounds of taxpayer's money has been wasted. The confusion over the re-building of Wembley Stadium and the subsequent withdrawal of London as host to the World Athletics Championships in 2005 also poses questions about the competence of the UK and its government agencies to handle massive projects.

London's transport is a notoriously complicated economic, technological and political issue, which is far from being resolved, with or without an Olympic Games. The ARUP (2002) report shows that London has the capacity to cope with an anticipated flow of some 500,000 extra passengers daily during the Games, but in reality it will take more than the provision of schedules, buses and underground carriers to enable smooth movement across the city. The co-operation of Londoners and its visitors in changing their travel habits will be vital to the implementation of any transportation plan.

Security has for some time been a concern, particularly in connection with major events. The history of the Olympics justifies a concern for security, and particularly since 11 September 2001 a more intense focus has been placed on the threats posed by terrorists. Security therefore becomes an expensive issue and the projected Games income will only cover the immediate Olympic zone. Elsewhere in London the public sector will bear the cost of security and experts also consider that there would be a need to seek assistance from the USA, Australia and other countries.

## Legacy of the Games

The Olympic Games lasts for 16 days but takes seven years of meticulous planning and preparation, thousands of paid and voluntary staff, countless organisations and billions of pounds to deliver. It is therefore crucial that the Games be organised so as to provide a lasting legacy to the host city, the country and the rest of the world. This is not an easy task as it is not possible to quantify all the benefits that can accrue from hosting an Olympic Games. The main potential benefits and legacies of an Olympic Games in London in 2012 can be summarised as follows:

- tourism
- cultural
- social
- economic
- sports development.

These are considered below, with some counter-arguments raised by various parties.

### Tourism

It is expected that the Games will bring an additional £160 million of income to an established tourist destination. The global exposure of the city provided by the Olympics will also act as a catalyst for the long-term development of tourism in Britain. Critics, however, warn of the recent tourism policy of diverting tourists away from London to other parts of Britain. There is evidence from Sydney and other former Olympic cities that whilst the host city enjoys a short-lived boom in tourism, other parts of the country experience a decline.

### Cultural

London is a multicultural city with over 100 different nationalities and some very well established ethnic communities. Organisers are promoting the idea that an Olympic Games would bring people together and contribute to greater cultural integration.

Critics argue that the Games can do very little to tackle long-standing problems of racism, religious intolerance and nationalism.

### Social

The Games also carry the substantial social responsibility of regenerating a whole region of London by building some 4000 housing units and other infrastructure. It is projected that this will contribute to models of behaviour, educational programmes, community links, greater inclusion and increased participation opportunities.

Additionally, it is expected that the Games would boost national prestige and the 'feel-good factor'. Indeed, playing host to the Olympics brings subtle advantages, which are difficult to quantify. For example, South Korea won 6 gold medals at the 1984 Los Angeles Olympics and 12 in Seoul in 1988; Spain won only 1 gold medal in Seoul (1988) but 13 in Barcelona in 1992. Australia won 9 gold medals in Atlanta and 16 four years later in Sydney.

Less optimistic voices raise concerns that the Olympics are an elitist project promoted by powerful multinational companies and media conglomerates in their quest for world domination, and will not benefit ordinary people. Neither is it certain whether an Olympic gold medal won by a British athlete at home would be more stimulating for national prestige than if the same medal had been won abroad.

### Economic

Owing to the IOC marketing programmes (global sponsorship, tickets and TV rights sales), since 1984 staging the Games has not been an unbearable financial burden as it comes with a guaranteed income for the host city.

However, the economic benefits associated with a London Olympics would be more diverse and uncertain. These would include the creation of 9000 full time jobs, of which 3000 would be in the East End economy. Other British cities are also expected to benefit economically by hosting holding-camps for overseas athletes. The quantified economic benefits from tourism and business activities are estimated at between £349 million and £679 million. Inward and outward investments would increase, as would the export of 'know-how' and expertise to organisers of future global sporting events.

Conversely, those who disagree that resources earmarked for sport should be used for the re-generation of the East End of London feel that this will inevitably divert cash flows from other areas and projects in need.

New sports facilities and infrastructure can easily become a burden without sustainable investment alongside them. House and services prices, which at present are already beyond the reach of millions of Londoners, will certainly increase, making the situation even worse.

### Sports development

The Olympic Games are perceived as a generator of public interest and an inspiration for young people in particular to take up sport. The Games will leave

256

a modern sporting infrastructure and range of technologies behind them. There is little doubt that athletes competing in London in 2012 will enthuse youngsters to follow in their footsteps. However, the Olympic sports facilities are highly specialised and difficult to adapt to the needs of ordinary recreational users. Moreover, enthusiasm is only one of many ingredients required to produce future sporting stars.

**IN BRIEF**

### SPORT ENGLAND POSITION ON LONDON OLYMPICS 2012

Sport England is broadly supportive of a London Olympic Games on the basis of certain assumptions. It is essential that any bid for 2012:

- does not divert investment from grass-roots sport
- has a robust, achievable business plan
- delivers a substantial and sustainable sporting, social inclusion and regeneration legacy
- is not reliant on Sport England Lottery funding
- contributes to the overall government objectives of increasing participation in sport
- recognises the role and success of volunteers
- has broad public, political and business support from the start.
    (Sport England written statement to the Culture, Media and Sport
        Select Committee London Olympic Inquiry, 2003)

A sustainable sports development needs quality programmes, qualified staff, facilities and professional management. Staging the Olympics does not automatically provide these elements. They have to be developed as part of a coherent national strategy and backed by long-term public and private investments.

One would expect that the leading sports organisations in Britain would support a London Olympic bid without reservation. However, the position of Sport England is indicative of the high demands which sports development places on the Olympics and for the adverse effects it may suffer if they are organised at the expense of the wider needs of sport.

## CASE STUDIES

1   Examine and compare the organisational models of the Olympic Games in Sydney 2000, Salt Lake City 2002 and Barcelona 1992. What conclusions can you draw about the role of the central and local governments and the private sector?

2   Discuss the economic and environmental impact of the Olympic Games in Sydney 2000 and Salt Lake City 2002 on the Mission of the Olympic Movement.

3   Consider the environmental legacy of the Olympic Games in light of the IOC's environment policy (see Chapter 8). Use available information on previous Olympic Games.

4   Identify the main stakeholders involved in London's bid for the 2012 Olympics and discuss the tensions that this project provokes.

5   Look at the websites of the main contenders to host the 2012 Olympics and evaluate the advantages and disadvantages of London's bid:

   ■   Paris <http://www.parisjo2012.fr>
   ■   New York <http://www.nyc2012.com>
   ■   Madrid <http://www.madrid2012.es>
   ■   London <http://www.london2012.org.uk>

# BIBLIOGRAPHY

Anthony, D. (ed.) (1999) *Minds, Bodies and Souls: An Anthology of the Olympic Heritage Network*, BOA, London.

Anthony, D. (2000) 'The British International Olympians', a paper presented at the British Olympic Academy, Lilleshall National Sports Centre, 7–9 April 2000.

AOCOG (1997) *Centennial Olympic Games Report*, Atlanta Organising Committee of the Olympic Games.

ARUP (2002) *London Olympics 2012*, 2.

Atkinson, S. (1997) 'Sydney 2000: physical impact and environment', in *Environment and Sport: An International Overview*, Da Costa (ed.), University of Porto, Porto, p. 275.

Auberger, A. *et al.* (1994) 'Sport, Olympism and disability', in *For a Humanism of Sport: After a Century of Olympism*, CNOSF-Editions, Paris.

Barnett, S. (1987) *Games and Sets: The Changing Face of Sport on Television*, British Film Institute, London.

Baskau, H. (1987) 'Methods of Olympic education' in *Report of the 27th Session of the International Olympic Academy*, 141–149.

Best, D. (1978) *Philosophy and Human Movement*, Allen & Unwin, London.

Best, D. (1980) 'Art and sport', *Journal of Aesthetic Education*, **14**(1), 69–80.

Borotra J. (1983) 'Olympism and fair play', in *Proceedings of the International Olympic Academy*, 84–94.

Botella, M. (1995) 'The political games: agents and strategies in the 1992 Barcelona Olympic Games', in *The Keys to Success: The Social, Sporting, Economic and Communications Impact of Barcelona '92*, De Moragas, M. and Botella, M. (eds), Centre d'Estudis Olympics I de l'Esport, Universitat Autonoma de Barcelona, Barcelona, 139–148.

Bovee, C. and Arens, W. (1989) *Contemporary Advertising*, 3rd edn, Irwin, Homewood.

Bowra, C.M. (1969) *The Odes of Pindar*, Penguin Books, Harmondsworth.

Bramley, P. *et al. Leisure Policies in Europe*, CAB International, Wallingford.

Briggs, A. and Cobley, P. (1998) *The Media: An Introduction*, Longman, London.

Brown, D.A. (1996) 'Pierre de Coubertin's Olympic exploration of Modernism, 1894–1914: aesthetics, ideology and the spectacle', *Research Quarterly for Exercise and Sport*, **67**(2), 121–135.

Brown, W.M. (1988) 'Paternalism, drugs and the nature of sports', in *Philosophic Enquiry in Sport*, Morgan, W. and Meier, K. (eds), Human Kinetics, Urbana, 297–306.

Brundage, A. (1963) 'The Olympic philosophy', *Proceedings of the International Olympic Academy*, 29–39.

Brunet, F. (1995) 'An economic analysis of the Barcelona '92 Olympic Games: resources, financing and impact', in *The Keys to Success: The Social, Economic and Communications Impact of Barcelona '92*, de Moragas, M. and Botella, M. (eds), Centre d'Estudis Olimpics I de l'Esport, Universitat Autonoma de Barcelona: Barcelona, 209.

Burke, D.B. and Roberts, T.J. (1997) 'Drugs in sport: an issue of morality or sentimentality?', *Journal of Philosophy of Sport*, **XXIV**, 99–113.

Burns, F. (1999) William Denny, quoted in, 'Robert Dover's Cotswold Olympick Games', in *Minds, Bodies and Souls. An Anthology of the Olympic Heritage Network*, Anthony, D. (ed.), BOA, London.

Cantelon, H. and Letters, M. (2000) 'The making of the IOC environmental policy as the third dimension of the Olympic Movement', *International Review for the Sociology of Sport*, **35**(3), 294–308.

Carl-Diem-Institut (1966) *The Olympic Idea: Pierre de Coubertin – Discourses and Essays*, Olympischer Sportverlag, Stuttgart.

Chappelet, J.-L. (2000) 'Management of the Olympic Games – the lessons from Sydney', *Olympic Review*, **35**, 43–47.

Chappelet, J.-L. (2001) 'Risk management for large-scale events: the case of the Winter Olympic Games', *European Journal for Sport Management*, **8**, 6–22.

Clapes, A. (1995) 'The volunteers of Barcelona '92: the greatest festival of participation', in *The Keys to Success: The Social, Sporting, Economic and Communications Impact of Barcelona '92*, De Moragas, M. and Botella, M. (eds), Centre d'Estudis Olympics I de l'Esport, Universitat Autonoma de Barcelona, Barcelona, 165–180.

Clark, K. (1969) *Civilisation*, BBC, London.

Clark, K. (1970) *The Nude*, Penguin, Harmondsworth.

Coakley, J. (1990) *Sport in Society. Issues and Controversies* (4th edn), Times Mirror/Mosby, St Louis, p. 287.

Cochrane, A., Peck, J. and Tickell, A. (1996) 'Manchester plays Games: exploring the local politics of globalisation', *Urban Studies*, **33**(8), 1319–1336.

Collins, M. (1999) 'The economics of sport and sports in the economy: some international comparisons', in *Progress in Tourism, Recreation and Hospitality Management*, Vol. 3, Cooper (ed.), Belhaven Press, London, 184–214.

Collins, M. and Jackson G. (1981) 'The economic impact of sport tourism', in *Sport Tourism*, Standeven and De Knop (eds), Human Kinetics, Champaign, 182.

Cox, R. (2003) *Landmarks in British Sport*, Frank Cass, London.

Craven, P. (2003) 'IPC focuses on development', *The Paralympian*, **1**, 1.

Creedon, P. (ed.) (1994) *Women, Media and Sport*, Sage, USA.

Crompton, J. (1995) 'Economic impact analysis of sports facilities and events: eleven sources of misapplication', *Journal of Sport Management*, **9**, 14–35.

Davis, K. (1994) *Sport Management: Successful Private Sector Business Strategies*, Brown & Benchmark, 1994.

De Coubertin, P. (1894a) Speech at the Paris Congress, in *The Olympic Idea: Pierre de Coubertin – Discourses and Essays*, Carl-Diem-Institut (1966) Olympischer Sportverlag, Stuttgart, 6–7.

De Coubertin, P. (1894b) 'Athletics in the modern world and the Olympic Games', in *The Olympic Idea: Pierre de Coubertin – Discourses and Essays*, Carl-Diem-Institut (1966) Olympischer Sportverlag, Stuttgart, 7–10.

De Coubertin, P. (1906) Opening Address to the Conference of Arts, Letters and Sports, in *The Olympic Idea: Pierre de Coubertin – Discourses and Essays*, Carl-Diem-Institut (1966) Olympischer Sportverlag, Stuttgart, 16–18.

De Coubertin, P. (1908) 'The "Trustees" of the Olympic Idea', in *The Olympic Idea: Pierre de Coubertin – Discourses and Essays*, Carl-Diem-Institut (1966) Olympischer Sportverlag, Stuttgart, 18–20.

De Coubertin, P. (1928) Message . . . to the athletes . . . of the IXth Olympiad, in *The Olympic Idea: Pierre de Coubertin – Discourses and Essays*, Carl-Diem-Institut (1966) Olympischer Sportverlag, Stuttgart, 105–106.

De Coubertin, P. (1929) 'Olympia', in *The Olympic Idea: Pierre de Coubertin – Discourses and Essays*, Carl-Diem-Institut (1966), Olympischer Sportverlag, Stuttgart, 106–119.

De Coubertin, P. (1931) *Mémoires Olympiques*, Bureau International de Pédagogie Sportive, Lausanne, 77.

De Coubertin, P. (1934) 'Forty years of Olympism' (1894/1934), in *The Olympic Idea: Pierre de Coubertin – Discourses and Essays*, Carl-Diem-Institut (1966) Olympischer Sportverlag, Stuttgart, 126–130.

De Coubertin, P. (1934b) 'All Games All Nations', in *The Olympic Idea: Pierre de Coubertin – Discourses and Essays*, Carl-Diem-Institut (1966), Olympischer Sportverlag, Stuttgart, 127.

De Coubertin, P. (1935) 'The philosophic foundations of modern Olympism', in *The Olympic Idea: Pierre de Coubertin – Discourses and Essays*, Carl-Diem-Institut (1966) Olympischer Sportverlag, Stuttgart, 130–134.

De Coubertin, P. (1997) *Olympic Memoirs*, IOC, Lausanne.

De Moragas Spa, M. *et al.* (1995) *Television in the Olympics*, John Libbey, London.

De Moragas Spa, M. *et al.* (2001) 'Internet and the Olympic Movement', Paper presented at the 11th International Association for Sport Information World Congress, Lausanne, Centre d'Estudis I de l'Esport (UAB), Barcelona.

DePauw, K. and Gavron, S. (1995) *Disability and Sport*, Human Kinetics, Champaign.

Diem, C. (1952) Exhibition catalogue at the XVth Olympiad. Preparatory note 9: Frankfurt on Main.

Diem, C. (1970) 'Art and amateurism', in *The Olympic Idea: Discourses and Essays*, Verlag Karl Hoffman, Schorndorf.

Dominick, J. (1990) *The Dynamics of Mass Communication*, McGraw-Hill, London.

Donnely, P. (1996) 'Prolympism: sport monoculture as crisis and opportunity', *Quest*, **48** (1), 25–43.

Drees, L. (1968) *Olympia: Gods, Artists and Athletes*, Praeger, New York.

Dubi, C. (1996) 'The economic impact of a major sports event', *Olympic Message*, **3**, 88.

During, B. and Brisson, J.F. (1994) 'Sport, Olympism and cultural diversity', in *For a Humanism of Sport*, Jeu, B. et al. CNOSF, Paris, Ch. 19.

Durry, J. (1998) 'The cultural events at the Olympic Games and Pierre de Coubertin's thinking', *Proceedings of the 38th Session of the International Olympic Academy*, 56–66.

Eichberg, H. (1984) 'Olympic sport – neo-colonialism and alternatives,' in *International Revue for the Sociology of Sport*, **19**(1), 97–104.

Elstad, B. (1996) 'Volunteer perception of learning and satisfaction in a mega-event: the case of the XVII Olympic Winter Games in Lillehammer', *Festival Management and Event Tourism*, **4**(1), 75–83.

Essex, S. and Chalkley, B. (1998) 'Olympic Games: catalyst of urban change', *Leisure Studies*, **17**(3), 187–207.

Eyler, M.H. (1981) 'The Right Stuff' *Proceedings of the International Olympic Academy*, 159–168.

Filaretos, N. (1987) 'The International Olympic Academy', in *Proceedings of the 27th Session of the Olympic Academy*, 27–31.

Finley, M.I. and Pleket, H.W. (1976) *The Olympic Games: The First Thousand Years*, Chatto & Windus, London.

Flognfieldt, T. (1998) 'A spectator's view of the results of the development of an Olympic host town, before and after the Games', *Festival Management and Event Tourism*, **5**(1/2), 93.

Foley, P. (1991) 'The impact of major events: a case study of the World Student Games and Sheffield', *Environment and Planning*, **C9**, 65–69.

Ford and Ford (1993) *Television and Sponsorship*, Focal Press, London.

Fraleigh, W. (1984) *Right Actions in Sport: Ethics for Contestants*, Human Kinetics, Leeds.

Fraleigh, W.P. (1994) 'Performance-enhancing drugs in sport; the ethical issue', *Journal of Philosophy of Sport*, **XI**, 23–29.

French, D. and Hainsworth, J. (2001) '"There aren't any buses and the swimming pool is always cold!": obstacles and opportunities in the provision of sport for disabled people', *Managing Leisure*, **6**, 36.

Gardiner, N.E. (1925) *Olympia, its History and Remains*, Clarendon Press, Oxford.

Gardiner, N.E. (1955) *Athletics of the Ancient World*, Clarendon Press, Oxford.

Georgiadis, K. (1992) 'International Olympic Academy: the history of its establishment, aims and activities', in *Report of the 32nd Session of the International Olympic Academy*, 62–71.

Georgiadis, K. (2004) *Olympic Revival*, Ekdotike Athenon S.A., Athens.

Goodhart, P. and Chataway, C. (1968) *War without Weapons*, W.H. Allen, London.

Gratton, C. and Taylor, P. (2000) *Economics of Sport & Recreation*, E & FN Spon, London, 181.

Gueorguiev, N. (1995) *Analyse du Programme des Jeux Olympiques d'hiver 1924–1998*, IOC, Lausanne.

Gueorguiev, N. (1995) *Analyse du Programme Olympique 1896–1996*, IOC, Lausanne.

Gutmann, A. (1988) 'The Cold War and the Olympics', *International Journal for the Sociology of Sport*, **43**(3), 554–568.

Healy, V. and Herder, R. (2002) 'A walk-up-and-use information system for the Sydney Olympics: a case study in user-centered design', *International Journal of Human–Computer Interaction*, **14**(3&4), 335–347.

Heinemann, K. (1992) 'The economic impact of the Olympic Games', in *Proceedings of the 32nd Session of the International Olympic Academy*, IOC, Lausanne, 147–156.

Henderson, P. (1989) 'Toronto's 1996 bid', in *The Olympic Movement and the Mass Media: Past, Present and Future Issues*, Jackson, R. and McPhail, T. (eds), International Conference Proceedings, Hurford Enterprises, Calgary, 10.9–10.11.

Henley Centre for Forecasting (1986) *The Economic Impact and Importance of Sport in the UK*, Study 30, The Sports Council, London.

Henry, I. (ed.) (1992) *Management and Planning in the Leisure Industries*, Macmillan, London, Chs 6 and 7.

Hill, C. (1996) *Olympic Politics*, Manchester University Press, Manchester.

Hoberman, J. (1984) 'Sport ideology in the post-Communist Age', in *The Changing Politics of Sport*, Allison, L. (ed.), Manchester University Press, 4,17.

Hoberman, J. (1984) *Sport and Political Ideology*, Heinemann, London.

Hoberman, J. (1988) 'Sport and the technological image of man', in *Philosophic Enquiry in Sport*, Morgan, W. and Meier, K. (eds), Human Kinetics, Urbana, 319–327.

Hollway, S. (2002) 'Enduring benefits of the Olympic Games for Australia', *Olympic Review*, 28–33.

Holt, R. (1990) *Sport and the British: A Modern History*, Oxford University Press, Oxford.

Houlihan, B. (1991) *The Government and Politics of Sport*, Routledge, London.

Hulme, D. (1990) *The Political Olympics: Moscow, Afghanistan, and the 1980 U.S. Boycott*, Praeger, London.

Huntington, S. (1981) 'Trans-national organisations in world politics', in *Perspectives on World Politics*, Smith, M. and Shackleton, M. (eds), Croom Helm, London, 198.

Huot, R. (1996) 'Olympic coins – collectibles with a mission', *Olympic Message*, **3**, 99.

IOC (1989) *National Olympic Academy – Foundation, Perspectives, Activities*, IOC, Lausanne.

IOC (1996) 'The Olympic Games and music', *Olympic Message*, April–June.

IOC (2001) *Sydney 2000 Marketing Report: Games of the XXVII Olympiad*, IOC, Lausanne, 44.

IOC (2003) *The Olympic Charter*, IOC, Lausanne.

IOC (1976) 'Great Britain and Olympism', *Olympic Review*, **99–100**, 54–91.

Jeu, B. *et al.* (1994) *For a Humanism of Sport*, CNOSF, Paris,

Jobling, I. (1994) 'Olympic proposals and bids by Australian cities', *Sporting Traditions*, **11**(1), 37–56.

Jobling, I. (2000) 'Bidding for the Olympics: site selection and Sydney 2000', in *The Olympics at the Millennium: Power, Politics and the Games*, Schaffer, K. and Smith, S. (eds), Rutgers University Press, New Brunswick.

263

Jones, H. (1989) *The Economic Impact and Importance of Sport: A European Study*, Council of Europe, Strasbourg.

Joynt, J. *et al.* (1989) 'The XV Winter Olympic Games Organising Committee (OCO '88)', in *The Olympic Movement and the Mass Media: Past, Present and Future Issues*, Jackson, R. and McPhail, T. (eds), International Conference Proceedings, Hurford Enterprises, Calgary, 15.3–15.7

Kartalis, K. (2000) 'The environment and the Olympic Games', in *Proceedings of the 40th Session of the International Olympic Academy*, IOC, Lausanne, 105–106.

Kee, S. *et al.* (eds) (1984) *Olympics and Politics*, Hyung-Seoul Publishing, Seoul.

Kidane, F. (1997) 'The Olympic Movement and the environment', in *Environment and Sport: An International Overview*, Da Costa (ed.), University of Porto, 251.

Kidd, B. (1992) 'The culture wars of the Montreal Olympics', *International Review for the Sociology of Sport*, **27**(2), 151–161.

Kidd, B. (1992) 'The Toronto Olympic Committee: towards a social contract for the Olympic Games', *Olympika*, **1**, 154–167.

King, T. (1993) *Implication of a Successful Olympic Bid*, Potter Warburg, Melbourne.

Kitto, H.D. (1951) *The Greeks*, Penguin, Harmondsworth.

Landry, F. (1984) 'The Olympic Games and competitive sport as an international system', in *Proceedings of the International Olympic Academy*, **24**, 157–167.

Landry, F. (1995) 'Paralympic Games and social integration', in *The Key to Success*, De Moragas, M. and Botella, M. (eds), Centre d'Estudis Olimpics I de l'Esport, Barcelona.

Laswell, H. (1936) *Politics: Who gets What, When, How*, McGraw-Hill, New York.

Lavin, M. (1987) 'Sport and drugs: are the current bans justified?', *Journal of Philosophy of Sport*, **XIV**, 34–43.

Lawrence R. and Budd, A. (2003) *Sport and International Relations: An Emerging Relationship*, Frank Cass, London.

Leibold, M. and Zyl, C. (1996) 'The Summer Olympic Games and its tourism marketing – city tourism market experiences and challenges, with specific reference to Cape Town, South Africa', *Festival Management & Event Tourism*, **4**, 39–47.

Lekarska, N. (1986) *Tenth and Eleventh Olympic Congress: Comparative Studies and Essays*, Sofia Press, Sofia.

Lenk, H. (1964) 'Values, aims, reality of the modern Olympic Games', *Proceedings of the International Olympic Academy*, 205–211.

Lenk, H. (1982) 'Towards a philosophical anthropology of the Olympic athlete', *Proceedings of the International Olympic Academy*, IOC, Lausanne, 163–177.

Lenskyj, H. (1994) 'Buying and selling the Olympic Games: citizen participation in the Sydney and Toronto bids', in *Critical Reflections on Olympic Ideology*, Barney, R. and Meier, K. (eds), Second International Symposium for Olympic Research, London, Ontario, Centre for Olympic Studies, 70–77.

Lenskyj, H. (1996) 'When winners are losers: Toronto and Sydney bids for the Summer Olympics', *Journal of Sport and Social Issues*, **20**(4), 392–410.

Lesjo, J. (2000) 'Lillehammer 1994: planning, figurations and the "green" Games', *International Review for the Sociology of Sport*, **35**(3), 282–293.

264

Lines, M. and Moreno, A. (1999) 'The history of radio and television coverage of the Olympic Games', in *Television in the Olympic Games: The New Era*, Proceedings from an International Symposium, IOC, Lausanne.

Liponski, W. (1994) 'The influence of Ancient Greek sport on international culture, literature and art', in *Report of the 34th Session of the International Olympic Academy*, IOC, Lausanne, 66–80.

Lowes, M. (1997) 'Sports Page: A case study in the manufacture of sports news for daily press', *Sociology of Sport Journal*, **14**, 143–159.

Lucas, J. (1992) *Future of the Olympic Games*, Human Kinetics, Champaign.

MacAloon, J.J. (1984) 'The revival of the Olympic Games,' in *Report of the 24th Session of the International Olympic Academy*, IOC, Lausanne, 169–182.

MacAloon, J.J. (1996) 'On the structural origins of Olympic individuality', *Research Quarterly for Exercise and Sport*, **67**(2), 136–147.

Macintosh, D. and Hawes, M. (1992) 'The IOC and the World of Interdependence', *Olympika*, **1**, 29–45.

MacIntyre, A. (1981) *After Virtue*, Duckworth, London.

MacNeill, M. (1996) 'Networks: producing Olympic ice hockey for a national television audience', *Sociology of Sport Journal*, **13**, 103–124.

Mandell, R. (1972) *The Nazi Olympics*, Souvenir Press, London.

Mangan, T. (2000) *Athleticism in the Victorian and Edwardian Public School*, Frank Cass, London.

Marks, J. (1981) 'Political abuse of Olympic sport – De Frantz v. United States Olympic Committee', *Journal of International Law and Politics*, **14**(1), 155–185.

Martyn, S. (1998) 'An uncomfortable circle of knowledge: an examination of the Nairobi Treaty on the Protection of the Olympic Symbol', in *Global and Cultural Critique: Problematizing the Olympic Games*, Barney, R. et al. (eds), International Centre for Olympic Studies, The University of Western Ontario, London, Ontario, Canada, 87–97.

Mason, T. (ed.) *Sport in Britain: A Social History*, Cambridge University Press, Cambridge.

Masterson, D. (1973) 'The contribution of the fine arts to the Olympic Games', in *Proceedings of the 13th Session of the International Olympic Academy*, Athens, 200–213.

Masterson, D. (1979) 'The influence of sport on the fine arts', *Proceedings of the 19th Session of the International Olympic Academy*, Ancient Olympia, 177–191.

Matbis, P. (2003) 'Behind the scenes at the Olympics', *Public Roads* (Mar/Apr), 8.

May, V. (1995) 'Environmental impact of the Winter Olympic Games', *Tourism Management*, **16**(4), 269–275.

Mbaye, K. (1995) *The International Olympic Committee and South Africa*, IOC, Lausanne.

McIntosh, P. (1979) *Fair Play: Ethics in Sport and Education*, Heinemann, London.

McLatchey, C. (2003) 'Building and supporting a legacy', Paper presented at the British National Olympic Academy, Edinburgh, 14 March 2003.

Meadow, R. (1987) 'The architecture of Olympic broadcast', in *The Olympic Movement and Mass Media*, Proceedings of an International Conference, Calgary, 6–19.

Mechikoff, R. (1984) 'The Olympic Games: sport as international politics', *Journal of Physical Education, Recreation and Dance*, **55**(3), 23–25.

Mezo, F. (1958) 'The arts in the Olympic Games', in *Sport and Society*, Natan, A. (ed.), London, 114.

Modden, J. (2002) 'The economic consequences of the Sydney Olympics: The CREA/Arthur Andersen Study', *Current Issues in Tourism*, **5**(1), 7–21.

Moore, J. (1996) 'The Olympic consumer opportunity', *Olympic Message*, **3**, 64

Morgan, W. and Meier, K. (1988) *Philosophic Enquiry in Sport*, Human Kinetics, Urbana.

Morrow, D. (1987) 'Newspapers: selected aspects of Canadian sport journalism and the Olympics', in *The Olympic Movement and Mass Media*, Proceedings of an International Conference, Calgary, 2-13-2-33.

Muller, N. (1976) 'The Olympic idea of Pierre de Coubertin and Carl Diem and its materialization in the Olympic Academy', in *Report of the 16th Session of the International Olympic Academy*, 94–105.

Mullin, B. (1983) *Sport Marketing, Promotion and Public Relations*, National Sport Management, Amherst, Massachusetts, Ch. 12.

Mullins, S.P. (1984) 'Pierre de Coubertin and the Wenlock Olympian Games', in *Report of the 24th Session of the International Olympic Academy*, 99–112.

Munthe, C. (2000) 'Selected champions', in *Values in Sport*, Tamburrini, C. and Tännsjö, T. (eds), Routledge, London, 217–231.

Neal-Lunsford, J. (1992) 'Sport in the land of television: the use of sport in network prime-time schedules 1946–50', *Journal of Sport History*, **19**(1), 59–60.

Nichols, P. (ed.) (1996) *Atlanta '96, The Official British Olympic Team Handbook*, BOA, London.

Nicholson, R. (1987) 'Drugs in sport: a re-appraisal', *Institute of Medical Ethics Bulletin*, Supplement 7.

Nisetich, F.J. (1980) *Pindar's Victory Songs*, Johns Hopkins University Press, Baltimore.

Nissiotis, N. (1983) 'Psychological and sociological motives for violence in sport', *Proceedings of the Intenational Olympic Academy*, 95–108.

Nissiotis, N. (1984) 'Olympism and today's reality', *Proceedings of the International Olympic Academy*, 57–74.

O'Donnell, H. (1994) 'Mapping the mythical: a geopolitics of national sporting stereotypes', *Discourse and Society*, **5**(3), 345–380.

O'Keeffe, P. (1997) 'A behind-the-scene look at Olympic management', *Workforce*, Feb 26–29.

Olympic Congress (1989) *The Olympic Movement and the Mass Media: Past, Present and Future Issues*, Hurford Enterprises, Calgary.

Orr, G. (1995) 'Marketing Games: the regulation of Olympic indicia and images in Australia', *European Intellectual Property Journal*, **17**(3), 161–162.

Osterhoudt, R.G. (1984) 'Modern Olympism' in Segrave J.O. and Chu, O. (eds), *Olympism*, Human Kinetics, Leeds, 347–362.

Palaeologos, C. (1964) 'The Ancient Olympics', in *Report of the 4th Session of the International Olympic Academy*, 61–78.

Palaeologos, C. (1966) 'First thoughts and acts for the revival of the Olympic Games in Greece', in *Report of the 6th Session of the International Olympic Academy*, 121–125.

Palaeologos, C. (1982) 'Hercules, the ideal Olympic personality', *Proceedings of the International Olympic Academy*, 54–71.

Palaeologos, C. (1985) 'Olympia of myth and history', in *Report of the 25th Session of the International Olympic Academy*, 64–70.

Parry, J. (1986) 'Sport, art and the aesthetic', *Proceedings of the 26th Session of the International Olympic Academy*, 90.

Parry, J. (1987) 'The devil's advocate', *Sport and Leisure*, Nov/Dec.

Parry, J. (1988) 'Olympism at the beginning and end of the twentieth century', *Proceedings of the International Olympic Academy*, 81–94.

Parry, J. (1998) 'Aggression and violence in elite competitive sport', in *Ethics and Sport*, McNamee, M.J. and Parry, S.J. (eds), Routledge, London, 205–224.

Persson, C. (2002) 'The International Olympic Committee and site decisions: the case of the 2002 Winter Olympics', *Event Management*, **6**, 143–147.

Polley, M. (2002) *Sport and British Diplomacy 1986–2000*, Frank Cass, London.

Poole, L. and Poole, G. (1963) *History of the Ancient Olympic Games*, Vision Press, London.

Preuss, H. (2001) 'The economic and social impact of the Sydney Olympic Games', in *Proceedings of the 41st Session of the International Olympic Academy*, IOC, Lausanne, 94–109.

Preuss, H. (2003) 'Winners and losers of the Olympic Games', in *Sport and Society: A Student Introduction*, Houlihan, B. (ed.), Sage, London.

Puijk, R. (ed.) (1997) *Global Spotlights on Lillehammer. How the World Viewed Norway during the 1994 Winter Olympics*, John Libbey, Luton.

Ratnatunga, J. and Muthaly, S. (2000) 'Lessons from Atlanta Olympics and organisational considerations for 2000', *International Journal of Sports Marketing & Sponsorship*, Sep/Oct, 342.

Real, M. (1996) 'The postmodern Olympics: technology and the commodification of the Olympic Movement', *Quest*, **48**, 15.

Redmond, G. (1986) *Sport and Politics – The 1984 Olympic Scientific Congress Proceedings*, Vol. 7, Human Kinetics, Champaign.

Redmond, G. (1988) 'Toward modern revival of the Olympic Games', in *The Olympic Games in Transition*, Segrave, J.O. and Chu, O. (eds), Human Kinetics, Leeds, 71–88.

Reid, L.A. (1970) 'Sport, the aesthetic and art', *British Journal of Educational Studies*, **18**(3), 245–258.

Ritchie, J.B. and Smith, B. (1991) 'The impact of mega event on host region awareness: a longitudinal study', *Journal of Travel Research*, **30**(1), 3–10.

Rivenburgh, N. (1999) 'The Olympic Games as a media event', in *Television in the Olympic Games: The New Era*, Proceedings from an International Symposium, IOC, Lausanne, 143–144.

Roesch, H.-E. (1979) 'Olympism and religion', *Proceedings of the International Olympic Academy*, 192–205.

Ruhl, J. and Keuser, A. (1999) 'The history of the Liverpool Olympics in 19th century England', in *Minds, Bodies and Souls: An Anthology of the Olympic Heritage Network*, Anthony, D. (ed.), BOA, London.

Rutheiser, C. (1996) 'How Atlanta lost the Olympics', *New Statesman*, No. 125 (19 July), 28–29.

Samaranch, J. (1995) 'The Olympic Movement and politics', *Olympic Review*, **XXV**(5), 3.

Samaranch, J.A. (1995) 'Olympic ethics', *Olympic Review*, **XXV-1** (Feb–Mar), 3.

Sansone, D. (1988) *Greek Athletics and the Genesis of Sport*, University of California Press, Berkeley.

Schaffer, K. and Smith, S. (2000) 'The Olympics of the everyday', in *The Olympics at the Millennium: Power, Politics and the Games*, Schaffer, K. and Smith, S. (eds), Rutgers University Press, New Brunswick.

Schantz, O. and Gilbert, K. (2002) 'An ideal misconstrued: newspaper coverage of the Atlanta Paralympic Games in France and Germany', *Sociology of Sport Journal*, **18**(1), 69–94.

Schell, L. and Duncan, M. (1999) 'A content analysis of CBS coverage of the 1996 Paralympic Games', *Adapted Physical Activity Quarterly*, **16**, 29.

Schiavone, N. (1989) 'Audience response, research and strategies of broadcasting in the Olympic Games', in *Television in the Olympic Games: The New Era*, Proceedings from an International Symposium, IOC, Lausanne, 82–83.

Schneider, A.J. and Butcher, R.B. (2000) 'A philosophical overview of the arguments on banning doping in sport', in *Values in Sport*, Tamburrini, C. and Tännsjö, T. (eds), Routledge, London, 185–199.

Scruton, J. (1999) *Stoke Mandeville Road to the Paralympics*, Peter House Press, Aylesbury.

Segrave, J. (2000) 'The (neo)modern Olympic Games', *International Review for the Sociology of Sport*, **35**(3), 278.

Segrave, J. O. and Chu, D. (eds) (1984) *Olympism*, Human Kinetics, Leeds.

Segrave, J.O. and Chu, D. (eds) (1988) *The Olympic Games in Transition*, Human Kinetics, Leeds.

Senn, A. (1999) *Power, Politics, and the Olympic Games*, Human Kinetics, Champaign.

Sherill, C. and Williams, T. (1996) 'Disability and sport: psychological perspectives on inclusion, integration, and participation', *Sport Science Review*, **5**(1), 42–64.

Sherrill, C. (1997) 'Paralympic Games 1996: feminist and other concerns. What's your excuse?' *Palaestra*, **13**(1), 32–38.

Shibli, S. (2003) 'Analysing performance at the Summer Olympic Games: beyond the final medal table', in *Proceedings of the 11th European Sport Management Congress*, Stockholm.

Shone, A. (2001) *Successful Event Management: A Practical Handbook*, Continuum, London, 17–22.

Siedentop, D. (ed.) (1994) *Sport Education: Quality PE through Positive Sport Experiences*, Human Kinetics, Leeds.

Simon, R L. (1988) 'Good competition and drug-enhanced performance', in *Philosophic Enquiry in Sport*, Morgan, W. and Meier, K. (eds), Human Kinetics, Urbana, 289–296.

Simson, V. and Jennings, A. (1992) *The Lords of the Rings*, Simon and Schuster, London.

Slack, T. (ed.) (2002) *The Commercialisation of Sport*, Frank Cass, London.

Smith, M.D. (1983) *Violence and Sport*, Butterworth, Toronto.

SOC (1913) *Stockholm Olympic Games Official Report*, Stockholm Organising Committee.

Sport England (1999) *The Value of Sport*, Sport England, London.

Spotts, J. (1994) 'Global politics and the Olympic Games: separating the two oldest games in history', *Dickson's Journal of International Law*, **13**(1), 115–119.

Steadward, R. (2001) 'The Paralympic Movement: a championship future', *Proceedings of the 40th Session of the International Olympic Academy 2000*, Olympia, Greece, IOC, Lausanne.

Swaddling, J. (1980) *The Ancient Olympic Games*, British Museum, London.

Tamburrini, C. (2000) 'What's wrong with doping?', in *Values in Sport*, Tamburrini, C. and Tännsjö, T. (eds), Routledge, London, 200–216.

Tamburrini, C. and Tännsjö, T. (eds) (2000) *Values in Sport*, Routledge, London.

Thomas, N. (2003) 'Sport and disability', in *Sport and Society: A Student Introduction*, Houlihan, B, (ed.), Sage, London, 105–124.

Thomas, N. and Smith, A. (2003) 'Preoccupied with able-bodiedness? An analysis of the British media coverage of the 2000 Paralympic Games', *Adapted Physical Activity Quarterly*, **20**, 166–181.

Toohey, K. and Veal, A. (2000) *The Olympic Games: A Social Science Perspective*, CABI, London.

Townshend, N. (19950 The British Olympic Association, nationally and internationally', a paper presented at the British Olympic Academy, Bath.

Varley, D. (1992) 'Barcelona's Olympic facelift', *Geographical Magazine*, **LXIV**(7), 20–24.

Waitt, G. (2001) 'The Olympic spirit and civic boosterism: the Sydney 2000 Olympics', *Tourism Geographics*, **3**, 249–278.

Wang, P. and Irwin, R. (1993) 'An assessment of economic impact techniques for small sporting events', *Sport Management Quarterly*, **II**(3), 33–37.

Weiler, I. (1984) 'Reasons for the decline of the Ancient Olympic Games', in *Report of the 24th Session of the International Olympic Academy*, 121–129.

Wenn, S. (1994) 'An Olympic squabble: the distribution of Olympic television revenue, 1960–1966', *Olympika*, **III**, 27–42.

Wenner, L. (1989) *Media, Sport and Society*, Sage, Thousand Oaks.

Wertz, S.K. (1984) 'A response to best on sport and art', *Journal of Aesthetic Education*, **18**(4), 105–107.

West, G. (1753) 'Dissertation on the Olympick Games', in *The Odes of Pindar*, R. Dodsley, London, vol. 2, 1–206.

West, G. (1753) *The Odes of Pindar*, R. Dodsley, London.

Whannel, G. (1992) *Fields in Vision: Television Sport and Cultural Transformation*, Routledge, London.

Whannel, G. (1992) *Profiting by the Presence of Ideals: Sponsorship and Olympism*, International Olympic Academy, Lausanne, 7.

Wigglesworth, N. (2002) *The Evolution of English Sport*, Frank Cass, London.

Winnick, J. (ed.). (1995) *Adapted Physical Education and Sport*, Human Kinetics, Champaign.

Yalouris, N. (1971) 'The art in the sanctuary of Olympia', *Proceedings of the 11th Session of the International Olympic Academy*, IOC, Lausanne, 90.

Young, D.C. (1984) *The Olympic Myth of Greek Amateur Athletics*, Ares, Chicago.

# INDEX

271

LIBRARY, UNIVERSITY OF CHESTER